MARK MAHANEY

Frederick Seidel

POEMS 1959–2009

These are the collected poems of a master whose
work includes many of the most compelling, sav-
age, and tender poems in the language. Frederick
Seidel is, in the words of the critic Adam Kirsch,
"the best American poet writing today."

POEMS 1959–2009

POEMS
1959–2009

Frederick Seidel

FARRAR, STRAUS AND GIROUX
NEW YORK

Farrar, Straus and Giroux
18 West 18th Street, New York 10011

Distributed in Canada by D&M Publishers, Inc.
Printed in the United States of America
Published in 2009 by Farrar, Straus and Giroux
First paperback edition, 2010

Evening Man originally appeared as a limited-edition chapbook.

The Library of Congress has cataloged the hardcover edition as follows:
Seidel, Frederick, 1936–
  [Poems. Selections]
  Poems 1959–2009 / Frederick Seidel.— 1st ed.
    p.   cm.
  Includes indexes.
  ISBN: 978-0-374-12655-1 (alk. paper)
    1. American poetry.   2. Poetry.   I. Title.

PS3569.E5 P64 2009
811'.54—dc22

                                        2008047161

Paperback ISBN: 978-0-374-53219-2

Designed by Peter A. Andersen

www.fsgbooks.com

1   3   5   7   9   10   8   6   4   2

CONTENTS

EVENING MAN (2008)

OOGA-BOOGA (2006)

THE COSMOS TRILOGY (2003)

The Cosmos Poems (2000)

Life on Earth (2001)

Area Code 212 (2002)

GOING FAST (1998)

For a New Planetarium

MY TOKYO (1993)

THESE DAYS (1989)

SUNRISE (1980)

FINAL SOLUTIONS (1963)

EVENING MAN (2008)

BOYS

Sixty years after, I can see their smiles,
White with Negro teeth, and big with good,
When one or the other brought my father's Cadillac out
For us at the Gatesworth Garage.
RG and MC were the godhead,
The older brothers I dreamed I had.
I didn't notice they were colored,
Because older boys capable of being kind
To a younger boy are God.
It is absolutely odd
To be able to be with God.
I can almost see their faces, but can't quite.
I remember how blazingly graceful they were,
And that they offered to get me a girl so I could meet God.

I have an early memory of a black chauffeur,
Out of his livery,
Hosing down a long black Packard sedan, sobbing.
Did it happen? It took place
In Portland Place.
I remember the pink-soled gum boots
That went with the fellow's very pink gums
And very white teeth, while he washed
The Packard's whitewalls white
And let them dry, sobbing,
Painting on liquid white with an applicator afterward.
Later that afternoon he resumed his chauffeur costume,
A darky clad in black under the staring sun.
Franklin Delano Roosevelt had died.

On the other hand, Ronny Banks was light-skinned.
He worked as a carhop at Medart's drive-in.
He was well-spoken, gently friendly.
He was giving a party, but I didn't go.
I actually drove there, but something told me no.
I suddenly thought he was probably a homo.
I drank my face off, age fifteen.
I hit the bars

In the colored section to hear jazz.
I raved around the city in my father's cars,
A straight razor who, wherever he kissed, left scars.
I was violently heterosexual and bad.
I used every bit of energy I had.
Where, I wonder, is Ronny Banks now?

I remember a young man, whose name I have forgotten,
Who was exceedingly neat,
Always wearing a white shirt,
Always standing there jet-black in our living room.
How had this been allowed to happen?
Who doesn't hate a goody-goody young Christian?
My father and uncle underwrote the boy's education.
He was the orphaned son of a minister.
He sang in the church choir.
He was exemplary, an exemplar.
But justice was far away, very far.
Justice was really an ashtray to display
The lynched carcass of a stubbed-out cigar,
Part brown, part black, part stink, part ash.

When I was a little boy,
My father had beautiful manners,
A perfect haughty gentleman,
Impeccable with everyone.
In labor relations with the various unions,
For example, he apparently had no peer.
It was not so much that he was generous,
I gather, but rather that he was fair.
So it was a jolt, a jolt of joy,
To hear him cut the shit
And call a black man Boy.
The white-haired old Negro was a shoeshine boy.
One of the sovereign experiences of my life was my joy
Hearing my father in a fury call the man Boy.

Ronny Banks, faggot prince, where are you now?
RG and MC, are you already under headstones
That will finally reveal your full

Names, whatever they were?
RG, the younger brother, was my hero who was my friend.
I remember our playing
Catch in the rain for hours on a rainy weekend.
It is a question
Of when, not a question of whether,
The glory of the Lord shall be revealed
And all flesh shall cease together.
A black woman came up to my father.
All the colored people in this city know who you are.
God sent you to us. Thank God for your daddy, boy.

AMERICAN

My face had been sliced off
And lay there on the ground like a washcloth
With my testicles and penis
Next to it.

The car had Wyoming plates.
I'd been to Colorado but not Wyoming,
Which I gather is beautiful.
The other one I hadn't seen was Utah.

Someone had carefully cut under it and lifted it off,
I suppose to obliterate the identity,
Except had left it out in the open.
It looked like a latex glove but also someone's face.

She told me she had always loved me.
I was the happy ending of a fairy tale.
She would recognize my penis anywhere,
Even on the ground.

FROM *Evening Man*

IN THE MIRROR

I'm back at Claridge's, room 427,
And in the mirror find a bit of heaven.
It isn't plastic surgery that makes
Me look like you—two heartless dashing rakes!

You're me, not you—you're me but modified
To look like you and in the throes of. Why'd
I ever think that we were ocean waves?
We're stingrays winging through the warmth with raves

From every mermaid who reviews us. *Hush!*
There's someone coming! Hamlet talking lush
Escape routes to the upper world. The ray,
Whose stinger walks behind, doth kneel and pray.

Art deco Claridge's is Fred Astaire's
Lighthearted bee sting love affairs. She cares!
The stinger sticking out from Baudelaire's
Check trousers is a poem that despairs.

His pain is palpable. It can't be pain,
This gentle sound of sweetly London rain.
I wouldn't dream of plastic surgery
Unless it somehow helped the poetry.

Prince Hamlet's dressed in flowing black. The black
Is doubled over, having an attack.
The man is standing up, but bent in two
To put his contacts in. He looks at you

Because you're looking in the mirror, too.
You want to see what Baudelaire will do.
Lenticular astigmatism makes
His fangs squirt sperm and what a pair of snakes,

Blue eyes that bite through lenses tinted blue!
When I'm goose-stepping down the avenue,
My other self is with me. Here's a clue—
The one with the umbrella is the Jew.

PORTIA DEW

Freddy Dew was Portia's younger brother.
Lord Dew was just eighteen.
Last year they lost their father and their mother,
A cousin of the queen.

They had the house in Mayfair on their own,
Right out of Henry James.
A brother/sister strangeness set the tone,
Blonds wrapped in icy flames.

The English are so goddamn glamorous,
Too fucking much to bear.
The women are both cold and amorous.
One almost doesn't dare.

"Dewy" had the most amazing tits
And lots of love down there.
One-size-fits-all loved lots of boys to bits,
And coldly couldn't care.

Of course she had her ignorance to thank.
Her sort was all she knew.
Freddy's friends read Chairman Mao and drank
Champagne from her shoe.

"Bloodies" were aristocratic brutes—
Not Freddy's cut of meat!
They liked to beat up whores and beat up fruits,
And drink and barf and eat.

To Portia they were lovely penises,
Fox hunters fucking fox.
She thought of them as English Venuses,
But with outrageous cocks.

FROM *Evening Man*

A SONG FOR COLE PORTER

The tennis ball is in the air to be struck. *Thwock.*
The dove is in the air to be shot. *Bam.*
The fuzz will come off the white, off-white.
You always leave me.
Soft is whack.

It's completely a sign of age
That suddenly I have breasts.
Mine are as big as my girlfriend's.
Yes, hers are small.
I have so many girlfriends.

It's endocrinal. It's disgusting. It's de-lovely.
She always says, "You always leave me."
True, me and my breasts leave town.
I have so many girlfriends.
But one's the one.

I for years was unable to decide,
Tits or ass? And don't forget legs.
Which one do you think is the best?
My choice would vary. Who would *you* choose?
It was all too good to be true. Then came you!

Everyone's a sexual object.
Everyone is something to use.
Everyone is something good.
I'm her vibrator—but believe me,
Everyone is something unphysical also.

I'm so cool—I'm so *hot!*
I make her oink when we fuck.
Me and my breasts, we're leaving town.
We're going to Montana to throw the houlihan.
Ride around, little dogies, ride around them slow.

For everyone's a sexual object.
Everyone is something to use.
Everyone is something good.
I oink when I fuck but have feelings and wings.
Pigs can fly.

FROM *Evening Man*

"SII ROMANTICO, SEIDEL, TANTO PER CAMBIARE"

Women have a playground slide
That wraps you in monsoon and takes you for a ride.
The English girl Louise, his latest squeeze, was being snide.
Easy to deride
The way he stayed alive to stay inside
His women with his puffed-up pride.
The pharmacy supplied
The rising fire truck ladder that the fire did not provide.
The toothless carnivore devoured Viagra and Finasteride
(Which is the one that shrinks the American prostate nationwide
And at a higher dosage grows hair on the bald) to stem the tide.
Not to die had been his way to hide
The fact that he was terrified.
He could not tell them that, it would be suicide.
It would make them even *more* humidified.
The women wrapped monsoon around him, thunder-thighed.
They guide his acetone to their formaldehyde.
Now Alpha will commit Omegacide.
He made them, like a doctor looking down a throat, open wide,
Say Ah; and *Ah*, they sighed;
And out came sighing amplified
To fill a stadium with cyanide.
He filled the women with rodenticide.
He tied
Their wrists behind them, tried
Ball gags in their mouths, and was not satisfied.
The whole room when the dancing started clapped and cried.
The bomber was the bomb, and many died.
The unshod got their feet back on and ran outside.
The wedding party bled around the dying groom and bride.

BIPOLAR NOVEMBER

I get a phone call from my dog who died,
But I don't really.
I don't hear anything.
Dear Jimmy, it is hard.
Dear dog, you were just a dog.
I am returning your call.

I have nothing to say.
I have nothing to add.
I have nothing to add to that.
I am saying hello to no.
How do you do, no!
I am returning your call.

I rode a bubble to the surface just now.
I unthawed the unthawed.
I said yes. Yes, yes,
How do you do?
I called to say hello
But am happy.

Today it is spring in November.
The weather opens the windows.
The windows look pretty dirty.
I go to my computer to see.
The six-day forecast calls
For happy haze for six days.

The trees look like they're budding.
They can't be in late November.
It is mucilaginous springtime.
It is all beginning all over.
The warplanes levitate
To take another crack at Iraq.

FROM *Evening Man*

Hey, Mr. Big Shot!
I bet you went to Harvard.
Leaves are still on the trees.
The trees are wearing fine shoes.
Everything is handmade.
Everything believes.

MIAMI IN THE ARCTIC CIRCLE

And the angel of the Lord came to Mary and said:
You have cancer.
Mary could not think how.
No man had been with her.

And then there was the other time.
Remember how happy we were.
You were in my arms.
I still had arms.

The rain fell on upturned faces.
Stars rained down on the desert.
Everybody was body temperature.
Everywhere was temperate.

It was raining and global warming.
Spiritual renewal made it beautiful.
Desertification turned into desert.
The sky above was shooting stars.

The Martians rode across the desert
In their outfits and their armbands,
Clanging cymbals and banging a big drum.
Boom! Boom!

I am in favor of global warming.
I don't care about great-grandchildren.
I won't be here.
I won't be there.

Angel, I can see your mouth wide open,
But can't hear what you are singing.
The shaking roar of the liftoff
Does a vanishing act straight up.

Fiddles and viols, let me hear your old gold.
Trumpets, the petals of the antique rose unfold.
This is the end.
Testing, one, two, three, this is a test.

FROM *Evening Man*

COCONUT

A coconut can fall and hit you on the head,
And if it falls from high enough can kind of knock you dead.
Dead beneath the coconut palms, that's the life for me!
And green jungle and white beaches and the blue South China Sea.

That New York night at Café Lux when Cathy Hart was there,
I knew that I was not prepared, but how does one prepare?
When the coconut that kills you smiles and says, Please, Fred, have a seat—
And feeds you fresh coconut milk to drink and sweet coconut meat to eat.

I learned it was her birthday—which meant of course champagne!
I ordered up the best Lux had with my extinguished brain.
Do not resuscitate the zombie under the coconut tree!
It's me on my Jet Ski painting a contrail on the blue South China Sea!

Happy birthday, Doctor Hart.
You stopped my heart.
You made it start.
You supply the Hart part. I'll supply the art part.

MARRIAGE

It was summer in West Gloucester.
It was winter in West Gloucester.
The birds sang in the brambles.
Hands cut off for stealing.

Hands cut off for stealing wings and song.
New Eden 1960.
Jack Kennedy campaigning.
Every morning showered sparks of frost and freshness.

Our fifty-acre magic carpet flew
Out over the Atlantic.
The birds sang in the brambles till
The total-whiteout blizzard stopped everything but lust.

ODE TO SPRING

I can only find words for.
And sometimes I can't.
Here are these flowers that stand for.
I stand here on the sidewalk.

I can't stand it, but yes of course I understand it.
Everything has to have a meaning.
Things have to stand for something.
I can't take the time. Even skin-deep is too deep.

I say to the flower stand man:
Beautiful flowers at your flower stand, man.
I'll take a dozen of the lilies.
I'm standing as it were on my knees

Before a little man up on a raised
Runway altar where his flowers are arrayed
Along the outside of the shop.
I take my flames and pay inside.

I go off and have sexual intercourse.
The woman is the woman I love.
The room displays thirteen lilies.
I stand on the surface.

HOME

The homeless are blooming like roses
On every corner on Broadway.
I am unclean.
I bathe in their tears.

The homeless are popping like pimples.
They're a little dog's little unsheathed erection sticking out red.
It makes us passersby sing.
Ho ho. It's spring.

West Siders add fresh water
But feed the flowers with urine.
Sir, can you spare some change?
Can you look at me for a change?

Uncooked hamburger
Erupts when he lowers his trousers.
It's his song.
It's raw oozing out of a grinder.

He looks like a horrible burn from Iraq.
His wound ripples
In a hot skillet.
America doesn't look like that.

He bends down to eat garbage.
I bend down with a bag to clean up after the dog.
I take the shit out of the bag
And stuff it back up inside the dog

And sew the anus closed,
And put the dog in a two-fifty oven to scream for three hours.
The homeless are blooming like roses.
I'm hopeless.

I bathe in their screams.
I dress for the evening.
My name is Fred Seidel,
And I paid for this ad.

FROM *Evening Man*

I OWN NOTHING

I own nothing. I own a watch.
I own three watches.
I own five motorcycles.
It's all I do.

The undercarriage of the plane, whining to the down position for landing,
Locks in place, sick of sex.
My fancy life
Is plain and strange.

I always select Map
On the monitor at my seat.
It constantly displays where I am in my trip.
It refreshes the truth minute by minute.

You're over an ocean with the other people in the cabin.
You're far from your destination.
It will be hours at this altitude
Without sex.

I remember rushing out to an airport in Paris that morning on a whim,
Trying to get on any flight to divided Berlin
So I could watch the Wall coming down, which it did.
Which I did. I suppose it did some good.

I take my watch off at night but first thing in the morning slip
The platinum jail cell on my wrist like a noose and close the clasp.
Meanwhile, time is passing.
Sometimes I shave twice—

On waking as usual and then again
In the evening to be smooth,
Don't ask for whom.
My new motorcycle goes a thousand miles an hour.

The plane has touched down in the rain
In a country I don't know.
Talk about plain and strange.
I don't speak their singsong ugly language. Having arrived,

I am ready to leave already.
I love it out on the runway.
It's late at night. I love an empty airport.
They stamp my passport.

FROM *Evening Man*

I'M HERE THIS

My dog is running in his sleep.
He's yipping, his paws twitching, fast asleep.
Hey, wait a minute, he's been dead two years.
The sunlight's pouring down outside.

Salt Lake City, how exotic, here I come!
I can't believe how far it is to here.
I can't accept, Get on a plane and go,
Just pack and leave yourself behind and fly,

And take the free trolley three stops to the Mormon Temple.
It turns out there's nothing much to see.
The girl guides are darling, but watch it, they're sinister.
They're programmed to save you right there in the Visitors' Center.

Welcome to Saudi Arabia in the middle
Of snow-capped Switzerland!
No yodeling, no alcohol—and I'm forbidden even
To *think* about the inside of the Temple.

Picture a blue-eyed sky
Above a white man waiting on God.
I mean a waiter.
I mean serving a meal.

Here I am, cooked through.
Here I am, covered with snow.
The prehistoric lakebed is sunbaked in a crust of prayer, salt, lies,
Gold, silver, copper, lead, zinc.

Here we are at the Grand America Hotel
On Main Street, opposite the Little America Hotel
On Main Street. My room the size of a ballroom
Stares at the mountains.

The owner of Sinclair Oil and his wife
Designed their Taj Mahal and bought the best.
Handloomed English woolen carpets on every floor
Guarantee a blue-flash shock.

Bush and an army of Secret Service stayed here last week—
I'm here this.
I get the afternoon tea pianist to play Bach
When I get back from my motorcycle race.

It's *L'année dernière à Marienbad*, dude.
It's Mr. Sinclair Oil's idea of classy wow.
It's the Ice Age—spa for the tuxedoed dead.
Joy ahoy!

ITALY

TO JONATHAN GALASSI

My last summer on earth
I spent admiring Milan,
But they were having a heat wave.
The Japanese were everywhere.
They eat lice.
They order *risotto milanese*.
They eat everything.
My cell phone has changed my life.
I never talk to anyone.

I spent the summer in Bologna.
Bologna is my town.
Bologna is so brown.
I ate shavings
Of tuna roe on buttered toast
Despite the heat,
Brown waxy slices of fishy salt
As strong as ammonia, Bologna.
Bologna, it takes a prince to eat *bottarga*.

Italy, your women are Italian!
Your motorcycles are women.
Milan, your men are high-heeled women.
Bologna, your brown arcades
Are waterfalls of shade.
Fascist Italy was ice cream in boots.
Its *crema* straddled the world.
It licked south in the heat.
It licked its boot.

Fascisti! They take American Express!
Comunisti! You forgot to sign!
I have my table at Rodrigo in Bologna.
I always eat at Bice in Milan.
It is sweet to eat at Bibe, outside Florence,
To walk there from Bellosguardo through the fields.
Montale's little Bibe poem is printed on the menu.
I write my own.
Islam is coming.

MR. DELICIOUS

I stick my heart on a stick
To toast it over the fire.
It's the size of a marshmallow.
It bubbles and blackens to
Campfire goo—
Burnt-black skin outside
Gooey Jew.
From the twentieth century's
24/7 chimneys, choo-choo-
Train puffs of white smoke rise.
The trains waddle full of cattle to the camps.
The weightless puffs of smoke are on their way to the sky.
Ovens cremate fields of human cow.
Ovens cremate fields of human snow.
The snow turns into sleet.
The sleet turns into smoke.
Eat a heart for a treat.
It is sweet.
It tastes like meat.
I turn toward the east and bow five times.
One puff of white smoke signifies the College of Cardinals
Has found a new pontiff.
The vote flutters like a moth
Above the roofs of Rome.
Venice looks like an atoll from the air.
It rises like a ring seal from the sea.
It rises like the famous *corno ducale*,
The hydrocephalic jeweled hat the doge wore.
His swelled head is a helmet made of brocade but hard as horn.
Mr. Delicious has started his descent with tray table stowed.
Seatback restored to its original upright position.
Finally he is standing again
On one of the many bridges,
On the arched back of a footbridge filigree,
After all the years away,
After all the terrible miracles
And heart attacks of joy.
The Venetian canal water
Is hydraulic-green brake fluid

That runs through the veins
And embalms this exalted dead city.
It is incredible that they have to die.
The Nazis appear to know why.
The evidence suggests that they do.
Oh the smokestacks.
Oh the smokestacks in full view.
No one knew.
Oh the chimneys spew Jew.
Let me take a moment to talk about sex sounds.
These are the sounds Germans make when they are making love
When they are about to come.
This completes, thank you very much,
This year's
Report of the Paris Cricket Club.

MU'ALLAQA

FOR IMRU' AL-QAYS

The elephant's trunk uncurling
From the lightning flashes
In the clouds was Marie Antoinette,
As usual trumpeting.
The greedy suction
Was her tornado vacuuming across the golden Kansas flatness.

Meanwhile, the count was talking to the swan.
The swan liked what he was saying and got
Right out of the pond.
Meanwhile, grown men in Afghanistan.
The count had fought in Algeria.
Meanwhile, neon in Tokyo.

Madame la Comtesse waved to us from the top step,
Waved to her count, their swan, their ornamental pond, *et moi*.
We were a towering cornucopia
Of autumn happiness
And *gourmandise* rotating counterclockwise,
Backwards toward the guillotine.

I kept a rainbow as a pet and grandly
Walked the rainbow on a leash.
I exercised it evenings together with the cheetah,
A Thorstein Veblen moment of conspicuous consumption:
A dapper dauphin in a T-shirt that said FRED
Parading with his pets decked out in T-shirts that said FRED'S.

I left my liver in the Cher.
I ate my heart out *en Berry*.
We drank and ate
France between the wars,
And every morning couldn't wait.
It felt sunshiny in the shadow of the château.

And when the rainbow leapt from there to here,
It landed twenty years away from the Cher.
The place it landed was the Persian Gulf.
It landed twinkling stardust where I'm standing in my life
With one-hump Marie Antoinette, my wife,
Who resembles that disarming camel yesterday.

In fact, the camel yesterday was smitten.
She left the other camels to come over.
You have a lovely liquid wraparound eye.
She stood there looking at me sideways.
They feed their racing camels caviar in Qatar.
The ruler of Dubai has said that he will try to buy Versailles.

A refrigerated ski slope, five stories high,
Lives improbably inside a downtown shopping mall in Dubai.
Arab men, wearing sneakers under their robes, hold hands.
Faceless black veils stop shopping to watch through the glass.
Seeing the skiers emphasizes the desert,
Like hearing far-off thunder at a picnic.

Both the word *thunder* and the word *picnic* are of course Arabic.
Indeed, Arabic was the language of French aristocrats
Before the Terror, bad body odor perfumed.
It is the language of the great Robert Frost poems,
Which have the suicide bomber's innocence
Walking safely past the checkpoint into the crowd.

They pay payola to Al Qaeda to stay away from Doha.
The emir was in his counting-house, counting out his oil and gas.
Another sunny Sunni day in the UAE!
A candidate for president
Who wants to manumit our oil-dependent nation
First has to get the message to every oily girl and boy

To just say no to up and down and in and out, labanotation
Of moaning oil rigs extracting oil joy.
My fellow Americans, I see a desert filled with derricks
Pumping up and down but never satisfied:
Obsessional hydraulics and Jimi Hendrix has hysterics.
I smash my guitar to bits onstage and that's all, folks!

FROM *Evening Man*

It isn't.
I contemplate the end of the world. It isn't.
I have my croissant and café and the *Trib* and walk the rainbow
Around the block.
The young North African hipsters in the bitter *banlieues*
Contemplate the end of the world.

I contemplate the end of the world but in my case
It's not.
There are still things to buy.
I walk the rainbow in the dark.
The world is the kiosk where I get my *Herald Tribune*.
The world is my local café where my café au lait is quadroon.

I go to the strange little statue of Pierre Mendès-France
In the jardin du Luxembourg, in Paris, France.
I make a pilgrimage to it.
My quaint political saint and I visit.
The young North African hipsters in the bitter *banlieues*
Contemplate the end of the world, which isn't

The end of the world, though yes, quite true,
In Algeria and Afghanistan
Jihad is developing a dirty nuclear bomb
That smells like frangipani in flower
To keep Frangipani in power.
Ayatollah Frangipani has returned from his long exile in France

To annihilate vice.
I stomp the campfire out and saddle up my loyal *Mayflower*—
Who is swifter than a life is brief under the stars!
My prize four-wheel-drive with liquid wraparound eyes!
We ski the roller-coaster ocean's up and down dunes.
We reach land at last and step on Plymouth Rock.

DARKENING IN THE DARK

I woke in the middle
Of the night in Nevers, Frawnse.
Nuhvair.
I was a tornado funnel spinning across
The American Midwest in the center of France,
In the dark with my jet lag and my childhood.

I wrote in a bedside notebook, with the light on:
"The song is singing.
Meanwhile, grown men do their work.
The animals that live outdoors go on.
The rest of us won't even cross the street to vote."
With that, I turned back into fleshless smoke and slept.

No one my age can go on living for long.
No one the color of a turnip
Can be anything but
Caucasian with a problem—
With his liver or his sunblock—
Or a chameleon Caucasian darkening in the hotel room dark.

My metabolism was a lot younger in the Cher,
Near here, when I lived there.
I breathed away the lovely tons of alcohol
From the night before in the freezing morning air.
There was the crisp sweet of wood smoke from the château.
My dog and I barked frost when we laughed.

Never spend the night in Nevers,
Unless you came with the team for the race at Magny-Cours.
The hotel is unspeakable,
But the circuit is nearby. Manny Coor.
Many languages there were barking frost,
And not all of them in English.

FROM *Evening Man*

Life is a *tour dechauffe* for the living.
Life is a warm-up lap,
As if it were never too late.
Nehvur.
You rode the wheels off,
And now it is time to start.

THE DEATH OF ANTON WEBERN

I attend a concert I can ruin
In hear-a-pin-drop Zankel Hall, a Webern program I'll turn blue in
Trying not to cough. I suck on cough drops, sips of bottled water.
Webern's pinpricks sound a lot like silence, waiting for the slaughter.
These days I gasp for air. I can't control my cough.
So far no friend of mine has died. So far. Whoever's first will start us off.

The cough is like a barking guard dog, lunging on a chain, frantic to attack.
I'm coughing hard enough to break my back.
I lived for thirty years on Kools, unfiltered Camels, and Gauloises.
I'm coughing on a tightrope high above the *oohs* and *ahs*.
For thirty years a prince inhaled the razor arrows in his quiver,
And then he felt her arms around him and her hot breath made him shiver.

You smoke your face off for three decades and it nearly guarantees
Non-small cell lung Ca with some emphysema, please.
I'm crazy about big breasts—real or fake—the opposite of pinpricks.
My subject has always been death and breasts and politics.
An American G.I. shot Webern dead in Allied-occupied Austria just after the war.
Poor Webern had stepped outside at night to smoke a cigar.

I hear the pin drop. It is a miracle that one can hear at all.
It's almost comical the way the subway rumbles under Zankel Hall.
The N and the R throb through the pinpricked silence everyone hears.
The riders on the trains are presumably in tears.
The children on the trains hear the Webern and start sobbing.
The women on the trains passing under us are throbbing.

The pin drops. The Lord be with you. I hear it.
The man who killed him starts to drink too much. And with thy spirit.
The war is over and there's no more war.
His son-in-law has given him a fine cigar.
He's going to step outside for nicotine and tar.
The door's ajar.

WEIRDLY WARM DAY IN JANUARY

I'm waiting in my urine specimen in the cup provided.
The busyness of dizziness sweep-second-hands the waiting room.
Every time I see God it's the same shock of sight.
The same violin of feeling.

Such a shock to see that God the Father is a goddess.
She stands unstained inside a long white coat.
I'm waiting in the abattoir.
I'm waiting for spring to come.

It walks in off the street. Spring, please have a seat.
The doctor will be with you shortly.
The music starts to play
The violin I'm playing.

I want to feel your breasts, Lord.
I want to start the stem cells.
The White House is prepared
To fly me Mach 3 to an undisclosed secure location.

PAIN MANAGEMENT

I'm a liar with a lyre. Kiss me, life!
Even if I vomit
When you try to bring me back with mouth-to-mouth.
Even if the mouth-to-mouth
Vomits in my mouth, it's life!
A fellow in the elevator
Jokes about global warming and it being 84°
Outside. *But what did you expect? It's late October!*
The corpses put out leaves.
Leaves don't leave the trees. New Guinea in New York.

The Caribbean nannies in the park are savage sausages
On cell phones.
Boudins noirs. Blood inside a casing. Caretakers.
The children stand around in little cages, waiting whitely.
The Caribbean nurses at the hospital are expressionless bone
Nose rings behind the white Formica counter
When bed 229B calls the Nurses Station a second time, a third time.
It is too early to give the poor woman more morphine.
The masks hide the heart
Inside each human being's head. A liar with a lyre.

The nurses in the park ignore the ruin they've got slumped
Next to them on the bench—and talk on their nonstop tom-toms,
On their cell phones that are jungle drums.
The old on their walkers inch forward inside their cages
With their nurses. The nurses at the hospital are expressionless
Behind the Formica in 5 Central when 229B
Howls this time, but really howls.
She will get something
When the pain management guy
Rounds with his team.

And the dog walker doesn't walk the dogs.
He sits on the curb not doing the job.
His innocence flotilla on leashes surrounds him
Like a parachute on the ground

FROM *Evening Man*

After a landing, panting.
The pure of heart stare at Adolf Hitler with their honest eyes.
Poor United States of America.
The nurses stand outside the hospital on their break
Where they can smoke.
These ones are mostly white, wearing green.

There's something about the sight of nurses lighting up.
Do nurses think nurses are protected?
They inhale the horn of the charging rhino.
I also do impersonations
Of righteous persons.
My righteous fall like rain,
And grow like grass.
I impersonate myself. I'm a liar with a lyre.
Sto mentendo.
(I'm lying.)

A man still wearing his solar topee
Is being boiled alive in a jungle pot.
Needless to say, the man is white.
With one chop, the Aztec priest splits open the Spanish captive's chest
And, reaching inside, yanks out the still-beating heart,
Which he sets on an alabaster plate, and which God starts to eat,
Who, needless to say, is wearing a solar topee.
Needless to say, needless to say,
Never mind what I'm saying,
I'm lying.

It's my physical therapist friend at the other end of the telephone trying.
To tell me something crying.
Her husband is back in the hospital, not dying.
But with his whole left side suddenly paralyzed.
The doctors at New York-Presbyterian don't know why.
It is exactly as if he'd had a stroke—though he is young.
But his speech and cognition are unimpaired.
But he can't even use a bedpan or sit up in bed.
Art throws the dog a bone.
I am ashamed of my poem.

DO YOU DOHA?

A river of milk flows gently down the Howard Street gutter
Because it's a fine warm day in Sag Harbor
And someone upstream is washing a car.
I picture a Texan—Christian name Lamar—
Who snips off the end of a Cuban cigar
And lovingly lights up in Doha, Qatar,
Which young oilmen like him pronounce Doha, *Cutter*.
It's the Salt Flats of Utah in the Persian Gulf, but utter.
The emir is richer than melted butter.
Bumps and bubbles of white snot in the bone marrow look like an ice flow of hot,
The way the universe was just before it expanded a lot.
You never know what disease you'll get, or you've already got.
It's your asteroid coming to get you, only for now it's smaller than a dot.
I'm an aging boy. I never grew up. I'm glued to the spot.

Adam in Eden is summertime Gloucestershire,
But riding to hounds in winter is really the glory here.
If it's strictly speaking illegal these days to chase a fox, they do not care.
If life is a matter of daring to do, they dare.
Lamar flies like the wind on the one he likes, the fiery mare.
She jumps a fence.
She doesn't care if it makes sense.
She leaps a ditch behind the pack.
Her thundering insolent brilliance will only attack.
I am thinking of your bad back and the stunning diagnosis.
I google *multiple myeloma*. I brace for the prognosis.
Yesterday you found out.
The sun rose today and the birds in the trees woke with a shout.
The Sag Harbor Tree Fund will plant many more memorial trees, no doubt.

I wouldn't recommend Stage III multiple myeloma.
The patient ends up screaming or in a coma.
Yes, the remissions can be quite exciting.
The question is, who is doing the accepting and who is doing the inviting.
Irrepressible plasma cells chitter-chatter away on their cell phones
While malignantly breaking your bones.
I personally would rather have non-small cell lung Ca.
Isn't that a wonderful name, itself a medical-language holiday?
Here's a pun—*It took my breath away!* Lung cancer? Breath away?

FROM *Evening Man*

Outside, I can see through the window it is actually a nice day.
In the American manner, a visitor leaving the Visitors elevator says, Have a nice day!
I think of the Stradivarius fiddle I held this morning that made me want to pray.
I used to play.
That's what I'm trying to say.

Act your age!
I don't have to. I won't. You can't make me. I'm in an absolute rage.
I walk on stage.
The other *ELVES* are Gentry Shelton,
Raymond Sunderman, Harry Monteith, Harry Mathews, Alex Netchvolodoff,
James Hearne, Monroe Roberts III,
Paul Chandeysson, John Neiger III.
BEARS are Henry Pflager, Neil Horner, John Curtis, John Sutter, John Lewis,
Jan Bosman, Norfleet Johnston, George von Schrader.
BUNNIES: Teddy Simmons, Billy Crowell, Walter Shipley.
BLUEBIRDS: Nat Green, Joe Larimore.
ROBINS: Hord Hardin, August Busch III, Ralph Sansbury.
DANDELIONS, VIOLETS, ROSES: Little girls in various poses.
Titless teases and their diseases.

Boys and girls in Pakistan,
Iraq, Iran, Afghanistan,
Are sweeter far than marzipan,
And that includes the Taliban.
Sunni and Shia fulfill God's plan.
Afghanistan, Iraq,
Children on timers go tock-tick, tick-tock.
A boy is instructed by his parents, who are not peasants.
They pray with the child and give him compliments and presents.
Their son is sweeter to them than honey.
The parents receive martyr money.
We are ten thousand miles from my childhood in St. Louis.
St. Louis didn't do this.
St. Louis never knew this.

I know it was you who vomited on the chintz, Seidel.
You will never be invited to this house again, and just as well.
My wife and myself wish you well.
It will not end well.
She will follow you to hell.

The butler has gone to answer the front doorbell.
We are gentlemen here. No one here is a Jew or a queer.
I value sincerity. I know you are sincere.
Warren Beatty told Mary Kirby he liked candor.
Mary Kirby told Warren Beatty she gave good candor.
I remember dirt roads for the horsemen and the maroon perfume of summer roses.
Little girls grown up, and little boys, in various poses,
My music shows ye have your closes,
And all must die.

La Cina è vicina. China is near.
The butler returns to say the hearse is here. The ushers for the groom appear.
I give a toast, so brief that I sit down before anyone knows
I've given it, to no applause. God knows
It's odd to cry, with no one listening, my seagull cry.
Children wonder why one has to die.
It doesn't mean gulls are really crying when they cry in the sky.
Lamar can try to live forever. It's a poem. Why not try?
I flip a switch. The flowers wake with a shout. The trees immediately turn green.
Night dives like a submarine
As day breaks through the surface with its conning tower and power to preen.
On all sides of Sag Harbor Village is water—my little darling Doha in the desert!
Do you Doha? Do you knowa how to Doha?
La Cina è vicina. It is time to say Aloha.

SUNLIGHT

There is always hope except when there isn't—it is everywhere.
The pigeons above Broadway fly left to right in their underwear.
They skydive down to the sidewalk to sup.
They land like paratroopers, standing up,
Hauling in their parachutes of light.
I look down on the trees from my superior height.

I look down at the snapshot of a friend and I think,
This man will be dead pretty soon, and I think,
How weird that I'm thinking that.
My mood has made the photograph's brain waves flat.
I don't really mean that the way it sounds.
I don't really think he ought to die because he's put on a few pounds.

If you consent to life, as I do, condescendingly,
It seems you get to fuck unendingly.
The woman in my bed plays Mozart heartrendingly.
I drank too much last night—as usual—mind-bendingly.
The body on the bed is all eyes as I prepare to mount it.
There's the body's usual hopefulness. The thing is to surmount it.

I'm standing at the window, after, looking out and looking back,
Looking past my floaters, my swimming specks of black.
I'm shitting on the ledge outside, moaning in my awful way.
I rap on the window to make myself fly away.
The body on the bed gets up, smiling at the gorgeous day.
The winter sunlight sparkles diamonds down on Broadway.

IN A PREVIOUS LIFE

The smell of rain about to fall,
A sudden coolness in the air,
Sweetness wider than the Mississippi at its muddy brownest.
I didn't steal his pencil, Mrs. Marshall, honest!
It's CAPTAIN MIDNIGHT . . . brought to you by OVALTINE!
I travel backwards in a time machine
And step inside a boy who's four feet tall.
How dare he have such curly hair!
Now that's a happy dog as boy and dog go rafting down the river!
They have a message to deliver
To the gold-toothed king.
Sire, we have a message that we bring.
Little boy, approach the throne.
Ow! I hit my funny bone.

The thing to do at night in the heat was drive to Peveley Dairy
And park and watch the fountain changing colors.
The child sat in the back, slurping the last drops of an ice cream soda,
Sucking the straw in the empty glass as the noisy coda.
Sometimes on Sunday they drove to the Green Parrot.
There was the sideways-staring parrot to stare at.
The chickens running around were delicious fried, but nothing was sanitary.
BO was the scourge of the age—and polio—and bathroom odors.
If you forgot to wash your hands,
It contributed—as did your glands.
His father always had gas for their cars from his royal rationing cards.
The little boy went to see the king at one of the king's coal yards.
The two of them took a train trip to tour the dad's wartime coal mine.
It was fun. It was fine.

The sweetness of the freshness of the breeze!
The wind is wiggling the trees.
The sky is black. The limousine trees deep green.
The man mowing the enormous lawn before it rains makes goodness clean.
It's the smell of laundry on the line

FROM *Evening Man*

And the smell of the sea, brisk iodine.
Nine hundred miles inland from the ocean, it's that smell.
It makes someone little who has a fever feel almost well.
It's exactly what a sick person needs to eat.
Maybe it's coming from Illinois in the heat.
Watch out for the crows, though.
With them around, caw, caw, it's going to snow.
I think I'm still asleep. I hope I said my prayers before I died.
I hear the milkman setting the clinking bottles down outside.

EVENING MAN

The man in bed with me this morning is myself, is me,
The sort of same-sex marriage New York State allows.
Both men believe in infidelity.
Both wish they could annul their marriage vows.

This afternoon I will become the Evening Man,
Who does the things most people only dream about.
He swims around his women like a swan, and spreads his fan.
You can't drink that much port and not have gout.

In point of fact, it is arthritis.
His drinking elbow aches, and he admits to this.
To be a candidate for higher office,
You have to practice drastic openness.

You have to practice looking like thin air
When you become the way you do not want to be,
An ancient head of ungrayed dark brown hair
That looks like dyed fur on a wrinkled monkey.

Of course, the real vacation we will take is where we're always headed.
Presidents have Air Force One to fly them there.
I run for office just to get my dark brown hair beheaded.
I wake up on a slab, beheaded, in a White House somewhere.

Evening Man sits signing bills in the Oval Office headless—
Every poem I write starts or ends like this.
His hands have been chopped off. He signs bills with the mess.
The country is in good hands. It ends like this.

FROM *Evening Man*

MY POETRY

I sat in my usual place with my back to the corner, at the precious corner table,
Where everyone wanted to sit, to see and be seen.
Even the celebretariat were not automatically able
To sit at that particular table, never mind how desperately keen.
I sat in my solitude, a songbird that can't be bought.
Look at my solitude, white meat deep in thought.

This was the look of fat dressed slenderly by Savile Row,
My tailor in those days being Huntsman, in those days long ago.
But can Mr. Rilke be alone if there are always servants in the castle? Not really. No.
In a minute, I would be visited by the restaurant owner, the superb madman Elio,
Who'd been a Marxist once: "Shit, at the five other front tables tonight sit
A billion dollars! And then there's you. I just noticed it."

I sit at my regular table in a restaurant I favor,
Napkin tucked into my collar, eating dirt and a stone,
Stooped over in a La Tache stupor. I know it's disgusting but I savor
My African-American antipode with her hand out outside the window, my clone,
Begging just outside on the sidewalk. I'll buy her and take her home. We'll eat dirt.
We'll grovel in the grass and bat our eyes and flirt.

Look at this poem, a set of dingy teeth hailing a cab.
Look at this poem, kissing the hand of that woman's brown frown.
I'm always ready to use my mouth, though my teeth may be drab.
Lord Above—starless sky above the high-rise—here I am, look down.
But first open your eyes. The cruel overseer is brutally whipping a slave
While the slave yawns over an after-dinner poire. Don't behave. Be brave.

POEM BY THE BRIDGE AT TEN-SHIN

This jungle poem is going to be my last.
This space walk is.
Racing in a cab through springtime Central Park,
I kept my nose outside the window like a dog.
The stars above my bed at night are vast.
I think it is uncool to call young women Ms.
My darling is a platform I see stars from in the dark,
And all the dogs begin to bark.
My grunting gun brings down her charging warthog,
And she is frying on white water, clinging to a log,
And all the foam and fevers shiver.
And drink has made chopped liver of my liver!
Between my legs it's Baudelaire.
He wrote about her Central Park of hair.

I look for the *minuterie* as if I were in France,
In darkness, in the downstairs entrance, looking for the light.
I'm on a timer that will give me time
To see the way and up the stairs before the lights go out.
The so delicious Busby Berkeley dancers dance
A movie musical extravaganza on the staircase with me every night.
Such fun! We dance. We climb. We slip in slime.
We're squirting squeezes like a wedge of lime!
It's like a shout.
It's what *minuterie* is all about.
Just getting to the landing through the dark
That has been interrupted for a minute is a lark.
And she's so happy. It is grand!
I put my mobile in her ampersand.

The fireworks are a fleeting puff of sadness.
The flowers when they reach the stars are tears.
I don't remember poems I write.
I turn around and they are gone.
I do remember poor King Richard Nixon's madness.
Pierre Leval, we loved those years!
We knocked back shots of single malt all night.
Beer chasers gave *dos caballeros* double vision, second sight—

Twin putti pissing out the hotel window on the Scottish dawn.
A crocodile has fallen for a fawn.
I live flap copy for a children's book.
He wants to lick. He wants to look.
A tiny goldfinch is his Cupid.
Love of cuntry makes men stupid.

It makes men miss Saddam Hussein!
Democracy in Baghdad makes men think
Monstrosity was not so bad.
I followed Gandhi barefoot to
Remind me there is something else till it began to rain.
The hurricane undressing of democracy in Baghdad starts to sink
The shrunken page size of *The New York Times*, and yet we had
A newspaper that mattered once, and that is sad,
But that was when it mattered. Do
I matter? That is true.
I don't matter but I do. I lust for fame,
And after never finding it I never was the same.
I roared into the heavens and I soared,
And landed where I started on a flexing diving board.

I knew a beauty named Dawn Green.
I used to wake at the crack of Dawn.
I wish I were about to land on Plymouth Rock,
And had a chance to do it all again but do it right.
It was green dawn in pre-America. I mean
Great scented forests all along the shore, which now are gone.
I've had advantages in life and I pronounce Iraq "Irrock."
The right schools taught me how to tock.
I'm tocking Turkey to the Kurds but with no end in sight.
These peace tocks are my last. Goodbye, Iran. Iran, good night.
They burned the undergrowth so they could see the game they hunt.
That made the forest a cathedral clear as crystal like a cunt.
Their arrows entered red meat in the glory
Streaming down from the clerestory.

Carine Rueff, I was obsessed—I was *possessed!* I liked your name.
I liked the fact Marie Christine Carine Rue F was Jewish.
It emphasized your elegance in Paris and in Florence.
You were so blond in rue de l'Université!

The dazzling daughter of de Gaulle's adviser Jacques Rueff was game
For anything. I'm lolling here in Mayfair under bluish
Clouds above a bench in Mount Street Gardens, thinking torrents.
Purdey used to make a gun for shooting elephants.
One cannot be the way one was back then today.
It went away.
I go from Claridge's to Brands Hatch racing circuit and come back
To Claridge's, and out and eat and drink and bed, and fade to black.
The elephants were old enough to die but were aghast.
The stars above this jungle poem are vast.

To Ninety-second Street and Broadway I have come.
Outside the windows is New York.
I came here from St. Louis in a covered wagon overland
Behind the matchless prancing pair of Eliot and Ezra Pound.
And countless moist oases took me in along the way, and some
I still remember when I lift my knife and fork.
The Earth keeps turning, night and day, spit-roasting all the tanned
Tired icebergs and the polar bears, which makes white almost contraband.
The biosphere on a rotisserie emits a certain sound
That tells the stars that Earth was moaning pleasure while it drowned.
The amorous white icebergs flash their brown teeth, hissing.
They're watching old porn videos of melting icebergs pissing.
The icebergs still in panty hose are lesbians and kissing.
The rotting ocean swallows the bombed airliner that's missing.

OOGA-BOOGA (2006)

KILL POEM

Huntsman indeed is gone from Savile Row,
And Mr. Hall, the head cutter.
The red hunt coat Hall cut for me was utter
Red melton cloth thick as a carpet, cut just so.
One time I wore it riding my red Ducati racer—what a show!—
Matched exotics like a pair of lovely red egrets.
London once seemed the epitome of no regrets
And the old excellence one used to know
Of the chased-down fox bleeding its stink across the snow.

We follow blindly, clad in coats of pink,
A beast whose nature is to run and stink.
I am civilized in my pink but
Civilized is about having stuff.
The red coats are called "pinks." Too much is almost enough.
No one knows why they are. I parade in the air
With my stuff and watch the disappearing scut
Of a deer. I am civilized but
Civilized life is actually about too much.

I parade in the air
And wait for the New Year
That then will, then will disappear.
I am trying not to care.
I am not able not to.
A short erect tail
Winks across the winter field.
All will be revealed.
I am in a winter field.

They really are everywhere.
They crawl around in one's intimate hair.
They spread disease and despair.
They rape and pillage
In the middle of Sag Harbor Village.
They ferry Lyme disease.
The hunters' guns bring them to their knees.
In Paris I used to call the Sri Lankan servants "Shrees."
I am not able not to.

Winter, spring, Baghdad, fall,
Venery is written all
Over me like a rash,
Hair and the gash,
But also the Lehrer *NewsHour* and a wood fire and Bach.
A short erect tail
Winks across the killing field.
All will be revealed.
I am in a killing field.

I remember the *chasse à courre* in the forest in the Cher.
I remember the English thoroughbreds ridden by the frogs.
I remember the weeping stag cornered by the dogs.
The stag at bay in the pond literally shed a tear.
A hunt servant in a tricorn hat waded out to cut its throat.
Nelson Aldrich on his horse vomited watching this.
The huntsman's heraldic horn sounded the *hallali*.
The tune that cuts off the head. *L'hallali!*
Back to the château to drink the blood. *L'hallali!*

I am in Paris being introduced at Billy's,
1960, avenue Paul-Valéry.
One of her beautiful imported English Lillys or Millys
Is walking around on her knees.
It is rather like that line of Paul Valéry's.
Now get down on all fours, please.
We are ministers of state and then there is me chez Billy.
Deer garter-belt across our field of vision
And stand there waiting for our decision.

Our only decision was how to cook the venison.
I am civilized but
I see the silence
And write the words for the thought balloon.
When the woods are the color of a macaroon,
Deer, death is near.
I write about its looks in my books.
I write disappearing scut.
I write rut.

The title is *Kill Poetry*,
And in the book poetry kills.
In the poem the stag at bay weeps, literally.
Kill poetry is the *hallali* on avenue Paul-Valéry.
Get rid of poetry. Kill poetry.
Label on a vial of pills. Warning: Kill kill kill kills.
Its title is *Kill Poem*,
From the *Book of Kills*.
The antlered heads are mounted weeping all around the walls.

John F. Kennedy is mounted weeping on the wall.
His weeping brother Robert weeps nearby.
Martin Luther King, at bay in Memphis, exhausted, starts to cry.
His antlered head is mounted weeping on the wall.
Too much is almost enough, for crying out loud!
Bobby Kennedy announces to a nighttime crowd
That King has died, and then quotes Aeschylus, and then is killed.
Kill kill kill kills, appalls,
The American trophies covered in tears that deck the American halls.

FROM NIJINSKY'S DIARY

And when the doctor told me that I could have died.
And when I climbed up from the subway to the day outside.
White summer clouds were boiling in the trees.
I felt like falling to my knees.
Stand clear of the closing doors, please! Stand clear of the closing doors, please!

And when the camel knelt to let me mount it.
Winged angels knelt in silhouette
To worship at the altar made of blue
That the sun was fastened to.
It all came down to you. It all comes down to you.

In New York City "kneeling" buses kneel for the disabled.
My camel kneels. We fly into the desert.
I flee in terror to my tranquilizer the Sahara.
I stroll slowly down sweet Broadway.
It is as you say. We are here to pray.

VIOLIN

I often go to bed with a book
And immediately turn out the light.
I wake in the morning and brush and dress and go to the desk and write.
I always put my arm in the right sleeve before I slip into the left.
I always put on my left shoe first and then I put on the right.

I happen right now
To be walking the dogs in the dangerous park at night,
Which is dangerous, which I do not like,
But I am delighted, my dog walk is a delight.
I am right-handed but mostly I am not thinking.

(CHORUS)
A man can go to sleep one night and never wake up that he knows of.
A man can walk down a Baghdad street and never walk another drop.
A man can be at his publisher's and drop dead on the way to the men's room.
A poet can develop frontotemporal dementia.
A flavorful man can, and then he is not.

The call girls who came to our separate rooms were actually lovely.
Weren't they shocked that their customers were so illegally young?
Mine gently asked me what I wanted to do. Sin is Behovely.
Just then the phone rang—
Her friend checking if she was safe with the young Rambo, Rimbaud.

I am pursuing you, life, to the ends of the earth across a Sahara of tablecloth.
I look around the restaurant for breath.
I stuff my ears to sail past the siren song of the rocks.
The violin of your eyes
Is listening gently.

NECTAR

A rapist's kisses tear the leaves off.
Aiuto!
The world looks so white on the white pillow.
I think I know you. I don't think so.

Winter is wearing summer but it wants to undress for you, Fred.
Oh my God. Takes off the lovely summer frock
And lies down on the bed naked
Freezing white, so we can make death.

Joel and I were having lunch at Fred's,
The restaurant on the ninth floor of Barneys
Where Joel likes to eat when he is in New York,
Who had just landed, and when I ask him what astonishment

He is carrying around with him this time,
He takes out of his jacket pocket
A beige *pochette*,
And out pops a stupefying diamond ring I know from Paris.

It opens its big eye.
It went nonstop to Florida in his pocket on the plane.
Now returns with a stop in Manhattan to the JAR safe, place Vendôme.
I have to try it on.

It is incredible what travels
Unprotected in that pocket through the time zones.
I look down at my finger
And field-trip an alternate universe.

Don't I know you? I don't think so. It is not for sale.
Diane von Furstenberg in those sweet bygone days
Got it in her head I had to meet her friend
The jeweler to the stars.

Two hummingbirds hummed across the pont des Arts,
And through the cour du Louvre, to Joel's JAR.
At her old apartment at 12, rue de Seine,
We lived like hummingbirds on nectar and oxygen.

FROM *Ooga-Booga*

ON BEING DEBONAIR

Shirts wear themselves out being worn.
Suits fit perfectly,
But a man does
Decades of push-ups and no longer fits.
I take myself out to dinner.
It is a joy to sit alone
Without a book.
I use myself up being fine while I dine.
I am a result of the concierge at the Carlyle.
I order a bottle of Bordeaux.
I am a boulevard of elegance
In my well-known restaurants.

The moon comes over to my table.
Everything about her is typical.
I like the way she speaks to me.
Everything about me is bespoke.
You are not
Known, and you are not no one.
I remember you from before.
Sometimes I don't go out till the end of the day.
I simply forget till
I rush out, afraid the day will end.
Every sidewalk tree is desperate
For someone.

The desert at this time of year
Is troops in desert camouflage.
Bring in the unmanned drones.
I dine with my Carlyle smile.
She tells me spring will come.
The moon stops by my table
To tell me.
I will cut your heart out
And drink the rubies and eat the coral.
I like the female for its coral.
I go to Carnegie Hall
To make her open her mouth onstage and scream.

HOMAGE TO PESSOA

I once loved,
I thought I would be loved,
But I wasn't loved.
I wasn't loved for the only reason that matters—
It was not to be.
I unbuttoned my white gloves and stripped each off.
I set aside my gold-knobbed cane.
I picked up this pen . . .
And thought how many other men
Had smelled the rose in the bud vase
And lifted a fountain pen,
And lifted a mountain . . .
And put the shotgun in their mouth,
And noticed that their hunting dog was pointing.

FROM *Ooga-Booga*

FOR HOLLY ANDERSEN

What could be more pleasant than talking about people dying,
And doctors really trying,
On a winter afternoon
At the Carlyle Hotel, in our cocoon?
We also will be dying one day soon.

Dr. Holly Andersen has a vodka cosmopolitan,
And has another, and becomes positively Neapolitan,
The moon warbling a song about the sun,
Sitting on a sofa at the Carlyle,
Staying stylishly alive for a while.

Her spirited loveliness
Does cause some distress.
She makes my urbanity undress.
I present symptoms that express
An underlying happiness in the face of the beautiful emptiness.

She lost a very sick patient she especially cared about.
The man died on the table. It wasn't a matter of feeling any guilt or doubt.
Something about a doctor who can cure, or anyway try,
But can also cry,
Is some sort of ultimate lullaby, and lie.

FOG

I spend most of my time not dying.
That's what living is for.
I climb on a motorcycle.
I climb on a cloud and rain.
I climb on a woman I love.
I repeat my themes.

Here I am in Bologna again.
Here I go again.
Here I go again, getting happier and happier.
I climb on a log
Torpedoing toward the falls.
Basically, it sticks out of me.

At the factory,
The racer being made for me
Is not ready, but is getting deadly.
I am here to see it being born.
It is snowing in Milan, the TV says.
They close one airport, then both.

The Lord is my shepherd and the Director of Superbike Racing.
He buzzes me through three layers of security
To the innermost secret sanctum of the racing department
Where I will breathe my last.
Trains are delayed.
The Florence sky is falling snow.

Tonight Bologna is fog.
This afternoon, there it was,
With all the mechanics who are making it around it.
It stood on a sort of altar.
I stood in a sort of fog,
Taking digital photographs of my death.

FROM *Ooga-Booga*

A RED FLOWER

The poet stands on blue-veined legs, waiting for his birthday to be over.
He dangles from a muse who works the wires
That make a puppet move in lifelike ways onstage.
Happy birthday to a *semper paratus* penis!
His tiny Cartier wristwatch trumpets it!
He dares to wear a tiny thing that French and feminine.
Nose tilted up, arrogance, blue eyes.
He can smell the ocean this far inland.

We are in France. We are in Italy. We are in England. We are in heaven.
Lightning with a noose around its neck, feet on a cloud,
Drops into space, feet kicking, neck broken.
The parachute pops open . . . a red flower:
Plus ne suis ce que j'ai été,
Et plus ne saurais jamais l'être.
Mon beau printemps et mon été
Ont fait le saut par la fenêtre.

DICK AND FRED

His dick is ticking . . .
Tick tick tick tick . . .
The bomb looks for blonde.
It smiles like a dog.

Werner Muensterberger liked to say to his patients
A stiff prick has no conscience . . .
Tick tick tick tick . . .
Fred Astaire in a tuxedo is doing a blind man with a white cane.

He is looking for blonde.
He looks for brunette.
He licks to play golf.
A bomb is blind.

There was a king.
His name was King Wow.
Anyhow,
In the kingdom of Ebola,

It was on his mind
Constantly. Be kind,
King, be a kind king.
The oceans rose.

About the queen his mother, Gertrude.
Shit with a cunt!
The prince was blunt.
Shit with a cunt.

Cunt with a dick!
Judith slew Holofernes.
Cut his head off.
Slew slime.

Cunt with a dick
Cut the monster's head off.
Holofernes' startled head farts blood
And falls off.

FROM *Ooga-Booga*

Man delights not me; no, nor woman neither.
Viagra has caused blindness
In thirty-eight impotent men
Who paid for their erections with their eyes.

One man in his eighties took the pill
For the first time and went blind
When his penis started to rise
For the first time in years.

Imagine his double surprise!
The joyous, fastidious, perfectionist
Fred Astaire flies!
Astaire,

Debonair,
Tap-dances the monomania and mania
Of Napoleon Bonaparte's tiny penis, the up.
Fred flies, fappingly, bappingly,

Tick-tick-tick-tick-tappingly,
That athletic nonchalance that Fred Astaire defined.
A penis in a tuxedo is flying all over the place
With the white cane of the blind!

Fred is dancing on a tilting dance floor on the ocean floor
In a sunken ocean liner
In 1934—lighter than air!—Fred Astaire!—
In the depths of the Great Depression.

White people froze the world markets to a great whiteness.
The world will end tomorrow.
They walk around like penguins in their tuxedos.
The planet is frozen.

NEW YEAR'S DAY, 2004

It used to be called the Mayfair.
Leonardo Mondadori used to stay there.
The lobby was the bar.
Fancy Italians were on display.
They sat in the lobby for years.
They seduced from the lavish armchairs.
They told their driver and car to be waiting outside
On their European cell phones.

I was a Traveller then upon the moor.
I walked directly through and down the three stairs.
Their women were theirs.
The Milanese women wore couture.
They smoked cigarettes and smiled and did not blink.
They were going to eat at Le Cirque.
Who could have been kinder than Leonardo?
It was a long time ago.

FROM *Ooga-Booga*

THE ITALIAN GIRL

Monsoon is over but it's raining.
The rain keeps coming down. It gets you down. It's draining.
The sticky heat in Singapore is really not that entertaining.
The boutique hotel air-conditioning is aquaplaning.
The rain stops just inside the door and the fashion show goes on.

So they board the little tram at the zoo to do the "Night Safari"
To experience wild animals who are separate but equal.
The Chinese tour guide puts her finger to her lips: "Let us be quiet."
They hear the silence roar
In humid Singapore.

Nobody has hair like this Italian girl, in this humidity!
She came three days ago to do the fashion show.
She hadn't cut her mane in weeks.
She loves the hippos bathing in the perspiring water.
Her curls are African lions exploding from a thicket.

THE BIG GOLCONDA DIAMOND

The Master Jeweler Joel Rosenthal, of the Bronx and Harvard,
Is Joel Arthur Rosenthal of JAR, place Vendôme.
The greatest jeweler of our time
Has brought to Florida from his safe
A big Golconda diamond that is matchless,
So purely truthful it is not for sale, Joel's favorite, his Cordelia.
His mother in Florida can keep it
If she wants, and she doesn't want.
Love is mounted on a fragile platinum wire
To make a ring not really suitable for daily wear.

I wore the bonfire on a wire, on loan from Joel,
One sparkling morning long ago in Paris.
I followed it on my hand across the pont des Arts
Like Shakespeare in a trance starting the sonnet sequence.

FROM *Ooga-Booga*

WHAT ARE MOVIES FOR?

Razzle-dazzle on the surface, wobbled–Jell-O sunlight,
A goddess and her buttocks walk across a bridge,
Electrocute the dazed, people can't believe it's her.
The Seine sends waves toward Notre Dame.
She's here without an entourage, she stands there all alone.
A woman standing at the rail is jumping in broad daylight
From the pont des Arts, and thinks of jumping.
Her flames almost reach the Institut de France.
It bursts into flame.
A tenement suddenly collapsing vomits fireworks.
A soda jerk pulls the lever
That squirts the soda
That makes an old-time ice cream soda of flames.
A Pullman porter turns down the stateroom bed, white crisp sheets,
Clean as ice,
The clickety-click American night outside,
A Thousand and One Nights inside the star's head.
Miles of antebellum slums, old St. Louis hot at night,
Rows of antebellum houses of white trash in the Southern moonlight:
Developers took advantage of Title 1 funds to pulverize
The picturesque so they could put up miles of projects,
The largest undertaking of its kind in the United States,
So poorly constructed that a few years later
The whole hideous thing would have to be leveled.
I feel such joy.
I stare at sparkles. I don't care.
The carbonated bubbled bloodstream gushes out.
Kiss me here. *Ouf!* Kiss me there.
The crocodile of joy lifts the nostrils of his snout.
His eyes of joy stare at her eyes.
I want to eat between your eyes and hear your cries.
I don't care who lives or dies.
I am the crocodile of joy, who never lies.

THE OWL YOU HEARD

The owl you heard hooting
In the middle of the night wasn't me.
It was an owl.
Or maybe you were
So asleep you didn't even hear it.
The sprinklers on their timer, programmed to come on
At such a strangely late hour in life
For watering a garden,
Refreshed your sleep four thousand miles away by
Hissing sweetly,
Deepening the smell of green in Eden.
You heard the summer chirr of insects.
You heard a sky of stars.
You didn't know it, fast asleep at dawn in Paris.
You didn't hear a thing.
You heard me calling.
I am no longer human.

FROM *Ooga-Booga*

E-MAIL FROM AN OWL

The irrigation system wants it to be known it *irrigates*
The garden,
It doesn't water it.
It is a stickler about this!
Watering is something done by hand.
Automated catering naturally
Does a better job than a hand with a watering can can.
Devised in Israel to irrigate their orange groves,
It gives life everywhere in the desert of life it goes.
It drips water to the chosen, one zone at a time.
Drip us this day our daily bread, or, rather, this night,
Since a drop on a leaf in direct sunlight can make
A magnifying glass that burns an innocent at the stake.
The sprinkler system hisses kisses on a timer
Under an exophthalmic sky of stars.
Tonight my voice will stare at you forever.
I click on Send,
And send you this perfumed magic hour.

WHITE BUTTERFLIES

I

Clematis paniculata sweetens one side of Howard Street.
White butterflies in pairs flutter over the white flowers.
In white kimonos, giggling and whispering,
The butterflies titter and flutter their silk fans,
End-of-summer cabbage butterflies, in white pairs.
Sweet autumn clematis feeds these delicate souls perfume.
I remember how we met, how shyly.

II

Four months of drought on the East End ends.
Ten thousand windshield wipers wiping the tears away.
The back roads are black.
The ocean runs around barking under the delicious rain, so happy.
Traditional household cleaners polish the imperial palace floors
Of heaven spotless. THUNDER. Cleanliness and order
Bring universal freshness and good sense to the Empire. LIGHTNING.

III

I have never had a serious thought in my life on Gibson Lane.
A man turning into cremains is standing on the beach.
I used to walk my dog along the beach.
This afternoon I had to put him down.
Jimmy my boy, my sweetyboy, my Jimmy.
It is night, and outside the house, at eleven o'clock,
The lawn sprinklers come on in the rain.

FROM *Ooga-Booga*

THE CASTLE IN THE MOUNTAINS

I brought a stomach flu with me on the train.
I spent the night curled up in pain,
Agonizingly cold and rather miserable.
I went out for a walk earlier today:
Snow started falling
Like big cotton balls this morning
And the park looks beautiful.
I will try to eat tonight: steamed cauliflower.
You would love it here.
It is still quite nice somehow.

You would like the emperor.
Some days the joy is overpowering.
The last time I was here,
He told a story.
It was Christmas.
Snow kept falling.
The emperor held his hand up for silence and began.
His fingernails have perfect moons, which is quite rare.
You hardly see it anymore, I wonder why.

The emperor began:
"Prehistoric insects were
Flying around brainless
To add more glory to the infant Earth.
Instead of horrible they were huge and beautiful,
And, being angels, were invincible.
Say the Name, and the angel begging with its hand out would
Instantly expand upward
To be as tall as the building . . ."

The ruthless raw odor of filth in an enclosed space,
And the slime tentacles with religious suckers,
And the four heads on one neck like the four heads carved on Mount Rushmore,
Hold out a single hand.

Hold out your hand.
Take my hand.

A FRESH STICK OF CHEWING GUM

A pink stick of gum unwrapped from the foil,
That you hold between your fingers on the way home from dance class,
And you look at its pink. But you know what.
I like your brain. Your pink. It's sweet.

My brain is the wrinkles of the ocean on a ball of tar
Instead of being sweet pink like yours.
It could be the nicotine. It could be the Johnnie Walker Black.
Mine thought too many cigarettes for too many years.

My brain is the size of the largest living thing, *mais oui*, a blue whale,
Blue instead of pink like yours.
It's what I've done
To make it huge that made it huge.

The violent sweetness in the air is the pink rain
Which continues achingly almost to fall.
This is the closest it has come.
This can't go on.

Twenty-six years old is not childhood.
You are not trying to stop smoking.
You smoke and drink
And *still* it is pink.

The answer is you can drink and smoke
Too much at twenty-six,
And stink of cigarettes,
And stand outside on the sidewalk outside the bar to have a cigarette,

As the law now requires, and it is paradise,
And be the most beautiful girl in the world,
And be moral,
And vibrate into blank.

FROM *Ooga-Booga*

DANTE'S BEATRICE

I ride a racer to erase her.
Bent over like a hunchback.
Racing leathers now include a hump
That protects the poet's spine and neck.
I wring the thing out, two hundred miles an hour.
I am a mink on a mink ranch determined not
To die inside its valuable fur, inside my racesuit.

I bought the racer
To replace her.
It became my slave and I its.
All it lacked was tits.
All it lacked
Between its wheels was hair.
I don't care.
We do it anyway.

The starter-caddy spins its raving little wheel
Against the Superbike's elevated fat black
Rear soft-compound tire.
Remember: *racer*—
Down for second gear instead of up!
Release the clutch—the engine fires.
I am off for my warm-up lap on a factory racer
Because I can't face her.

I ride my racer to erase her.
I ride in armor to
Three hundred nineteen kilometers an hour.
I am a mink on a mink ranch about
To die inside its valuable fur,
Inside my leathers.
She scoops me out to make a coat for her.
She buttons up a me of soft warm blur.

Is this the face that launched
A thousand slave ships?
The world is just outstanding.
My slavery never wavers.
I use the word "slavers"
To mean both "drools"
And, changing the pronunciation, "trades in slaves."
I consider myself most of these.

Mark Peploe and I used to sit around
Cafés in Florence grading
Muses' noses.
Hers hooks like Gauguin's,
His silent huge hooked hawk prow.
I am the cactus. You are the hyena.
I am the crash, you the fireball of Jet-A . . .
Only to turn catastrophe into dawn.

BOLOGNA

My own poetry I find incomprehensible.
Actually, I have no one.
Everything in art is couplets.
Mine don't rhyme.

Everything in the heart, you meant to say.
As if I ever meant to say anything.
Don't get me wrong.
I do without.

I find the poetry I write incomprehensible,
But at least I understand it.
It opens the marble
And the uniforms of the lobby staff

Behind the doorman at 834 Fifth.
Each elevator opens
On one apartment to a floor.
The elevator opened

To the page.
The elevator opened on the little vestibule
On the verge of something.
I hope I have. I hope I don't.

The vagina-eyed Modigliani nude
Made me lewd.
I waited for my friend to descend
The inner staircase of the duplex.

Keyword: house key.
You need a danger to be safe in.
Except in the African bush where you don't,
You do.

The doorway to my childhood
Was the daytime doorman.
An enormously black giant wore an outfit
With silver piping.

He wore a visored cap
With a high Gestapo peak
On his impenetrably black marble.
Waits out there in the sun to open the car door.

My noble Negro statue's name was Heinz,
My calmly grand George Washington.
You'll find me
At my beloved Hotel Baglioni

In Bologna
Still using the word Negro.
I need a danger to be safe in,
In room 221.

George Washington was calmly kind.
The defender of my building was George Washington
With a Nazi name
In World War II St. Louis.

Heinz stood in the terrible sun after
The Middle Passage in his nearly Nazi uniform.
He was my Master Race White Knight.
I was his white minnow.

The sun roars gloriously hot today.
Piazza Santo Stefano might as well be Brazzaville.
The humidity is a divinity.
Huck is happy on the raft in the divinity!

They show movies at night on an outdoor screen
In the steam in Piazza Maggiore.
I'm about to take a taxi
To Ducati

And see Claudio Domenicali, and see Paolo Ciabatti,
To discuss the motorcycle being made for me.
One of the eight factory Superbike racers
Ducati Corse will make for the year,

Completely by hand, will be mine.
I want to run racing slicks
On the street for the look,
Their powerful fat smooth black shine.

I need them
To go nowhere fast and get there.
I need to begin to
Write the poem of Colored Only.

When Heinz took my little hand in his,
Into the little vestibule on the verge
Of learning to ride a bicycle,
I began *Bologna.*

Federico Minoli of Bologna presides
In an unair-conditioned apartment fabulously
Looking out on the seven churches
In Piazza Santo Stefano, in the town center.

The little piazza opens
A little vestibule on the verge of something.
The incredible staircase to his place opens
On seven churches at the top.

The only problem is the bongo drums at night.
Ducati's president and CEO is the intelligent Federico.
Late tonight I will run into him and his wife
At Cesarina, in the brown medieval

Piazza, a restaurant Morandi
Used to lunch at,
Bologna's saintly pure painter of stillness.
I will sit outside in the noisy heat and eat.

RACER

FOR PAOLO CIABATTI

I spend most of my time not dying.
That's what living is for.
I climb on a motorcycle.
I climb on a cloud and rain.
I climb on a woman I love.
I repeat my themes.

Here I am in Bologna again.
Here I go again.
Here I go again, getting happier and happier.
I climb on a log
Torpedoing toward the falls.
Basically, it sticks out of me.

The F-16s take off in a deafening flock,
Shattering the runway at the airbase at Cervia.
They roar across horizontally
And suddenly go straight up,
And then they lean backwards and level off
And are gone till lunchtime and surprisingly wine.

So funny to see the Top Guns out of their G suits get so Italian
In front of the fire crackling in the fireplace.
Toasts are drunk to their guests, much use of hands.
They are crazy about motorcycles
In the officers' mess of the 23rd Squadron.
Over a period of time, one plane in ten is lost.

I hear the man with the silent chow chow
Tooting his saxophone
Down in the street, Via dell'Indipendenza, Independence Street.
The dog chats with no one.
The man chats with everyone
With gusto and delight, and accepts contributions.

At the factory,
The racer being made for me
Is not ready, but is getting deadly.
I am here to see it being born.
It is snowing in Milan, the TV says.
They close one airport, then both.

The Lord is my shepherd and the Director of Superbike Racing.
He buzzes me through three layers of security
To the innermost secret sanctum of the racing department.
I enter the adytum.
Trains are delayed.
The Florence sky is falling snow.

The man with the silent chow chow
Is tooting in the street
Below my room at the Hotel Baglioni—the Bag in Bo—
My marble home away from home, room 221.
He buzzes me through three layers of security,
Poetry, Politics, Medicine, into the adytum.

Tonight Bologna is fog.
This afternoon, there it was,
With all the mechanics who are making it around it.
It stood on a sort of altar.
I stood in a sort of fog,
Taking digital photographs of my death.

AT A FACTORY IN ITALY

The Man of La Mamma is a tenor as brave as a lion.
Everything is also its towering opposite.
Butch heterosexuals in Italy spend lavishly on fragrances.
The in thing was to shave your head, the skinhead look.
Guys spend more on beauty products here
Than in any other country in the world.
Everyone is also a boss.

The English executive assistant to the Italian CEO stays blondly exuberant
When sales to America plummet, when the dollar is weak.
Her name is Alice Coleridge. Her phone rings nonstop. *Pronto, sono Aleecheh!*
The world at the other end of the phone is a charging rhinoceros.
A descendant of Samuel Taylor Coleridge speaks Italian to the rhinoceros.
Poetry has power, as against the men and women actually making things
On the assembly line on the ground floor.

Someone had the brilliant idea of using
Factory workers in the ads,
And using a fashion photographer to add elegance and surprise.
They found an incredible face on the ground floor
With a nose to die for, and paid her to straddle
A motorcycle her assembly line had made and pose in profile.
So what did the Italian nose do? She ran with the money to get a nose job.

FROM *Ooga-Booga*

FRANCE FOR BOYS

There wasn't anyone to thank.
Two hours from Paris in a field.
The car was burning in a ditch.
Of course, the young star of the movie can't be killed off so early.

He felt he had to get off the train when he saw the station sign CHARLEVILLE—
Without knowing why—but something had happened there.
Rimbaud explodes with too good,
With the terrible happiness of light.

He was driving fast through
The smell of France, the French trees
Lining the roads with metronomic to stroboscopic
Bringing-on-a-stroke whacks of joyous light.

They were drunk. It had rained.
Going around the place de la Concorde too fast
On slippery cobbles, and it happened.
Three spill off the motorcycle, two into a paddy wagon.

Eeehaw, eeehaw, a midsummer night's dream
Down the boulevard along the Seine.
The most beautiful American girl in France
Has just stepped out of a swimming pool, even in a police van.

Eeehaw, Eeehaw,
In a Black Maria taking them to a hospital.
The beautiful apparently thought the donkey she had just met was dying
And on the spot fell in love.

The wife of the American ambassador to France
Took her son and his roommate to Sunday lunch
At a three-star restaurant some distance from Paris.
The chauffeur drove for hours to get to the sacred place.

The roommate proudly wore the new white linen suit
His grandmother had given him for his trip to France.
At the restaurant after they ordered he felt sick and left for the loo.
He dropped his trousers and squatted on his heels over the hole.

No one heard him shouting because the loo was in a separate building.
His pal finally came to find him after half an hour.
Since it was Sunday no one could buy him new pants in a store.
No one among the restaurant staff had an extra pair.

White linen summer clouds squatted over Điện Biên Phủ.
It must be 1954 because you soil yourself and give up hope but don't.
The boys are reading *L'Étranger* as summer reading.
My country, 'tis of thee, Albert Camus!

The host sprinted upstairs to grab his fellow Existentialist—
To drag him downstairs to the embassy's July Fourth garden party.
The ambassador's son died horribly the following year
In a ski lodge fire.

GRANDSON BORN DEAD

The baby born dead
Better lie down.
Better stand up.
Better get up and go out
For a walk.
He stands around in the rain
In the room.
Breathe two three four.
And down in the rain in the drain
In the floor.
Babies born dead
Drown in the main in the more.
Better a walk.
The head on a stalk
Laughs and waves.
It is the sun with its rays.
The sun wants to talk.
If you start to be sick,
If you start to be stuck,
If you have to sit down,
If one foot starts to drop,
If hope starts to stop,
You will drown
In the drain in the main in the more.
The rain is downtown.
Up here is happy.
Get up!
Get up, get out of bed!
Wake up!
Wake up, you sleepyhead!
All right. Go ahead.
Be dead.

DEATH

Dapper in hats,
Dapper in spats,
Espousing white tie and tails or a tailcoat and striped trousers
With dancing-backward Ginger Rogers and other espousers,

Singing with such sweet insincere
Dated charm and good cheer,
And his toupee of slicked-down dated hair;
Immortal date-stamped Fred Astaire!

EAST HAMPTON AIRPORT

East Hampton Airport is my shepherd.
It was smaller when I took lessons.
The shepherd's crook has high-tech runway lights now.
The shack became a terminal.
The private jets drop by to sleep.
I stand in the afternoon in the open field across the road.
The light planes come in low.
The dog doesn't even look up.
Their wings wave around frantically
Through the valley of the shadow of death.
They touch down calmly and taxi to a stop.

East Hampton Airport is my harbor.
I shall not want.
The harbormaster maketh me to lie down
In green pastures he has paved over.
He leadeth me beside the runway's still waters.
He keeps me in the air so I can land.
I stand in the open field on the far side of Wainscott Road
And watch the summer, autumn, winter sky.
It was my idea to take up flying,
To die doing something safer than motorcycling.
I went up with my instructor not to learn, just to fly.

I stand in the field opposite the airport.
I watch the planes flying in and the planes flying out.
My proud Irish terrier takes pills for his cardiomyopathy.
Before we bark our last,
Our hearts enlarge and burst.
George Plimpton went to bed
And woke up dead.
I write this poem thinking of the painter David Salle
Who wants to make a movie
About the poet Frank O'Hara.
A beach taxi on Fire Island hit Frank and he burst, roll credits.

I remember flying back from Montauk.
I was flying the plane.
The instructor asked me, "Notice anything?"
Yes. The plane was absolutely stuck—
Speechless—ecstatically still.
The headwinds were holding us in place in space.
We were flying, but not moving, visibility forever.
The ocean was down there waving.
The engine purred contentment.
I am flying, but not moving.
I stand in a field and stare at the air.

A WHITE TIGER

The golden light is white.
It is the color of moonlight in the middle of the night
If you suddenly wake and you are a child
In the forest and the wild
Animals all around you are sleeping.
You are in your bed and you are weeping
For no reason.
It is because it is tiger season.
The big-game hunters' guns are banging.
The corpse of a real beauty is hanging
From a tree in the darkness, waiting.
Of *course*, the Palestinians and the Jews are exaggerating!
The building is not a million stories high.
The moonlight is not going to die.
The Israelis and the Palestinians are by no means exaggerating.
The carcass is hanging from the darkness, waiting.
The building is a million human stories high.
The moonlight is going to die.
In the corners of your little room,
The large-bore guns go *boom boom*.
The tigers are field dressed where they fall, who used to roar.
The stomach and lungs are removed with the gore.
Tiger incisors get sold at the store.
Tiger canines ground into powder get sold at the store.
Tiger heart will also restore.
The tigers will end up a tiger skin on the floor.
Especially a rare white tiger is not safe anywhere anymore.
One escaped from the cage when they opened the door.

Rest in fierce peace, Edward, on the far shore.

CLOCLO

The golden person curled up on my doormat,
Using her mink coat as a blanket,
Blondly asleep, a smile on her face, was my houseguest
The Goat who couldn't get her set of keys to work, so blithely
Bedded down to wait in the apartment outside hall.
A natural animal elegance physically
Released a winged ethereal exuberance,
Pulling g's, then weightlessness, the charm of the divine,
Luxuriously asleep in front of the front door like a dog.
Dear polymorphous goddess who past sixty
Could still instantly climb a tree,
But couldn't get the metal key
To turn in any residence
In London or New York or Calabria or Greece or Florence.
Always climbing anything (why
Someone had dubbed her the Goat when she was young),
Climbing everywhere in a conversation,
Up the Nile, up the World Trade Center Twin Towers,
Upbeat, up late, up at dawn, up for anything,
Up the ladder to the bells.
A goat saint lived ravishingly on a rock,
Surrounded by light, dressed in a simple frock,
The last great puritan aesthete
In the Cyclades.
She painted away
Above the Greek blue sea.
She chatted away
Beneath the Greek blue sky.
Every year returned to London.
So European. So Jamesian.
Every year went back
To Florence, her first home.
To the thirty-foot-high stone room in Bellosguardo.
To paint in the pearl light the stone gave off.
Ten generations after Leonardo had painted on the same property.
She worked hard as a nun
On her nude landscapes of the south,
With their occasional patio or dovecote and even green bits,

FROM *Ooga-Booga*

But never people or doves, basking in the sun.
Believed only in art.
Believed in tête-à-têtes.
Believed in walks to the top of the hill.
Knew all the simple people, and was loved.
It comes through the telephone
From Florence when I call that she has died quietly a minute ago,
Like a tear falling in a field of snow,
Climbing up the ladder to the bells out of Alzheimer's total whiteout,
Heavenly Clotilde Peploe called by us all Cloclo.

LAUDATIO

A young aristocrat and Jew and German
The rise of Hitler sent to school in London.
St. Paul's School made a man a gentleman.
The gentleman grew up to be a boy.

The boy came to America to become a dashing OSS officer.
The boy slipped into Germany to meet the schoolboys plotting to kill Hitler.
The boy became a not bad postwar racecar driver.
The boy became a heterosexual clothes designer.

A Jewish boy donned the uniform of an SS officer,
Cross-dressing across Deathland in the final months of the war,
Urbane inside his skull-and-crossbones attire—
The first John Weitz fashion show, my dear!

When Weitz wanted to obliterate his SS tattoo,
He burned it off with a cigarette just like the real SS.
The underground network he would infiltrate had removed theirs.
A mysterious beautiful woman was involved. It gets better.

There is the story of how he needed publicity
For his fashion line and couldn't spend much money.
No one had thought of putting advertisements on the back
Of New York City buses back then.

Weitz wrote koans for the age of Warhol.
I DON'T UNDERSTAND JOHN WEITZ ADVERTISING
Went rolling down Fifth Avenue behind a bus.
He looked like a distinguished diplomat when he ate a wurst.

Weitz had the lofty friendliness of a duke.
He was full of goy.
He was not discreet.
He admired the great.

He could operate on automatic pilot
With his beautiful manners.
He had unreal good looks.
He used his mellifluous voice.

FROM *Ooga-Booga*

John Weitz belonged to clubs, loved boats,
Told lovely anecdotes, bad jokes, wrote cordial biographies
Of colorless Third Reich personalities.
He loved honors and he loved glory.

He kept the Iron Cross
Of his father from the First World War framed on the wall.
He denied that he was dying.
He never sighed until the moment after he died.

TO DIE FOR

The ants on the kitchen counter stampede toward ecstasy.
The finger chases them down while the herd runs this way and that way.
They are alive while they are alive in their little way.
They burst through their little ant outfits, which tear apart rather easily.

The little black specks were shipped to Brazil in ships.
The Portuguese whipped the little black specks to bits.
The sugar plantations on the horrible tropical coast where the soil was rich
Were a most productive ant Auschwitz.

The sugar bowl on the counter is a D-cup, containing one large white breast.
The breast in the bowl is covered by excited specks
That are so beyond, and running around, they are wrecks.
They like things that are sweet. That's what they like to eat.

The day outside is blue and good.
God is in the neighborhood.
The nearby ocean puts liquid lure in each trap in the set of six,
Paving the way to the new world with salt and sweet.

They sell them at the hardware store on Main Street.
Inside each trap is a tray that gives them a little to eat
And sends them back.
There is light in Africa, and it is black.

I was looking for something to try for.
I was looking for someone to cry for.
I was looking for something to die for.
There isn't.

FROM *Ooga-Booga*

BARBADOS

Literally the most expensive hotel in the world
Is the smell of rain about to fall.
It does the opposite, a grove of lemon trees.
I isn't anything.
It is the hooks of rain
Hovering with their sweets inches off the ground.
I is the spiders marching through the air.
The lines dangle the bait
The ground will bite.
Your wife is as white as vinegar, pure aristo privilege.
The excellent smell of rain before it falls overpowers
The last aristocrats on earth before the asteroid.
I sense your disdain, darling.
I share it.

The most expensive hotel in the world
Is the slave ship unloading Africans on the moon.
They wear the opposite of space suits floating off the dock
To a sugar mill on a hilltop.
They float into the machinery.
The machine inside the windmill isn't vegetarian.
A "lopper" lops off a limb caught
In the rollers and the machine never has to stop.
A black arm turns into brown sugar,
And the screaming rest of the slave keeps the other.
His African screams can't be heard above the roar.
A spaceship near the end of a voyage was becalmed.
Two astronauts floated weightlessly off the deck
Overboard into the equator in their chains and *splash* and drowned.

A cane toad came up to them.
They'd never seen anything so remarkable.
Now they could see the field was full of them.
Suddenly the field is filled with ancestors.
The hippopotamuses became friendly with the villagers.
Along came white hunters who shot the friendly hippos dead.
If they had known that friendship would end like that,
They never would have entered into it.
Suddenly the field is filled with souls.

The field of sugarcane is filled with hippopotamus cane toads.
They always complained
Our xylophones were too loud.
The Crocodile King is dead.
The world has no end.

The crocodile explodes out of the water and screams at the crowd
That one of them has stolen his mobile phone.
On the banks of the muddy Waddo, *ooga-booga!*
What about a Christmas tree in a steamy lobby on the Gulf of Guinea!
Because in Africa there are Africans
And they are Africans and are in charge.
Even obstipation
Can't stop a mighty nation.
The tragic magic makes lightning.
Some of the young captives are unspeakable
In their beauty, and their urine makes lightning, black and gold.
The heat is so hot
It will boil you in a pot.
Diarrhea in a condom is the outcome.

The former president completely loses it and screams from the stage
That someone fucking stole his fucking phone.
The audience of party faithful is terrified and giggles.
This was their man who brought the crime rate down
By executing everyone.
The crocodile staged a coup
And ended up in prison himself
And then became the president.
He stood for quality of life and clitorectomy.
But in his second term, in order to secure those international loans,
The crocodile changed his spots to free speech.
Lightning sentences them at birth to life without parole
With no time off for good behavior.
At that point in the voyage the ocean turns deeper.

People actually suffered severe optical damage from the blinding effects
Of the white roads in full sunlight.
It is the island roads so white you can't see,
Made of crushed limestone snow.
It is the tropical rain the color of grapefruit

Hovering in the figure of the goddess Niscah
Above the tile roof of the plantation house.
She dangles her baited lines.
It is the black of the orchids in a vase.
The goddess overpowers the uprising
And *I* is the first one hacked to pieces.
The asteroid is coming to the local cinema.
It is a moonlit night with the smell of rain in the air.
Thump thump, speed bump.

The most expensive hotel in the world ignites
As many orgasms as there are virgins in paradise.
These epileptic foaming fits dehydrate one,
But justify the cost of a honeymoon.
The Caribbean is room temperature,
Rippling over sand as rich as cream.
The beach chair has the thighs of a convertible with the top down.
You wave a paddle and the boy
Runs to take your order.
Many things are still done barefoot.
Others have the breakout colors of a parrot.
In paradise it never rains, but smells as if it could.
Two who could catapulted themselves overboard into the equator.
I die of thirst and drown in chains, in love.

Into the coconut grove they go. *Into the coconut grove they go.*
The car in the parking lot is theirs. *The car in the parking lot is theirs.*
The groves of lemon trees give light. *Ooga-booga!*
The hotel sheds light. *Ooga-booga!*
The long pink-shell sky of meaning wanted it to be, but really,
The precious thing is that they voted. *Ooga-booga!* And there we were,
The cane toads and the smell of rain about to fall.
The crocodiles and spiders are
The hippos and their friends who shot them dead.
The xylophone is playing too loud
Under the coconut palms, which go to the end of the world.
The slave is screaming too loud and we
Can't help hearing
Our tribal chant and getting up to dance under the mushroom cloud.

CLIMBING EVEREST

The young keep getting younger, but the old keep getting younger.
But this young woman is young. We kiss.
It's almost incest when it gets to this.
This is the consensual, national, metrosexual hunger-for-younger.

I'm getting young.
I'm totally into strapping on the belt of dynamite
Which will turn me into light.
God is great! I suck Her tongue.

I mean—my sunbursts, and there are cloudbursts.
My dynamite penis
Is totally into Venus.
My penis in Venus hungers and thirsts,

It burns and drowns.
My dynamite penis
Is into Venus.
The Atlantic off Sagaponack is freezing black today and frowns.

I enter the jellyfish folds
Of floating fire.
The mania in her labia can inspire
Extraordinary phenomena and really does cure colds.

It holds the Tower of Pisa above the freezing black waves.
The mania is why
I mention I am easily old enough to die,
And actually it's the mania that saves

The Tower from falling over.
Climbing Everest is the miracle—which leaves the descent
And reporting to the world from an oxygen tent
In a soft pasture of cows and clover.

Happening girls parade around my hospice bed.
The tented canopy means I am in the rue de Seine in Paris.
It will embarrass
Me in Paris to be dead.

FROM *Ooga-Booga*

It's Polonius embarrassed behind the arras,
And the arras turning red.
Hamlet has outed Polonius and Sir Edmund Hillary will wed
Ophelia in Paris.

Give me Everest or give me death.
Give me altitude with an attitude.
But I am naked and nude.
I am constantly out of breath.

A naked woman my age is just a total nightmare,
But right now one is coming through the door
With a mop, to mop up the cow flops on the floor.
She kisses the train wreck in the tent and combs his white hair.

ORGANIZED RELIGION

Will you? Everything? Anything? Weird stuff, too?
I want to do anything you want me to.
I will meet you in an hour in the mirror.
I will meet you in front of the mirror.

When the cars have their lights on in the daytime when it's raining,
And the full-length bedroom mirror is the hostess entertaining,
And the summer downpour thrillingly thrashes the windows,
My naked in high heels shows me she can touch her toes!

The rainy city outside stretches around the world.
The rainy season inside the mirror gets whirled
Into a waterspout. No doubt
The dolphins in the mirror know what water is about!

You love it all.
I love it when you make me get down on all fours and crawl.
I put you on a leash and spank you.
I thank you.

The value of life which will end is unbearable,
And these are just some ways of bearing it. The joy is terrible.
The joy is actually terrible.
The sweetness of life is actually unbearable.

God looks up to His creation by dint of lying on the floor.
God lies there on His back on the carpet and looks. That's what you are for.
Hike your skirt up higher. There is nothing higher or more
Than Him you stand over and adore!

FROM *Ooga-Booga*

MOTHER NATURE

Mother Nature walked from Kenya.
Going faster is Italian.
Going fast got you nowhere.
Madagascar is impatiens.

Came the warriors of the nations,
Came the Delawares and Mohawks,
Came the Choctaws and Comanches,
Came the Mandans and Dacotahs,

Came the Hurons and Ojibways,
All the warriors drawn together
By the signal of the peace pipe.
And they stood there on the meadow,

With their weapons and their war gear,
Painted like the leaves of autumn,
Painted like the sky of morning,
Wildly glaring at each other.

The smiling Indian economy is running uphill inputting,
Outrunning a rising ocean of sweat.
The poor stay behind and drown
In their own brown.

Technology is the placenta
Feeding the fetus dreams.
It was high tide.
It was wet dreams.

Skira reproduced the paintings,
Mother Nature at Ajanta,
Her beauty, her big breasts,
Her athleticism, her shoreline, her high tides.

The orbit was Aryan.
Sanskrit debris floats by a boy in orbit in St. Louis.
Anything to see those breasts
In that art book!

By the shore of Gitche Gumee,
By the shining Big-Sea-Water,
Hiawatha liked the white man,
Liked Caucasians, liked their smell.

From the waterfall he named her,
Laughing Water, Minnehaha.
Mother Nature, you, my mother,
Help the paleface ask me for my colored hand in marriage!

And the great chief liked his odor,
And he offered him his daughter,
Redskin jewel from a giant, legend waiting for an answer,
And the frightened white man could not answer.

Mother Nature went to China,
China the vagina.
Wet dreams conceive there,
Where no one wants a daughter.

I pin the throttle on the straight
Toward China all night,
With the moon out and the stars,
And reach Kabul.

The nightclub bombing in Bali
Shattered Baghdad.
The hotel temple dancers hold the sky up.
The elephant lifts his friend the tiger to safety.

The satellite picks up a faint signal
From the Arabian Peninsula
From long before Islam
Of the immortal Imru' al-Qays declaiming his ode.

Whalesong surfaces in the desert and spouts.
The Arab Pindar pinpricks the emptiness.
A nanosecond of moisture
Irrigates ancient Arabia.

FROM *Ooga-Booga*

His she-camel is a Ferrari with a saddle
Who knows the desert by heart and is unafraid.
He praises her in his monorhymes of tribal twaddle
About this and that and the brevity of life.

The Prophet Muhammad
Acknowledged his fame
As the finest poet in hell
Where the pre-Islamic poets dwell.

Let shuttered windows shatter
To let the bomb-blast in.
Everyone is screaming.
The exits have been padlocked.

Everyone is screaming.
Muhammad took away their silliness.
Muhammad is the firestorm.
Everyone converts.

Her breast is bigger than I am.
Her nipple is bigger than my mouth.
Let me masturbate to death.
Let my hand fall off.

Islam is submission.
Behead the man
Who will not listen!
My head and hand are coming to an end.

I am coming in Manhattan
By the shining Big-Sea-Water.
I am coming to the end. I am coming to.
The predawn streets are empty.

This is what it feels like.
Everyone is screaming.
I am coming, Mother Nature.
I am coming, Mannahatta.

I am coming in Manhattan.
This is what it comes to.
Everyone is screaming. All the planes are grounded.
The exits have been padlocked.

The asteroid is really coming.
The president in Washington is speaking to the world.
The sea tilts up and down
Next to the silent dawn.

FROM *Ooga-Booga*

BROADWAY MELODY

A naked woman my age is a total nightmare.
A woman my age naked is a nightmare.
It doesn't matter. One doesn't care.
One doesn't say it out loud because it's rare
For anyone to be willing to say it,
Because it's the equivalent of buying billboard space to display it,

Display how horrible life after death is,
How horrible to draw your last breath is,
When you go on living.
I hate the old couples on their walkers giving
Off odors of love, and in City Diner eating a ray
Of hope, and then paying and trembling back out on Broadway,

Drumming and dancing, chanting something nearly unbearable,
Spreading their wings in order to be more beautiful and more terrible.

LOVE SONG

I shaved my legs a second time,
Lagoon approaching the sublime,
To cast a moonlight spell on you.
TriBeCa was Tahiti, too.

I know I never was on time.
I was downloading the sublime
To cast a moonlight spell on you.
TriBeCa was Tahiti, too.

The melanoma on my skin
Resumes what's wrong with me within.
My outside is my active twin.
Disease I'm repetitious in.

The sun gives life but it destroys.
It burns the skin of girls and boys.
I cover up to block the day.
I also do so when it's gray.

The sunlight doesn't go away.
It causes cancer while they play.
Precancerous will turn out bad.
I had an ice pick for a dad.

A womanizing father, he's
The first life-threatening disease.
His narcissistic daughter tried
To be his daughter but he died.

The richest man in Delaware
Died steeplechasing, debonair.
One company of ours made napalm.
That womanizing ice pick's gray calm

Died steeplechasing in a chair,
The jockey underneath the mare.
She posted and she posted and
Quite suddenly he tried to stand

And had a heart attack and died,
The ice pick jockey's final ride.
The heart attack had not been planned.
He saw my eyes and tried to stand.

My satin skin becomes the coffin
The taxidermist got it off in.
He stuffed me, made me lifelike. Fatten
My corpse in satin in Manhattan!

My body was flash-frozen. God,
I am a person who is odd.
I am the ocean and the air.
I'm acting out. I cut my hair.

You like the way I do things, neat
Combined with craziness and heat.
My ninety-eight point six degrees,
Warehousing decades of deep freeze,

Can burst out curls and then refreeze
And have to go to bed but please
Don't cure me. Sickness is my me.
My terror was you'd set me free.

My shrink admired you. He could see.
Sex got me buzzing like a bee
With Parkinson's! Catastrophe
Had slaughtered flowers on the tree.

My paranoia was revived.
I love it downtown and survived.
I loved downtown till the attack.
Love Heimliched me and brought me back.

You brought me life, glued pollen on
My sunblock. Happy days are gone
Again. My credit cards drip honey.
The tabloids dubbed me "Maid of Money."

Front-page divorce is such a bore.
I loathed the drama they adore.
You didn't love me for my money.
You made the stormy days seem sunny.

BREAST CANCER

The intubated shall be extubated and it rains green
Into the uptown air because it is almost raining.
You can smell the sidewalks straining.
The side streets are contagious but serene.
The disease is nutritious.
The bitter medicine delicious.
The beautiful breasts are repetitious.
The much older man you love is vicious.

The man will be even older by the time
She takes down the book to read the poem.

RILKE

As he approaches each tree goes on,
And the girls one by one
Glance down at their blouses. A nun,
Then six or seven, hop in
A cream station wagon,
White-beaked blackbirds baked in a pie.
In his mind is
The lid of an eye
The dark dilated closing behind him.

Rilke. Arched eyebrows and shadowed
Moist eyes. An El Greco. Swart, slim.
He's late to her. He thinks of her, waiting,
Limb by limb.

Her defenselessness and childlike trust!
Smiling to be combed out
And parted—and her lust
Touching the comb like a lyre.
To have been told by her not to trust her!

And he distrusts her.

And everywhere he sees
Hunchbacks and addicts and sadists
In braces in the cities,
Roosting in their filth,
Or plucking the trees,
In New York for true love,
In Boston for constancy.
You can be needed by someone
Or needy, thinks Rilke.

They clutch their loves like addicts
Embracing when they see
Hot May put out her flowers.
Or clutch themselves. They can't shake free.

He thinks of the time
He lived by her calendar
When she missed her time.

She gave the child a name.

When she bled, she laughed and gasped
Tears warm as pablum
On his wrists. But that is past.

Rilke feels his body
Moving in front of his last
Step. He sweats, and thinks
Of the rubble massed
On Creusa behind Aeneas's
White-hot shoulders and neck.

Addresses
And clothesline laundry swelled
Like pseudocyesis—
That's what he has to pass through.

His tie is her blue,
And a new lotion gives him an air
Of coolness. He combs his hair,
And tries to smooth his hair.

He'll be there,
The husband. She'll have left him asleep—
A nap, beyond the top stair,
In darkness.

Light, light is in the trees
Pizzicato, and mica
Sizzles up to his knees.
A dozen traffic lights
Swallow and freeze
And one by one relay red red
Like runners with a blank message.

I hate her, I hate her, he said
A minute ago. Curls cluster
Rilke's dark head.

CASANOVA GETTING OLDER

Do they think they are being original when they say
This is a new thing for me to ask, and ask
Do you love me?
Everyone these days keeps asking
Do you love me?
Everyone says
This is a new thing for me to ask.
The answer is yes.
This is a new thing for me to ask.

The answer is yes I don't.
Do you love me?
The answer is yes.
The eyes glisten with feeling.
The creature hath a purpose and its eyes are bright with it.
This sudden pecking of asking, of being asked, is this.
The answer is yes I don't.
The heart got the shot but got the flu anyway,
And the body aches, and fever and chills, and can't sleep.

The forest shivers with fever.
Their mother pulls their covers up.
The whippoorwill keeps calling *whippoorwill whippoorwill*.
Do you love me? Do you love me? I don't love you.
Not everyone is afraid.
Not everyone feels vulnerable.
Everyone is afraid of the terrible joy. I do.
Each other is Mecca,
The hajj to the Other.

FROM *Ooga-Booga*

IL DUCE

More than one woman at a time
Is the policy that got the trains running on time.
More than one at a time in those fascist days, and I climb
Into the clouds and then above—the sublime!—
And wag my wings and make it rhyme.

More than one woman at a time was enough.
On time because there were enough.
Mussolini in riding boots stood at his desk to stuff
Himself into the new secretary who was spread out on the desk. He goes *uff*.
He goes *uff wuff, uff wuff*, and even—briefly—falls in *luff*.

It's getting worse, and I don't like the way it sounds.
Down in the subway, while you are waiting, all those humming sounds.
In New York City, all the Lost-and-Founds.
All the towed-away-car pounds.
While you are waiting on the subway platform—God's wounds! Zounds!

Mussolini is standing on the little balcony
Above Italy, and Italy is looking up at Mussolini on the balcony,
Who is looking over at Ethiopia across a deep blue sea.
I never have enough for me.
I am getting on a girl motorcycle to go across the sea to see.

I AM SIAM

I saw the moon in the sky at sunset over a river pink as a ham.
I am the governess imported from England by me,
The widowed King of Siam.
I drop down on one knee.
I want to marry me.
Where you are I am.
Là où tu es je suis. Où tu es je suis.
I drop down on one knee.
I want to marry me.
I do a *saut de chat* at sunset over a silver spoon of jam.
Jam for the royal children, Felicity
And Sam.
I am the English governess imported from England by me.
I am the widowed King of Siam! The widowed King of Siam!

FROM *Ooga-Booga*

THE BIG JET

The big jet screamed and was hysterical and begged to take off,
But the brakes held it in place to force it to flower.
The runway was too short, that's why, kiddo.
Till the engines powered up to full power.

In a little school in what was then still called Burma, not yet cancered,
Carolyn was teaching English to the lovely brownish children.
The assignment was to use the word "often" in a sentence.
"Birds fly more often than airplanes," the boy answered.

Little sudden flowers in the desert after it rains,
Bearing gifts of frankincense and myrrh . . .
What thou lovest well remains.
Birds fly more often than airplanes.

Meat-eating seagulls shout their little cries *myanmar myanmar* above the airport,
Dropping razor clams on the runway to break them open.
Hard is soft inside.
The big jet has soft people inside for the ride.

THE BLACK-EYED VIRGINS

A terrorist rides the rails underwater
From one language to another in a packed train of London
Rugby fans on their way to the big match in Paris
And a flock of Japanese schoolgirls ready to be fucked
In their school uniforms in paradise.
This is all just after Madrid in the reign of terror.
This is the girls' first trip outside Japan.
The terrorist swings in the hammock of their small skirts and black socks.
The chunnel train stops in the tunnel with an announcement
That everyone now alive is already human remains.
The terrorists have seen to it that trains
Swap human body parts around with bombs.
The Japanese schoolgirls say so sorry.
Their new pubic hair is made of light.

FROM *Ooga-Booga*

EUROSTAR

Japanese schoolgirls in their school uniforms with their school chaperones
Ride underwater on a train
Every terrorist in the world would dearly love to bomb
For the publicity and to drown everybody.
The Eurostar dashes into the waves.
The other passengers are watching the Japanese girls eat
Little sweeties they bought with their own money
In London. President Bush the younger is making ice cream.
Ice cream for dessert
Is what Iraq is, without the courses that normally come before.
You eat dessert to start and then you have dessert.
One of them is a Balthus in her short school skirt standing on the seat.
She reaches up too high to get something out of her bag.
She turns around smiling because she knows where you are looking.

SONG: "THE SWOLLEN RIVER OVERTHROWS ITS BANKS"

The terrorists are out of breath with success.
And cancer is eating American women's breasts.
The terrorists are bombing Madrid
And everywhere serious and nice.
They put the backpacks on
Without a word and leave
The Italian premier talking to an empty room because
They leave the TV on and leave.
One of the many networks Mr. Berlusconi owns
Carries him live denouncing terror. The man
By now has reached Milan
Who has the man in London for Miami.
Both will board the train,
As in the swollen river overthrows its banks.

FROM *Ooga-Booga*

DRINKING IN THE DAYTIME

Anything is better than this
Bliss.
Nursing on a long-stemmed bubble made of crystal.
I'm sucking on the barrel of a crystal pistol
To get a bullet to my brain.
I'm gobbling a breast, drinking myself down the drain.

I'm in such a state of Haut-Brion I can't resist.
A fist-fucking anus swallowing a fist.
You're wondering why I talk this way, so daintily!
I'll tell you after I take a pee.
Now I'm back.
Oilcoholics love the breast they attack.

I'm talking about the way poetry made me free.
It's treated me very well, you see.
I climbed up inside the Statue of Liberty
In the days when you could still go up in the torch, and that was me.
I mean every part I play.
I'm drinking my lunch at Montrachet.

I'm a case of Haut-Brion turning into tar.
I'm talking about the recent war.
It's a case of having to raise your hand in life to be
Recognized so you can ask your question. *Mr. Secretary! Mr. Secretary!*
To the secretary of defense, I say:
I lift my tar to you at Montrachet!

I lift my lamp beside the golden door to pee,
And make a vow to make men free, and we will find their WMD.
Sir, I supported the war.
I believe in who we are.
I dedicate red wine to that today.
At Montrachet, near the Franklin Street stop, on West Broadway.

THE BUSH ADMINISTRATION

I

The darkness coming from the mouth
Must be the entrance to a cave.
The heart of darkness took another form
And inside is the Congo in the man.
I think the Bush administration is as crazy as Sparta was.
Sparta has swallowed Congo and is famished.
The steel Spartan abs turn to fevered slush
While it digests the good that it is doing
In the desert heat. I felt a drop of rain,
Which is the next Ice Age being born.

II

I stood on Madison. The sun was shining.
I felt large drops of rain as warm as tears.
I held my hand out, palm up, the way one does.
The sun was shining and the rain really started.
Maybe there must have been a rainbow somewhere.
I hailed a cab and as I hopped in
That was the first thing
The radio said:
They had beheaded an American.
There was a thunderclap and it poured.

III

The downpour drumming on my taxi gets the Hutu in me dancing.
Il rombo della Desmosedici makes machete music.
I crawl into a crocodile
And I go native.
The white cannibals in cowboy boots
Return to the bush
And the darkness of the brutes.
I am on all fours eating grass
So I can throw up because I like the feeling.
I crouch over a carcass and practice my eating.

FROM *Ooga-Booga*

IV

The United States of America preemptively eats the world.
The doctrine of eat lest you be eaten
Is famished, roars
And tears their heads off before its own is sawed off.
The human being sawing screams *God is Great!*
God is—and pours cicadas
By the tens of millions through the air.
They have risen from underground.
The voices of the risen make a summer sound.
It is pouring cicadas on Madison Avenue, making the street thick.

V

Every human being who has ever lived has died,
Except the living. The sun is shining and
The countless generations rise from underground this afternoon
And fall like rain.
I never thought that I would see your face again.
The savage wore a necklace made of beads,
And then I saw the beads were tiny human faces talking.
He started crying and the tears were raindrops.
The raindrops were more faces.
Everybody dies, but they come back as salt and water.

VI

I am charmed by my taxi's sunny yellow reflection
Keeping abreast of the speeding taxi I'm in,
Playful and happy as a dolphin,
All the way down York Avenue to the hospital,
Right up to the bank of elevators to heaven.
I take an elevator to the floor.
Outside the picture window, rain is falling on the sunshine.
In the squeeze-hush silence, the ventilator keeps breathing.
A special ops comes in to check the hoses and the flow.
A visitor holds out his palm to taste the radiant rain.

VII

The Bush administration likes its rain sunny-side up.
I feel a mania of happiness at being alive
As I write you this suicide note.
I have never been so cheerily suicidal, so sui-Seidel.
I am too cheery to be well.
George Bush is cheery as well.
I am cheeriest
Crawling around on all fours eating gentle grass
And pretending I am eating broken glass.
Then I throw up the pasture.

VIII

CENTCOM is drawing up war plans.
They will drop snow on Congo.
It will melt without leaving a trace, at great expense.
America will pay any price to whiten darkness.
My fellow citizen cicadas rise to the tops of the vanished Twin Towers
And float back down white as ashes
To introduce a new Ice Age.
The countless generations rise from underground this afternoon
And fall like rain.
I never thought that I would live to see the towers fall again.

FROM *Ooga-Booga*

THE DEATH OF THE SHAH

Here I am, not a practical man,
But clear-eyed in my contact lenses,
Following no doubt a slightly different line than the others,
Seeking sexual pleasure above all else,
Despairing of art and of life,
Seeking protection from death by seeking it
On a racebike, finding release and belief on two wheels,
Having read a book or two,
Having eaten well,
Having traveled not everywhere in sixty-seven years but far,
Up the Eiffel Tower and the Leaning Tower of Pisa
And the World Trade Center Twin Towers
Before they fell,
Mexico City, Kuala Lumpur, Accra,
Tokyo, Berlin, Teheran under the Shah,
Cairo, Bombay, L.A., London,
Into the jungles and the deserts and the cities on the rivers
Scouting locations for the movie,
A blue-eyed white man with brown hair,
Here I am, a worldly man,
Looking around the room.

Any foal in the kingdom
The Shah of Iran wanted
He had brought to him in a military helicopter
To the palace.
This one was the daughter of one of his ministers, all legs, a goddess.
She waited in a room.
It was in the afternoon.

I remember mounds of caviar before dinner
In a magnificent torchlit tent,
An old woman's beautiful house, a princess,
Three footmen for every guest,
And a man who pretended to get falling-down drunk
And began denouncing the Shah,
And everyone knew was a spy for the Shah.

A team of New York doctors (mine among them)
Was flown to Mexico City to consult.
They were not allowed to examine the Shah.
They could ask him how he felt.

The future of psychoanalysis
Is a psychology of surface.
Stay on the outside side.
My poor analyst
Suffered a stroke and became a needy child.
As to the inner life: let the maid.

How pathetic is a king who died of cancer
Rushing back after all these years to consult more doctors.
Escaped from the urn of his ashes in his pajamas.
Except in Islam you are buried in your body.
The Shah mounts the foal.
It is an honor.
He is in and out in a minute.
She later became my friend
And married a Texan.

I hurry to the gallery on the last day of the show
To a line stretching around the block in the rain—
For the Shah of sculptors, sculpture's virile king,
And his cold-rolled steel heartless tons.
The blunt magnificence stuns.
Cruelty has a huge following.
The cold-rolled steel mounts the foal.

The future of psychoanalysis is it has none.

I carry a swagger stick.
I eat a chocolate.
I eat brown blood.

When we drove with our driver on the highways of Ghana
To see for ourselves what the slave trade was,
Elmina was Auschwitz.
The slaves from the bush were marched to the coast
And warehoused in dungeons under St. George's Castle,
Then FedExed to their new jobs far away.

FROM *Ooga-Booga*

One hotel kept a racehorse as a pet.
The owner allowed it the run of the property.
Very shy, it walked standoffishly
Among the hotel guests on the walkways and under the palms.
The Shah had returned as a racehorse dropping mounds of caviar
Between a coconut grove and the Gulf of Guinea.

An English royal is taught to strut
With his hands clasped behind his back.
A racehorse in West Africa kept as a pet
Struts the same way the useless royals do,
Nodding occasionally to indicate he is listening.
His coat has been curried until he is glistening.

Would you rather be a horse without a halter
Than one winning races being whipped?
The finish line is at the starting gate, at St. George's Castle.
The starting gate is at the finish line for the eternal life.
God rears and whinnies and gives a little wave.
He would rather be an owner than a slave.

Someone fancy says
How marvelous money is.
Here I am, an admirer of Mahatma Gandhi,
Ready to praise making pots of money
And own a slave.
I am looking in the mirror as I shave the slave.
I shave the Shah.
I walk into the evening and start being charming.

A counterfeiter prints me.
(The counterfeiter *is* me.)
He prints Mohammad Reza Shah Pahlavi.

I call him Nancy.
He is so fancy.
It is alarming
He is so charming.
It is the thing he does and knows.
It is the fragrance of a rose.
It is the nostrils of his nose.

It is the poetry and prose.
It is the poetry.
It is a horse cab ride through Central Park when it snows.
It is Jackie Kennedy's hairpiece that came loose,
That a large Secret Service agent helped reattach.

I remember the Duck and Duckess of Windsor.
You could entertain them in your house.

Here I am, looking around the room
At everyone getting old except the young,
Discovering that I am lacking in vanity,
Not that I care, being debonair,
Delighted by an impairment of feeling
That keeps everything away,
People standing around in a display case
Even when they are in bed with you,
And laser-guided bombs destroy the buildings
Inside the TV, not that I care,
Not that I do not like it all,
Not that I am short or tall,
Not that I do not like to be alive,
And I appeal to you for pity,
Having in mind that you will read this
Under circumstances I cannot imagine
A thousand years from now.

Have pity on a girl, perdurable, playful,
And delicate as a foal, dutiful, available,
Who is waiting on a bed in a room in the afternoon for God.
His Majesty is on his way, who long ago has died.
She is a victim in the kingdom, and is proud.
Have pity on me a thousand years from now when we meet.
Open the mummy case of this text respectfully.
You find no one inside.

THE COSMOS TRILOGY (2003)

The Cosmos Poems (2000)

1. INTO THE EMPTINESS

Into the emptiness that weighs
More than the universe
Another universe begins
Smaller than the last.

Begins to smaller
Than the last.
Dimensions
Do not yet exist.

My friend, the darkness
Into which the seed
Of all eleven dimensions
Is planted is small.

Travel with me back
Before it grows to more.
The church bell bongs,
Which means it must be noon.

Some are playing hopscotch
Or skipping rope during recess,
And some are swinging on swings,
And seesaws are seesawing.

That she is shy,
Which means it must be May,
Turns into virgin snow
And walking mittened home with laughing friends.

And the small birds singing,
And the sudden silence,
And the curtains billow,
And the spring thunder will follow—

And the rush of freshness,
And the epileptic fit that foams.
The universe does not exist
Before it does.

2. MIRROR FULL OF STARS

A can of shaving cream inflates
A ping-pong ball of lather,
Thick, hot, smaller than an atom, soon
The size of the world.

This does take time to happen.
Back at the start
Again, a pinprick swells so violently
It shoots out

Hallways to other worlds,
But keeps expanding
Till it is all
There is. The universe is all there is.

Don't play with matches.
The candle flame follows her
With its eyes. The night sky is a mirror
On a wall.

What she stands in front of are the roaring afterburners
Of the distant stars a foot away
Leaving for another world. They have been summoned
To leave her

For another girl
In another world who stands there looking
In a mirror full of stars
At herself in her room.

The room is not really,
But it might be. If there is
Something else as beautiful
As this snow softly falling outside, say.

The universe begins
With a hot ball of lather expanding
In a hand
That should be in her bed asleep.

FROM *The Cosmos Trilogy*

3. WHO THE UNIVERSE IS

The opposite of everything
That will be once
The universe begins
Is who it is.

Laws do not apply
To the pre-universe.
None of it
Does not make sense.

Puffs to the size
Of an orange in one single stunned
Instant
From smaller than a proton.

Morning coffee black
Happiness so condensed
Had to expand to this,
Had to expand to this,

Had to expand to this
Universe of love
Of freezing old
Invisible dark matter

To give it gravity.
If the hot unbelievable
Nothingness feeds
Itself into a hole and starts,

None of this does not make sense
Once you understand
The stars are who it is,
The sisters and the brothers.

Set the toaster setting between Light and Dark
And the unimaginable
Pre-universe will pop up a slice of strings
In eleven dimensions which balloons.

4. UNIVERSES

Think of the suckers on the tentacles
Without the tentacles. A honeycomb
Of space writhing in the dark.
Time deforming it, time itself deformed.

Fifteen billion light-years later a president
Of the United States gives the Gettysburg Address.
Two minutes. The solar system
Star beams down on him.

Other special stars express themselves,
Not shy at all, particles
Of powder floating on the swirl, each
Vast—each a vast pillow covering

A hidden speck it murderously
Attempts to suffocate.
The speck will eat it up.
The speck of gravity is a hole.

Through that hole there is a way.
There are as many of these, there are as many of these
Invisible black caviar
Specks as it would take

To fill the inside of St. Peter's to the roof.
It is the number
Of grains of sand on the shores
Surrounding the continent of Africa times ten.

Each invisible eyelet is a black hole
Highway out of time.
Think of the universe as a beanbag
On a bobsled on a run under lights at night.

Inside are universes.
It is incompletely dark inside.
There is motion.
There is the possibility.

FROM *The Cosmos Trilogy*

5. BLACK STOVEPIPE HAT

The wobbly flesh of an oyster
Out of its shell on the battlefield is the feel
Of spacetime
In the young universe.

The petals of the rose
Of time invaded
The attitude of zero and made it
Soften its attitude.

Lincoln's black stovepipe hat
Was dusty when he sat down
To scant applause. Many in the crowd did not know
He had just delivered

The Gettysburg Address, but it is over,
And the stars keep on redshifting,
The universe keeps on expanding
The petals of the rose.

U. S. Grant's cigar's red tip
Pulsed the primal fireball out
Through the new universe
It was the creator of with shock waves.

Speckles of the stars
And baby's breath (the flower)
Activate infinity
And decorate the parlor.

Baby's breath is counting on the roses
With it in the vases.
It is difficult to understand
Why the universe began.

It is difficult to be
Robert E. Lee.
Why does the cosmos have to happen?
What is another way?

6. THE CHILDHOOD SUNLIGHT

Blessed is the childhood sunlight
The solar star emotes.
Darkly filled-up emptiness
And galaxies too far away

Are what we feel inside ourselves
That make us want to walk somewhere,
And then we run and jump and sing.
The universe is not enough,

We rock 'n' roll to other ones
Through black hole wormhole timeways,
But here right now the rain has stopped,
The air is warm.

The parking lot washed clean smells sweet,
And even has a rainbow that
A little girl tiptoes toward,
Hoping not to frighten it.

The neighbor's dog that won't go home
Is watching her—which she can't see—
With naked eyes of love and awe.
She feels that way herself sometimes.

When you are sure that you're alone,
Tell yourself to not be sure.
This universe is not the first.
The other ones are not the same.

Or anyway no one can know.
At night when she should be asleep
She lights a match and blows it out
To show she has the power to.

Computers crunch the numbers and
The other stars lie down and say
The sun exhausts itself with light.
So good night.

FROM *The Cosmos Trilogy*

7. BEYOND THE EVENT HORIZON

And isn't it
The presence of a thing
That can't be seen
More massive than the universe?

And isn't it the strings
Of its own gut beneath infinity the bow
Who vibrate musically to make
The Primal Scene?

You realize this means
The massless spin-2 particle whose
Couplings at long distances
Are those of general relativity.

It means
Strings of an instrument that are
Ten to the minus thirty-two centimeters
In diameter in the Theory of Everything.

It means the temple
Is of a size
Too small for belief—indeed, whose
Dimensions do not begin.

O instrument.
O scene that moves the bow.
We could be everything that
Could be otherwise,

Reversed inside the tiny walled whirlpool
Of a black hole, but can't.
Even infinity is stuck and can't stop.
We could be

Playing with the toys
In another space,
Generating the video
Of something else.

8. BLUE AND PINK

The very young universe has reached
The size of a BB.
The idiopathic
Rheostat dialed up the expansion.

Suddenly it sticks out
A hair of spacetime.
It is of course the size of the universe
Inside the tiny BB.

All this happened long ago,
But still is happening
In my mind as I look for the runway
In the fumes.

Oxygen
Is not in the atmosphere
Of this particular planet.
The mother-of-pearl means that

If we decide to land,
We will slide. The ammonia park
Is the innocent summer's day
Colors of a Della Robbia terra-cotta statue.

The oil derrick–like devices pumping
Are the creatures.
We do a flyby
And decide better not.

Baby blanket blue and baby blanket pink we were warned
To watch out for when we were launched.
The good ship *Gigabyte*
Sails the seas of space.

Girls and boys, every planet we visit is different.
Some are made of ice cream and some are the blue and pink
Of the sign in front of the movie star's house:
ARMED RESPONSE.

FROM *The Cosmos Trilogy*

9. GALAXIES

Everyone knows that the moon
Is made of rice,
But how many of you know
That the jellyfish

You see in the picture on page 8—
Everybody open your book—
Is eleven million light-years wide?
It is beautiful, to boot.

It is beautiful to kick
The ball into the goal.
It is beautiful to know how
To answer the phone.

The jelly that looks like frog spawn
You see in the back pond
Is so many stars.
No, stars are different from Mars.

Everybody come to the window.
The blackness of space
Is simply the everything we are,
Subtracting the light.

The everything we are,
Minus the light,
Is what the battery acid is
Without the bulb.

But the bulb without the lens
To focus the heart
Is the spaceship we are all in
Without the artificially created gravity we need.

We all need
Our mothers and fathers who are dead.
We all need to be good
In case we will die too.

10. FEMINISTS IN SPACE

The stars are happy flowers in a meadow.
The grass is green and sweetly modest.
The burble of the brook
Is the thrust powered back.

Best friend, you walk with me through life,
Let's take a walk in space.
I'm suiting up, not easy, lots of laughter,
Squirming out of the girl suit, floating into the other.

We will be feminists in space,
Flying toward the stars,
With our backpack portable life-support,
All a grownup needs,

Even if there is a tether back to the mother
Ship we came from.
Leave your dolls behind.
Opening the hatch.

Two gentlemen are out taking a stroll
In their space suits big as polar bears.
That blue-eyed snowball is the planet Earth.
Oh, there's America, my earth, my ground.

Cars and factories and rain forests burning have farted
The cloud cover that suffocates the ball,
Which up here we jet away from
With our jet nozzles, squirting around like squids.

We can do anything we want.
We can turn somersaults all day long.
I also want to star in a movie but I want to sing
By being a scientist and being my brain.

Women of the world unite
Already at ten years old.
Two friends are skipping home from school,
Each with her own thoughts.

FROM *The Cosmos Trilogy*

11. THIS NEW PLANETARIUM

The universe roars an expletive
Starburst in every direction
Like the U.S. Navy Blue Angels
Flying their routine.

Everyone talks about the silence of light
But no one talks about the sound
Beyond decibels that
Is equally uncontainable,

And which the heavens declare the glory
Of as the jets explode
In joys expanding at a rate
That is increasing.

It is the candles
On a birthday cake blowing out
But lighting up—it is after the fast
A feast of spacetime

Faster and faster, uncontainable,
As the whole thing breathes out,
The rib cage of the universe expanding
Quite a bit faster than at the beginning.

Everyone talks about the silence
But no one talks about the sound.
I hear the light.
I hear the mighty organ bellowing heaven through

The bars of my playpen and I
Stand up, wobbling, age one,
Holding on to the sunshine
That is falling outside my window.

The light roars through this new planetarium.
Most of the universe is
The dark matter we are not made of,
But we stand.

12. INVISIBLE DARK MATTER

It is the invisible
Dark matter we are not made of
That I am afraid of.
Most of the universe consists of this.

I put a single normal ice cube
In my drink.
It weighs one hundred million tons.
It is a sample from the densest star.

I read my way across
The awe I wrote
That you are reading now.
I can't believe that you are there

Except you are. I wonder what
Cosmologists don't know
That could be everything
There is.

The someone looking at the page
Could be the everything there is,
Material that shines,
Or shined.

Dark matter is another
Matter. Cosmologists don't know.
The physicists do not.
The stars are not.

Another thing beside
The row of things is
Standing there. It is invisible,
And reads without a sound.

It doesn't matter
That it doesn't really.
I need to take its hand
To cross the street.

FROM *The Cosmos Trilogy*

13. A TWITTERING BALL

A twittering ball of birds
Repeatedly bursts in the sky,
Losing its shape but regaining it,
Making a fist and unfolding finger by finger

Time and galaxies and dust
Out of the little beginning herpes
Pimple swelling
Energy out, heat, huge,

Spacetime hiccuping
Itself outward into
Itself in exponential surges
According to the mathematics.

The mathematics prepares
The student stars.
It predicts a certain
Unevenness in the performance.

How to connect the very small
To the very large is the task
Ahead. The task ahead
Is the path of the mathematics not yet

Walked down to the place
Where we meet in a mirror,
Sit down together, raise a glass of wine
And smile, nodding in accord.

General relativity
And quantum theory at the same table at last
Lift a fork
The size of the universe to eat a pea.

The Planck length is the pea.
Hawking guiding his self-powered wheelchair
And Einstein riding his bicycle
Walk the Planck.

14. THE STAR

I was thinking about dogs
To fight death.
They get hold of it by the teeth and can
Go on forever.

Their eyes are pure
Fame and purity.
This was just an idea.
It came from thinking about the star.

I don't know its name.
It is very far away.
What does it say?
I was walking down by the water.

The night was warm,
The smell of spring.
In outer space the cold
Is fertile and freezes anything clean.

The star has the face
Of a flower.
It is burning and freezing
Immensity.

It has the power
To say a name.
When you look out the specially reinforced viewhole
Of the spaceship at the universe,

You are glancing down at the top
Of a tee as you prop a golf ball there
For the drive.
You look off in the distance toward the flag.

The black velvet lining of the box
That holds the stars is soft.
I let the dogs off the leash
And let them run and I pray.

FROM *The Cosmos Trilogy*

15. SPECIAL RELATIVITY

I am pushing the hidden
Pedals of my little car
To get somewhere I have
To get to.

The stars are everywhere, like tourists
At cherry blossom time.
A mist of cosmic dust
Drifts by for years.

Little Red Car to Earth:
I am up here. It's fun.
I'm doing all the things.
I'm signing off now to pedal.

The little boy pedaled
Through space in his car.
The birch canoe paddled
To avoid the black hole.

The stars stared,
Not being cool,
And stalked the celebrity cherry
Blossoms for an autograph.

And the very latest,
And the weather forecast,
And the Weather Channel,
And motorcycles are dangerous.

I was furiously pumping
The pedals of my little car
To get somewhere I had
To get to.

By the laws of special relativity,
I began to wrinkle and bend.
The universe has no end,
But I am getting there.

16. TAKE ME TO INFINITY

We are completely
In the dark with our eyes.
We listen with the radio
Telescope to the noise.

We repair the Hubble
Telescope in place in space because they hiss
It is head and shoulders above a 200-inch dish
On a mountaintop—but really

Astronomy is just like
Playing in the bath with a rubber duck
And looking at the universe all
At once and

We know so much nothing,
Why not know some more?
I say to the people
Of the United States,

Enough time has passed.
I say to the people of the world,
The time has come
And gone and now.

How did the universe begin?
I will count to ten.
How will it end?
I had the most amazing dream.

You were on all fours like a dog
And I was walking you
Around—
And you were me!

And I was reading me the riot act
Because I don't make sense.
Both of me say: Take me to infinity!
Take me to before the universe!

FROM *The Cosmos Trilogy*

17. POEM

Her hobby is laughter.
She plays the musical saw.
Her bunk is aft.
It's her turn to sleep.

Mission Control is working feverishly
Through the night
To solve the problem and needs her
Awake.

The international space crew
Floats in the dark
Composing final thoughts
And smelling the smoke.

She is the most popular
Mission Commander
In the history of the Shakespeare program ever—
Brave, Chinese, and brilliantly alive.

She is a wife and mother
And Girl Scout leader.
Suddenly the ship shakes violently.
Something has exploded.

Shakespeare 5 has been sent up
With all the world's hopes. One
Last chance to deflect the asteroid.
This is Mission Control. We're not reading you, *Shakespeare*. Over.

She wakes up in her crib
And is covered with moonlight.
She hears the nearby murmur
Of voices

Which must be the TV
One billion human beings
Are watching.
Someone softly covers her with her blanket.

18. SUPERSYMMETRY

You step into the elevator
To go down and it goes up,
And the surprise
Of the sensation of sudden

Happiness is weightless.
So is love.
The chemistry of intergalactic
Space is scarcely human,

But on the other hand we
Are all related.
So is love.
Einstein bicycled right here, didn't he?

The guru Edward Witten, talking
Along the same Princeton streets many years after
And into the grounds of the Institute
For Advanced Study, is not lost.

He zooms to a blackboard
Of equations about
The quantum mechanics
Of the central thing when it is raining outside.

He titters behind
The flutter of a geisha fan,
In heavy makeup, left, right, male, female,
Kabuki, kooky.

Over the ocean in France, the platinum meter stick
Under a glass bell is rational,
And meaningless,
And dissolving.

But Witten grasps it cheerily in one hand
And the geisha fan in the other,
Like the pots of gold at the ends of the rainbow
In the rain.

FROM *The Cosmos Trilogy*

19. EVERYTHING

And they overwhelm you and force
You to stay still till it is over.
Movies do.
I like the speed of light.

I like the speed
And the incomparably blurred
Sensation of being deformed
Into being and about to begin.

The starter is the inexhaustible
Appetite of the non-living
Miracle to grow a universe, so to speak,
So many digits

Every blink,
Tick tick tick tick
From the beginning.
I unlock the steamer trunk

From the days when they used to
Travel with steamer trunks. I lift the lid and inside
Find the original blast of spacetime
Growing outward toward a distant shore.

The stars are singing to the stars
In there, stars to stars.
It isn't over
When the galaxies cluster

And the audience is crying
And you are.
It overwhelms you and forces
You to stay till it is over.

The same poem over and over
You are witnessing, the swelling of the universe
Into the rose
Which it will give.

20. HAPPINESS

It isn't every day, but most,
That one inflicts this on oneself.
It is intolerable.
Such universality

Means there is no other place
So one must do it here, do
And be, and feel the joy
Most days bring.

We have scars
On our imagination that come from
Joy. I mean, the woman has
A huge star sapphire buried

In the middle of her forehead, yes?
And that is good.
And the universe she sits
On is.

Her third eye is.
However, it bleeds.
The universe is in a skillet
Cooking into something yum.

I say
Cimabue painted her without the sapphire
Holding the infant Jesus.
The dervish dancers swirl

In their white robes which whirl the stars
Into galaxies and the galaxies
Into cheese. The blue shoe is the Earth
Seen from space,

And its blade twirls on the ice of the skating rink
In the dark. There is no point
In trying to think about this
Bliss.

FROM *The Cosmos Trilogy*

21. THE ELEVEN DIMENSIONS

The images received are
One light-year old.
That has been confirmed.
On the monitor is

A wide boulevard of black
Lacquer in a capital.
A faint fuzz
Of spring blur coats the trees.

The headlights on in the rain must be
Their eyes.
The trees are the dogs
We know so little about

That they walked.
We have no idea what
Language they used
And did they use their mouths to excrete

What then was
Capitalized
To produce the malt
Which reproduced the songs?

They knew there were
More than three dimensions
To their wives.
Every year they called it spring.

They practiced herd individualism
And ran alone together.
Every headlight drank an evening cocktail
And didn't drive.

They knew there were
Eleven dimensions,
Which they didn't know
Were about to begin.

22. THE ROYAL PALM

The tiny octopus
Of galaxies and dust is
The universe taking up
Space.

The octopus also is
The black space around itself
Its octopus ink
Clones in clouds.

Its round human eye is looking
Out at nothing.
Its eight tentacles
Are fingering ink-jet spacetime.

It squirts the self
Around itself it floats in.
It opens its eight arms wide.
It opens its eye and mouth and suckers wide.

It is an eight-armed dome and does.
It is the universe and is.
It is the royal palm
Of consciousness slightly swaying above the beach.

Angels are swimming
In the sea.
Manta rays ripple by
Nearby.

The interstellar dust
Keeps incubating life.
The oral
Sharks are always having fun.

One tank at the aquarium
Of nothingness
Contains all this
Zest.

FROM *The Cosmos Trilogy*

23. FAINT GALAXY

I come from
Far away from you
And that is
Far away.

Hundreds of
Millions of stars in a
Galaxy and billions of galaxies and one
Billions of light-years away.

I came from
Far away from you
And that was
Far away.

My news is billions
Of light-years ago. When
I started to come toward
You.

And somewhere
Along the way. I
Forget
What I was going to say.

I came from
Far away from you and
That is far
Away.

The light
That reaches you now
Is I
Began far off.

That touches your eyes.
That enters your thought.
From afar.
From the start.

24. EDWARD WITTEN

Witten is designing
A baby's bib
With a little red
Sea horse raised

Embroidered emblem. Now
When baby spits out the baby food paste
The universe is spooning into her face
A little red sea horse will catch it.

A little red
Sea horse is eleven-dimensional
Spacetime. It unicycles
Upright in space

In all directions
At once.
A little thread sea horse
Is deaf,

Blind, can't smell,
Has no voice.
The universe
Is also raised

On a background of something else,
And the something else
Is there to catch something
Else.

It will catch hell
For the unfathomable inhuman
Daring of the theory
The heroic Edward Witten

At the Institute for Advanced Study
Has put forward in the Theory of Everything
To the effect
That we spill.

FROM *The Cosmos Trilogy*

25. THE BIRTH OF THE UNIVERSE

The perfect petals
Of the rose
Of time, of all three
Angels that prepare for this,

Of everything the blue
Warm water does
To magnify the August hour,
The perfect

Thunder mint
Between the thumb and finger
Makes, or the large smell of rain before it rains,
Grow from several storm cells

Violently,
While the hour
Hand sweeps as if it were barking seconds
And the day stands still,

In perfect bloom,
And so the universe
Was just conceived,
And just arrives,

And jets a rising fountain
Lit with many lights
And colors,
And a rushing sound,

And it is night,
And it is air,
And the ice cream is infinite
Above the cone

The small hand holds
Dripping, holds the torch
Of everything
Is good.

26. STARLIGHT

To return to the impossible
Is to be happy in the future
With what after all was the start
And continues to produce.

You know what that means?
It means you are in love.
It means to live your life
You have to.

The universe is ourself
Moving in sleep
Very slowly or in sudden
Seizures toward eternal life.

The universe is a single organism
Made of two
Or more individual,
Or many more than two, individual

Moving parts and blitzkrampf,
Explosive but balletic slow-mo
Of vast organs
Of ecstasy making sounds

The radio telescopes will hear
Billions of light-years from now,
The way whales croon
Whalesong through the ocean microphone

To an audience in darkness far away.
To live your life
You have to use it up.
A star performs its nuclear core.

Beautiful Kate Valk of the Wooster Group
Of actors does the male title role in *The Emperor Jones*
In blackface till she is so much
Starlight she stops.

FROM *The Cosmos Trilogy*

27. QUANTUM MECHANICS

It is raining on one side
Of the street and
A mother on the other.
Boy, it's hot!

Incandescence not making sense,
The ultimate
The weather will
Allow.

Of the energy
Of a supernova the
Undertow
Collapses to,

It has been said
There is no way to
Express the utterly
Unlighted

Out the other side.
It can appear out of nowhere
Outside your own front door.
Knock, knock.

Come in. It's open.
Delivery!
Come in, it's open.
Fifteen billion light-years is fast food

To the divine quantum equations
It is delivered to—
Which eat the delivery boy,
According to Heisenberg.

They have charm
And quark and spin.
They work both sides of the street.
They give good infinity.

28. IT IS THE MORNING
OF THE UNIVERSE

It is the morning of the universe:
Black children on their way to school to read.
The storefront metal gates on rollers rise
And all the shops are open now for praise.

It's hard to bear the beauty.
The traffic is sweet this early.
The old are up and listen,
Though the ones who don't get up don't listen.

Even in a universe this young
Things ask why
Enormous stars blow up
And more stars are born.

Born to burn,
They start to cry.
The young stars burn and shine.
That's the law.

As for the mania of being always
On,
It consumes the nuclear core
And beams truth through space

As deeply as a child reads his first real book.
When they assemble the biggest telescope ever
On the far side of the skin,
They will be able to see

A boy not moving his lips
And a book being read,
Free of the wobbles
Of earth atmosphere distortion.

Stars collide and explode
And their young are born.
The children arrive at school.
A billion years go by.

FROM *The Cosmos Trilogy*

29. FOREVER

The innocence of the tornado
Of the universe torridly
Twists the universe, the way a clay pot turns
On a potter's wheel languidly

Gaining form, the funnel and the rapturous
Waist swaying slowly
Like a belly dancer at ten million
Miles an hour, sways like an elephant's trunk

Of clots of rough and gray indigestible
That will be stars
And galaxies and strum and strums
The invisible cold dark matter,

Earsplitting odorless suction coming
Through time that stands
On its tail and the other force,
And is everything

Filling space,
And is space and everything,
Spacetime, everything.
What are we?

The everything looks
Out without eyes.
What are we?
Between everything and no.

The cobra sways
To the music
The belly dancer sways
To and the urge.

Gravity sings to the other force
And the other force sings back.
The hypnotized body floats in the air.
Love is God.

30. FOREVER

The surge of energy death can't
Protect itself against
Imagines everything
At once.

The surge protector
That a spike of energy
Can't avoid,
And that the spike of energy

Destroyed,
Fires its last distress flare forever,
Which is the aftermath
Till now, and is this place.

There is the tendency
Not to be
Which required
A singularity

To overcome
It, which made a blast which
Imaged everything
Just once,

The flash forever
That the flare flashes
Forever.
One consequence of the disappearance

Of nothingness
Is all the bandages eerily
Unwind and soon
The pharaoh finds the energy inside

The mummy case to lift
The lid. The flash of the universe
Goes out
To the eyes of time.

FROM *The Cosmos Trilogy*

31. FOREVER

I travel further than
I can to reach the place
I can. I reach
The place.

Stars testify.
The black is
Satisfied with that.
The black of space is old cold.

How cold it feels
When you remember warm.
I swim with winter wings
Beneath the royal palms.

Birth put a message
In a bottle and floated it away.
My DNA washed up on a shore, facelift smiling,
My plump green grape maturity flash-frozen.

I drank so much.
So many women
I touched.
The voyage to outer space parties forever.

The reading material is
Incinerated and
The mind gets so old cold
I ache but

Yes, those are stars.
Yes, in the vicinity of zero, the grape's now
Nearly fleshless face lifts
A trumpet to its lips.

American eternity
Swooningly crooning ballads on the red vinyl LP
From the 1950s on earth
Turns away wrath, swords into songs, undying rebirth.

32. THE LAST REMAINING ANGEL

Thinner than a fingerprint
And smaller than a postage stamp,
It looks like brains
Or softly scrambled eggs.

It moves in waves,
The latest Stealth technology.
It gets there fast.
The galaxies do the parallel processing.

Another miracle, the stars.
They give their lives when they fall.
The others pick up after them.
The implant keeps the bad things out.

It shocks the heart, restores the rhythm.
The operating system loves it.
The stars become so meek and mighty.
Sometimes things don't always crash.

A woman is a wingless angel flying.
The last remaining angel joined her.
The entire known universe
Is their high-wire act.

Everything there is is the trapeze, no net.
And now abideth faith, hope, gravity,
These three, but the greatest of these
Is the ground.

The universe is taking off
Its clothes and taking
Off in a hailstorm. The runway
Looks like brains. It looks like love

Is everything there is.
Things in boots
Are murdering the Jews on Mars
And other galaxies don't know.

FROM *The Cosmos Trilogy*

33. IN THE GREEN MOUNTAINS

Into the emptiness that weighs
More than the universe
Another universe is born
Smaller than the last.

Good tidings of great joy.
Adonai.
Glory be to God in the highest and likewise
To those of us who don't believe.

For Buddha
Is the advice
Of the stand-up comic
Hooded cobra god of the young, serene.

Unleashing the nourishing rain,
My lord Monsoon lashes the delta.
They sing from the Torah
The beginning of the universe

At the young woman's bat mitzvah. Behold.
I bring you good
Tidings of great joy.
Adonai.

My friend, the darkness
Into which the seed
Of all eleven dimensions
Is planted is small.

That she is shy,
Which means it must be May,
Turns into green and June
And the seedling synagogue in Bennington.

And the small birds singing,
And the sudden silence,
And the curtains of the Ark billow open,
And the Tibetan tubas in the echoing Green Mountains roar.

Life on Earth (2001)

34. BALI

Is there intelligent life in the universe?
No glass
In the windows of the bus
In from the airport, only air and perfume.

Every porch in the darkness was lighted
With twinkling oil lamps
And there was music
At 2 a.m., the gamelan.

I hear the cosmos
And smell the Asian flowers
And there were candles
Mental as wind chimes in the soft night.

Translucency the flames showed through,
The heavy makeup the little dancers wore,
The scented sudden and the nubile slow
Lava flow of the temple troupe performing for the hotel guests.

Her middle finger touches her thumb in the *vitarkamudra*,
While her heavily made-up eyes shift wildly,
Facial contortions silently acting out the drama,
And the thin neck yin-yangs back and forth to the music.

Announcing the gods,
The room jerked and the shower curtain swayed.
All the water in the swimming pool
Trampolined out, and in the mountains hundreds died.

The generals wanted to replace Sukarno.
Because of his syphilis he was losing touch
With the Communist threat and getting rather crazy.
So they slaughtered the Communists and the rich Chinese.

Gentle Balinese murdered gentle Balinese,
And, in the usual pogrom, killed
The smart hardworking Chinese,
Merchants to the poor, Jews in paradise.

35. FRENCH POLYNESIA

Drinking and incest and endless ease
Is paradise and child abuse
And battered wives.
There are no other jobs.

Everything else is either
Food or bulimia.
The melon drips with this.
It opens and hisses happiness.

A riderless horse sticks out,
Pink as an earthworm, standing on the beach.
Fish, fish, fish,
I feel fishish.

I develop
When I get below my depth.
I splinter into jewels, Cadillac-finned balls,
Chromed mercury no one can grab.

I care below the surface.
Veils in
Colors I haven't seen in fifty years nibble
Coral.

Easter Sunday in Papeete.
Launched and dined at L'Acajou.
The Polynesians set off for outer space
In order to be born, steering by the stars.

Specialists in the canoes chant
The navigation vectors.
Across the universe,
A thousand candles are lighted

In the spaceships and the light roars
And the choir soars. A profusion
Of fruit and flowers in tubs being offered
Forms foam and stars.

FROM *The Cosmos Trilogy*

36. THE OPPOSITE OF A DARK DUNGEON

Three hundred steps down
From the top
Pilgrims are
Looking up.

The temple is above
In a cave.
The stairs to it start next
To the standard frantic street.

Monkeys beg on
The stairs
All the way
Up to the entrance.

Vendors sell treats
To the pilgrims to feed to them.
Some people are afraid of monkeys
Because they think they might get bitten.

When you finally reach the top, somewhat
Out of breath, you enter
The heavy cold darkness
And buy a ticket.

The twenty-foot gilded figures recline.
There are trinkets you can buy to lay at their smiling feet.
They use up the universe with their size.
Their energy is balm and complete.

Everything in the cosmos
Is in the cave, including the monkeys
Outside. Everything is
The opposite of a dark dungeon. And so

A messenger from light arrived.
Of course they never know that they're a messenger.
Don't know they carry a message.
And then they stay awhile and then they leave.

37. STAR BRIGHT

The story goes one day
A messenger from light arrived.
Of course they never know that they're a messenger.
Don't know they carry a message.

The submarine stayed just
Below the surface with its engines off near the shore observing.
One day the world took off its shoes and disappeared
Inside the central mosque

And never came back out. Outside the periscope the rain
Had stopped, the fires on shore were
Out. Outside the mosque
The vast empty plaza was the city's outdoor market till

The satellite observed the changing
Colors of the planet
And reported to the submarine that
No one was alive.

A messenger from light arrived.
Of course they never know that they're a messenger.
Don't know they carry a message.
And then they stay awhile and then they leave.

Arrived, was ushered in,
Got in a waiting car and drove away.
Was ushered in,
Kowtowed to the Sacred Presence the required ten times

And backed away from the Sacred Presence blind,
And turned back into light.
Good night,
Blind light.

Far star, star bright.
And though they never know that they're a messenger,
Never know they carry a message,
At least they stay awhile before they leave.

FROM *The Cosmos Trilogy*

38. GOODNESS

In paradise on earth each angel has to work.
Jean-Louis de Gourcuff and his wife spend hours
Spreading new gravel in the courtyard and the drive.
The château swan keeps approaching its friend Jean-Louis to help.

Monsieur le Comte et Madame la Comtesse
Have faith, give hope, show charity.
This is the Château of Fontenay.
And this is the Gourcuffs' ancient yellow Lab, Ralph.

It's de rigueur for French aristocrats to name their dogs in English.
Something about happiness is expressed
By the swan's leaving the safety of its pond,
Given the number of English names around.

Ralph smiles and says *woof* and the swan smiles and says *hiss*
In a sort of Christian bliss.
What is more Christian than this?
You have entered the kingdom of the kind.

Old Count de Gourcuff lives in another wing, the father,
Tall big-boned splendor of an English gentleman, but French.
His small wife is even more grand and more France.
One has a whisky with him in the library.

Something about goodness is being expressed
At a neighbor's château nearby.
In the marble reception hall, ghosts are drinking champagne.
The host will be shot right afterward by the Nazis for something.

Blind Ralph barks at the hissing swan he waddles behind and adores.
It is left to the childlike to lead the sick and the poor.
Jean-Louis de Gourcuff, the saintly mayor of Fontenay,
Dons his sash of office, white, blue, and red.

Dominique de Gourcuff makes regular
Pilgrimages with the infirm, to refresh her heart, to Lourdes.
Dinosaurs on their way to being birds
Are the angels down here in heaven.

39. JOAN OF ARC

Even her friends don't like her.
Tears roll out of
Her tear ducts,
Boulders meant to crush.

She feels
Her own emptiness but oddly
It feels like love
When you have no insight at all

Except that you are good.
The tears crush even
That thought out and she is left happily
Undressed with her stupidity.

Nobody wants her
On their side in games at school
So the retard
Is wired to explode.

She smokes, gets drunk,
Gets caught, gets thrown out
As the ringleader when she was not since
She has no followers, this most innocent

Who is completely
Emptiness,
Who is a thrill no one wants and
Whom the cowed will kill.

The "Goddamns" (as the invading English are
Called) get in her France.
It made the Maid of Orleans a man and God
Hears her crewcut rapture screaming at the stake in pants.

For God's sake, the food is burning
On the stove!
You are the only one in the world.
You are my good girl.

FROM *The Cosmos Trilogy*

40. DOCTOR LOVE

It was a treatment called
Doctor Love, after the main character.
One of the producers discovered
To our horror a real

Dr. Love who, eerily, by
Pure coincidence, was also a woman
Oncologist trying to identify the gene that causes
Breast cancer. My

Fiction trampolined
Herself right off the treatment page,
Landing not on a movie set or a screen at the multiplex,
But at a teaching hospital in Los Angeles directing

Her lab. If you could identify the gene
That turns the cancer on,
Then maybe you could find a way to turn it off—
And make somebody rich.

She found a gene.
The villain needed to learn which.
He sets the innocent doctor up to
Commit a murder. The story was in such bad taste.

It never made sense.
I was doing rounds in a long white coat
To write the screenplay—playing doctor, doctor love.
Till death us do part, Dr. Catharine Hart,

I will remember you
On the street kissing me hello.
The cherry blossom petals blow—
White coats on rounds

In a soft East River breeze—like glowing fireflies of snow.
Dear Hart, it is spring.
Cutting a person open
Is possible without pain.

41. FEVER

Your pillow is pouring
You like a waterfall
You sleep through
In the middle of.

You shiver sweat
In the middle of
The rain forest chattering in
Darkness at midday.

You like heat because
It makes a reptile warm.
On the raft with you
Is your life.

You have everything
You have.
The crocodiles choo-chooing around
And around are the snouts

Of your ancestors
Which split and jaggedly yawn
Because it is time to
Read aloud

The story
Of the African slaves walking on water
In chains all the way to the United States
In 1776.

Two hundred–plus years later,
Islam overthrows the Shah.
NO MENSTRUATION WOMEN ALLOW,
A temple sign had said on Bali.

The temple monkeys had not been friendly.
The president of the rubber-stamp Iranian senate,
Sharif-Imami, the loathed Shah
Loved. The fever breaks.

FROM *The Cosmos Trilogy*

42. BLOOD

The yellow sunlight with
The milky moonlight makes
An egg without cholesterol
And I will live.

O tree of brains
And sound of leaves.
The day is green.
And now I pray.

I thank the cotton
For the shirt.
I thank the glass that holds me
In, that I see through into out there.

I'm driving to the car wash
And the dogs are getting haircuts
And the motorcycles drive by
And I ask for mine,

My body in your hands
To live.
The bay is blue
To me means that.

The saline breeze says that
The soft is firm enough today
To hold the water up
With gulls on top that won't

Sink in.
I don't know when.
I don't know how.
I don't know I.

I tell the cardiologist that
I'm in love.
The needle draws the champagne
Into crystal flutes the lab will love.

43. HOLLY ANDERSEN

I describe you.
I have a chart to.
I hold your
Heart. I feel.

The motor
Of your life
Is not diseased or weak
Or real until

I stress it from the
Outside, how
You test anyone before you
Find them true.

Totally in
Your power,
The stethoscope
Puts its taproot to your chest, and flowers.

The miles of
Treadmill agnostically
Takes core samples.
The bolus which jump-starts us back to life is love.

The light leaps and is living
On the screen
As the mine-detector mechanism
Looks for mines.

Take a deep breath.
You stopped smoking cigarettes.
Breathe out through your mouth.
How many years ago.

We are made of years
That keep on living.
We are made of tears
That as your doctor I can't cry.

FROM *The Cosmos Trilogy*

44. AT NEW YORK HOSPITAL

I enter the center.
I open the book of there.
I leave my clothes in a locker.
I gown myself and scrub in.

Anything is possible that I do.
Cutting a person open
Is possible without pain. An entourage rolls
In a murderous head of state with beautiful big breasts—

Who is already under and extremely nude
On the gurney. Her sheet has slipped off.
Her perfect head has been shaved
Bald. And now a target area

On the top of the skull will
Be painted magenta. Her body is rewrapped.
Her face gets sealed off. Her crimes against humanity
Will be lasered.

I am a Confederate scout, silence in the forest.
The all eyes and stillness
Of a bird watcher has stumbled on
A Yankee soldier asleep.

The dentist's drill drills a hole and
The drill slips and whines out of control,
But no matter. The electric saw cuts
Out a skullcap of bone.

The helicopter descends from Olympus to within an
Inch of touching down
On the wrinkled surface, when a tool falls incredibly
To the floor and I pick it up and am thanked.

The anesthesiologist for my benefit joyously
Declaims Gerard Manley Hopkins.
The surgeon recites a fervent favorite childhood hymn.
He slaps the monster tenderly to wake her up. Wake up, darling.

45. DRINKS AT THE CARLYLE

The pregnant woman stares out the spaceship window at space—
But is listening carefully.
The man is looking at the inward look on her face.
The man is answering her question while they leave the galaxy.

Why they are on this space voyage neither stranger quite knows.
There is something that
Someone watching them
Might feel almost shows,

But would not be able to say what.
She was describing the American child
She was, the athlete who played the violin,
Who grew up on Earth upstate.

He sees American thrust, the freckled ignition
Who vanished in a puff of smoke on stage—and the power and
Grandly pregnant happily married woman physician
There on stage when the smoke cleared. He looks at her left hand

And her bow hand. He sees the child lift the half-size violin
From its case, and take the bow,
And fit the violin to her shoulder and chin,
And begin to saw, sweetly, badly,

While she asks him what it is like to be him,
To be a space commander, revered.
He stares softly at her severed
Connection to him as she again looks inward

And very distantly smiles
While he tries to think what she is asking him and answer.
She is smartly dressed in black,
Blond midnight in the air-conditioned hot middle of summer.

She has smilingly said she is the only doctor in town on
Fridays in July, so she knows everything.
It is amazing what people actually do.
I am not possible to know.

FROM *The Cosmos Trilogy*

46. CHIQUITA GREGORY

Sagaponack swings the Atlantic around its head
Like an athlete in the windup for the hammer throw.
It is a hurricane and the radio
Predicts a tornado will follow.

The air violently
Smells fresh like nowhere else,
And I am just assuming it is
You calling to everyone lunch is ready.

We are heads bowed
At our place cards. Zeus is saying grace
When the chairs begin to shake and lightning outside
Shazams you back to life, tsunami

Light as a feather, the feather of life,
Very long legs,
Very short shorts, a chef's apron in front, so that from
Behind . . . Goddess,

You have returned to earth in a mood and
In a storm, and I have no doubt that
Irreplaceable trees on Sagg Main are davening
Themselves to the ground. They

Rend their clothes and tear their hair out out
Of joy. Chiquita, how can anyone be so
Angry who has died? The whirling light in
The drive is the police, here

To urge the last holdouts in houses near the
Ocean to leave. To help us
Decide, they suavely ask for the name of next of kin.
The ocean bursts into towering flames of foam.

The lobsters in the pot are screaming
Inside the reddening roar.
Your aproned ghost keeps boiling more, keeps boiling more,
And turns to serve the gore.

47. TO START AT END

To start at End
And work back
To the mouth
Is the start—

Back to the black hole
That ate the meal,
Back from the universe
And the book

To the illiteracy
Of the much too
Compressed pre-universe
To release. So it was

The hands of fingers on
The keyboard bringing up on the screen
The something thirteen
Billion light-years back that happened,

The *Gentlemen, start your engines!*
That made it start,
Which is the mouth
Of the music.

The uncontrollable
Is about to happen—
A gash in the nothingness invisibly
Appears.

The uncontrollable is about
To happen—the strings (of string theory)
Are trembling unseen ecstatically
Before they even are touched by the bow.

It all happened so fast.
The fall weather was vast.
At either end of spacetime the armies massed.
Youth was past.

FROM *The Cosmos Trilogy*

48. WE HAVE IGNITION

Infinity was one of many
In a writhing pot of spaghetti.
One among many
Intestines of time.

The
Trembling the size and color
Of boiled lobster coral
Was trying

More violently than anything
Could and still live. The
Subatomic particles
Were

The truth. One of them became
The universe at once
While the others fled.
And one—

Not our universe—
Became something else.
Don't think about it
And you won't.

The landmass of the continental
United States compared to an open
Manhole
On the bitter boulevard where citizens buy crack

Is how much bigger the human brain is
Than the entire universe was at the start,
When it was the prickle
Before the zit.

Godspeed, John Glenn.
Fly safely high
In your seventy-seven-year-old
Head thirteen billion years old.

49. ETERNITY

A woman waits on a distant star she is traveling to.
She waits for herself to arrive.
But first she has to embark.
3, 2, 1 . . . ignition.

All systems are go for the facelift.
Her face lifts off into space.
She heads for the distant star
And the young woman waiting for her there.

A man who wanted to look better
But not younger is red
Swells of raw.
Later they will remove the staples.

Ten weeks later
They are younger.
They pull over
Their head a sock of skin.

One day the girl sees in the mirror a girl
Laughing so hard her face falls off in her hands.
You can see the inside of the face.
The front of her head is an amputee's smooth stump.

Her old woman's body is a bag of spotted slop.
The gentleman at least is doing fine.
His face peeks through the shower curtains
Of his previous face.

In the tomb air
Of the spacecraft they get more perfumed
As they painstakingly near
The hot banks of the Nile, so green and fertile.

Heart is safe in a dish of preservative.
Face is a box for the telemetry for the journey.
Perishable slaves caravan the monumental blocks of stone to the site.
The faceless likeness deafens the desert.

FROM *The Cosmos Trilogy*

50. THE MASTER JEWELER
JOEL ROSENTHAL

What's Joel
Got to do but let the jewel
Hatch
The light and hook

It to the flesh
It will outlast
And point the staring
Woman at a mirror?

The stone alone was fireworks
But is Star Wars in his choker.
Of course Joel wears no jewelry himself but
Makes it for these reasons rhyme.

The staring woman is starving and
Eating her own face and
Stares with a raving smile
At her undying love.

The things they
Have to have
Are his
Designs on them.

The richest in the world stick out their necks
And hands and ears for JAR's gems—
Which they can ride through the eye of a needle
To heaven. His genius is his

Joy, is JAR, is
Agonized obsession, is death is double-parked
Outside the palace. Death is loading in the van
The women and camels of King Solomon it is repossessing.

Joel has designed a watch
In platinum.
This watch is the sequel
To anyone you have ever lost.

51. IN SPITE OF EVERYTHING

I had a question about the universe
On my way to my evening class,
Stuck between stations on the No. 3 Express,
And it was this.

You don't know what you mean
And that's what I mean.
God is playing peekaboo,
Not There behind the hands.

Then peekaboo and you
See face-to-face and bam.
I'm getting old.
I hid and I revealed myself.

All the way down to the wharf
All the way down to the wharf
All the way down to the wharf
He-wolf and she-wolf went walking.

Shut up, darling! I'll do the talking.
All the way down to the wharf
All the way down to the wharf
The stalker was stalking.

The talker was talking.
You want to talk
Until I droop.
The river runs by

Under the broken pier.
All the great ocean liners left for France from here,
Whose passengers are
Now ghosts mostly. Loup and Louve howl

To Neptune from their heaving gale-force stateroom—
Walk through drought, walk through dew,
Keep walking down the avenue,
For richer for poorer, for better for worse, malgré tout.

FROM *The Cosmos Trilogy*

52. SPRINGTIME

Sunset rolls out the red carpet
For Charlotte as she walks
To her appointment with life
In the awed soft-focus.

Charlotte sees the crimson trees
With her famous eyes.
Fat rises to the surface of the street in sunset flames.
The magnolias are vomiting brightness

In the mist. Spring in its mania refuses
To take its medication. It
Buys every newspaper left on the newsstand, then
Sobs in a café, sobs with laughter.

A car at a light rocks from side to side with the
Windows down, letting in red, letting out rhythm—
A pounding pulse of rap from the exophthalmic car radio.
She would give anything to be able to

Sleep in a shower of this fragrance.
She is talking on her fear
Phone to anyone in her mind. She is
Saying in a red city

I am alive at sunset.
Charlotte is beautiful but
Charlotte is so beautiful it is
Insolence.

A fan
Asks for her autograph outside a restaurant.
Horse carriages slowly carry
Honeymooners through a fog of love as thick as snow.

A slave to love
Kisses a real slave she bought to free.
The dominatrix is whipped by her slave—
Who has made a mistake on the new rug and wags.

53. SUMMER

Kitsy and Bitsy and Frisky and Boo
Stream by, memories of moist
Moss—green morphine—
On each bank of a stream.

Fronds as delicate
As my feelings present
Those summers.
You could drink the water you swam

In, clear, cold, sweet, but August,
But August in St. Louis,
But August and the heat
That slows the green smell of the lawns

To tar, lyric
Of humidity
That thickens to a halt, but sweet, that swells
Up, that you escaped to dreams

From. In one,
Beauty and kindness combined
To walk across a room.
The daughter of Colonel Borders, Kitsy,

Means God has found a way, walks in through a door.
The universe begins at once.
The stars erupt a sky
They can be stars in, that they can be

Unicorns in a pen in.
The perfect knight in armor to slay the fiery dragon
Has sex with it instead.
I wake from the dream in the dark.

I barely see above
The steering wheel at twelve years old.
The park at night is warm.
The air is sweet and moist and cool.

FROM *The Cosmos Trilogy*

54. FALL SNOWFALL

The book of nothingness begins
At birth.
The pages turn and there
Is far.

There is far from where
They start.
The pages turn into
The book.

And everything and everyone and
What is happening
Is blood in urine.
Ask the trees

The leaves leave.
They are left.
They remove their wigs.
They turn themselves in.

They stand there blank.
The now falls
On the fields white.
The smell of wood smoke stares and

The no falls,
Radios
Of blank now
On the fields.

A black crow shakes the no off.
Merrily we
Go around circling
The drain, life is but a dream.

The doctors in their white
No
Fall
On the fields.

55. CHRISTMAS

My Christmas is covered
With goosepimples in the cold.
Her arms are raised straight
Above her head.

She turns around slowly in nothing but a
Garter belt and stockings outdoors.
She has the powerful
Buttocks of a Percheron.

My beautiful with goosepimples
Climbs the ladder to the high diving board
In her high heels
And ideals.

The mirror of the swimming pool is looking up at her
Round breasts.
She bounces up and down
As if about to dive.

In her ideals, in her high heels,
The palm trees go up and down.
The mirror of the swimming pool is looking up at her
Bikini trim.

The heated swimming pool mirror is steaming
In the cold.
The Christmas tree is on.
A cigarette speedboat cuts the bay in two.

It rears up on its white wake.
Ay, Miami!
Ninety miles away
Is Mars.

The cigarette smokes fine cigars,
Rolls hundred-dollar bills into straws.
My Christmas
Is in his arms.

FROM *The Cosmos Trilogy*

56. COSMOPOLITANS AT THE PARADISE

Cosmopolitans at the Paradise.
Heavenly Kelly's cosmopolitans make the sun rise.
They make the sun rise in my blood
Under the stars in my brow.

Tonight a perfect cosmopolitan sets sail for paradise.
Johnny's cosmopolitans start the countdown on the launch pad.
My Paradise is a diner. Nothing could be finer.
There was a lovely man in this town named Harry Diner.

Lighter than zero
Gravity, a rinse of lift, the cosmopolitan cocktail
They mix here at the Paradise is the best
In the United States—pink as a flamingo and life-announcing

As a leaping salmon. The space suit I will squeeze into arrives
In a martini glass,
Poured from a chilled silver shaker beaded with frost sweat.
Finally I go

Back to where the only place to go is far.
Ahab on the launch pad—I'm the roar
Wearing the wild blazer, black stripes and red,
And a yarmulke with a propeller on my missile head.

There she blows! Row harder, my hearties!—
My United Nations of liftoff!
I targeted the great white whale black hole.
On impact I burst into stars.

I am the caliph of paradise,
Hip-deep in a waterbed of wives.
I am the Ducati of desire,
144.1 horsepower at the rear wheel.

Nights and days, black stripes and red,
I orbit Sag Harbor and the big blue ball.
I pursue Moby-Dick to the end of the book.
I raise the pink flamingos to my lips and drink.

57. SEX

The woman in the boat you shiver with
The sky is coming through the window at.
We will see.
Keep rowing.

You have
An ocean all around.
You are rowing on bare ground.
The greasy grassless clay is dead calm.

You love your life.
You love the way you look.
You watch a woman posing for you.
How awful for you. There's no one there.

Inside the perfume bottle life is sweet.
The glass stopper above you is the stars.
You smell the flowers,
Some far-off shore.

The slaves are chained in rows rowing.
The motion back and forth
Is the same as making love.
You fuck infinity and that takes time.

It's a certain way of talking to arthritis
That isn't heart disease or trust.
You can't remember why
Your hands are bleeding back and forth.

The thing about a man is that—
Is what?
One hand reaches for the other.
The other has a knife in it to cut the head off.

The fish flops back and forth
In the bottom of the boat.
The woman pulls the boat along
By its painter that the king slash slave is rowing.

FROM *The Cosmos Trilogy*

58. SONG

How small your part
Of the world is when
You are a girl.
The forests and deserts are full

Of the animals
We ride and eat
And the wind and the light
And the night,

But if you are
A girl you may
As well live in Boston
Or be a grain of white rice

Or be a fleck
Of mica in a sidewalk.
I wanted to have
A monocle and stick—

Put on my top hat,
And be a grain
Of radium,
And radiate a stadium with my act.

It's about holding
The wide-eyed bearded head of
Holofernes
Aloft. From the carrier deck

We climb to altitude
With an attitude, with
Our laser-guided bombs targeting
The white enormous whale.

We need the sperm oil to light
Our lamps, have to stop
The huge white life for whalebone stays to cage
Our corsets.

59. THE SEAL

What did the vomit of a god
Smell like? Like no one else
And there were clouds of it
In the White House.

It was an impeachable
U.S. bald eagle
Because it was barking and sporting
In the moisture like a seal.

Tubby smooth
Energy tube of seal seeks tender veal
For the White House mess and in a zoo
It smells like that.

To be slick
And sleek and swim
And in yours have hers,
Her hand, her heart.

Once it was a god,
Now they toss it fish
And watch it leap
And make it beg.

They're looking
At TV and look
It doesn't look that bad.
The ones from outer space are landing now.

A seal went out to play
In the middle of an enormous bay
All the cities surrounded,
The size of the Dust Bowl, as brown,

And sang of a 21st century that was lyrical
About effluents and landfill,
And set the presidential seal
On doing something about race and ass.

FROM *The Cosmos Trilogy*

60. HER SONG

I am presenting
Myself to
You for the punishment
I preserve.

Sometimes you seem to
Understand I am
Banished.
I am the emptiness of

Bandages
That wrap
The mummy. My heart
I preserve in a dish—

It is a dog collar on all fours.
Inside is the
Eloquence
Emptied out.

Your hand
Starts to thunder,
Starts to rain much
Harder.

You raised your hand
To touch my cheek.
You saw my eyes
Go berserk.

It is the terror.
It asks you
To make it more.
Don't fall

In love
With me and I won't either.
Don't stop when
I say stop.

61. GREEN DRESS, 1999

You want
To change your name to be new
For the
Millennium so do.

The trumpet sounds
Your smile.
You soar just
Sitting still.

Flapping wings of a
Flamingo, clouds
Of my angina
Blossom darkly into dawn.

Sunset follows
While they play
The songs one wants
To hear. Your

Legs made of eleven
Kinds of heaven
Leap to
Where they want to go.

But I don't know
How long I have the
Future for.
In the jungle of

The body is the beating of the
Tom-tom.
Living dot com—
How many hits on your site?

If dance is what you do, the bar
Is where you go to
Work. If what you do is drink,
You also hit the heart.

FROM *The Cosmos Trilogy*

62. LETTER TO THE EDITORS OF *VOGUE*

I'm seeing someone and
I really want to,
But I
Am stuck in glue.

I would go anywhere
To be near
The sky above
And smell the iodine

Wine of the port of Algiers,
Or for that matter the freezing
Nights on the dunes
Of the Sahara are blood

That you can drink till dawn
Under the terror of
Stars to
Make you blind.

I am drinking gasoline
To stay awake
In the midst of so much
Murder.

My daughter squeaks and squeaks
Like a mouse screaming in a trap,
Dangling from the cat who makes her come
When he does it to her.

Her killer goes out into
The streets to join his brothers
In the revolution
Who don't have jobs.

The *plastic* packed beautifully
Inside a tampons box that I carefully leave in the loo
At Café Oasis goes rigid and the
Unveiled meet God.

63. JAMES BALDWIN IN PARIS

The leopard attacks the trainer it
Loves, over and over, on every
Page, loves and devours the only one it allows to feed
It.

How lonely to be understood
And have to kill, how lovely.
It does make you want to starve. It makes an animal kill
All the caring-and-sharing in the cage.

Start with the trainer who keeps you alive
In another language,
The breasts of milk
That speak non-leopard. Slaughter them.

What lives below
The surface in a leopard will have to live above
In words. I go to sleep
And dream in meat and wake

In wonder,
And find the poems in
The milk
All over the page.

Lute strings of summer thunder, rats hurrying
Away, sunshine behind
Lightning on a shield of
Pain painting out happiness, equals life

That will have to be extinguished
To make way. The sound trucks getting out the vote
Drive the campaign song down every street.
Hitler is coming to Harlem.

Hitler is coming to Harlem!/There will be ethnic cleansing./
A muddy river of Brown Shirts/Will march to the Blacks.
Happiness will start to deface
Pain on the planet.

64. ST. LOUIS, MISSOURI

You wait forever till you can't wait any longer—
And then you're born.
Somebody is pointing something out.
You see what I'm saying, boy!

Can't find a single egg at his debutant
Easter egg hunt and has to be helped.
Jewish wears a little suit with a shirt with an Eton collar.
Blood cakes on the scratch on your little knee.

Excuse me a minute.
The angel is black as a crow.
The nurse comes back in the room.
It shakes the snow from its wings.

The waterfall hangs
Down panting in the humidity.
The roar at the top of the world
Is the icebergs melting in pain.

Don't play on the railroad tracks.
It is so hot.
The tracks click before you hear the train
Which the clicks mean is coming.

British consuls posted to St. Louis in those days
Before air-conditioning had to receive extra pay.
The congressman with a bad limp was bitter.
They had operated on the wrong leg, made it shorter.

My father's coal yards under a wartime heavy snow.
The big blue trucks wearing chains like S/M love.
Blessed are the poor, for they will have heat this Christmas.
The tire chains/sleigh bells go *chink chink*.

The crow at the foot of the bed caws you
Were the Age of Chivalry and gave my family coal.
And when it was hot your ice trucks delivered
To the colored their block of cold.

65. HAMLET

The horsefly landing fatly on the page
And walking through words from left to right is rage.
It walks, stage right to left, across the stage.
The play is called *The Nest Becomes a Cage.*

I'm reading *Hamlet*, in which a bulging horsefly
Soliloquizes constantly, played by
Me. He's getting old, don't ask me why.
His lines are not familiar. Then I die.

I have been thinking, instead of weeping, tears,
And drinking everybody else's, for years.
They taste amazingly like urine. Cheers!
I tell you this—(But soft! My mother nears.)

You wonder how I know what urine tastes like?
I stuck my finger in a hole in a dike
And made the heart near bursting burst. Strike
While it's hot. You have to seize the mike

And scream, "This is I! Hamlet the Dane!" True—
Too true—the lascivious iceberg you
Are cruising to, *Titanic*, is a Jew
Ophelia loved, a man she thought she knew.

One day I was bombing Belgrade, bombing Belgrade,
To halt the slaughter elsewhere, knowing aid
Arrives through the air in the form of a tirade
Hamlet stabs through the arras, like a man does a maid,

Only in this case it was the father of the girl,
Poor Polonius, her father. She is a pearl
At the bottom of a stream, and every curl
Of nothing but herself is drowned. I whirl

Around, and this is I! a fellow fanned
Into a flame. The horsefly that I land
On her has little legs—but on command
Struts back and forth on stage, princely, grand.

FROM *The Cosmos Trilogy*

66. FREDERICK SEIDEL

I live a life of laziness and luxury,
Like a hare without a bone who sleeps in a pâté.
I met a fellow who was so depressed
He never got dressed and never got undressed.

He lived a life of laziness and luxury.
He hid his life away in poetry,
Like a hare still running from a gun in a pâté.
He didn't talk much about himself because there wasn't much to say.

He found it was impossible to look or not to.
It will literally blind him but he's got to.
Her caterpillar with a groove
Waits for love

Between her legs. The crease
Is dripping grease.
He's blind—now he really is.
Can't you help him, gods!

Her light is white
Moonlight.
Or the Parthenon under the sun
Is the other one.

There are other examples but
A perfect example in his poetry is the what
Will save you factor.
The Jaws of Life cut the life crushed in the compactor

Out.
My life is a snout
Snuffling toward the truffle, life. Anyway!
It is a life of luxury. Don't put me out of my misery.

I am seeking more Jerusalem, not less.
And in the outtakes, after they pull my fingernails out, I confess:
I do love
The sky above.

Area Code 212 (2002)

67. I DO

I do
Standing still.
I do in my head.
I do everything to keep active.

Everything is excellent.
I do pablum. I do doo-doo. I do heroic deeds.
I do due
Diligence.

I do heroic deeds. I don't move.
I do love
The sky above
Which is black.

I do white gloves at the dances,
But I don't dance with the fascists.
I do beat and smash their stupid wishes.
I take you to be my.

The river is turning into
A place to drown.
The road lay down
In front of the car.

Everything in hell was
Talking English long ago.
I mean English.
I mean fruit bowl. I mean upper crust. I mean, really!

The ocean swings back into view in inland St. Louis.
The time is then.
My headmaster's exotic psychotic wife goes completely
Round the bend and maintains

The Mississippi is down there and up here
Is Berchtesgaden. I am shooting up on this.
Breast milk leaks from the insertion point.
His wife—my bride—wanders around the campus saying I do.

68. THE BATHROOM DOOR

Decapitated, he looks much the same,
The same homeless mind.
He watches a starving man
Eating his hiccups

Because he has nothing else to eat
In front of the mirror that is
Brushing his teeth.
Then he goes to bed headless. Then

He hears his wife get out of their bed
And lock the bathroom door
That they never lock.
Both of them are drunk.

He sleeps with his eyes shut in the dark
For a few minutes and then he gets up.
But he doesn't get up.
She comes back to bed.

She says I am so afraid.
She says I feel cold.
He asks her what she has done.
He makes her stand up and walk. He calls 911.

He will go to the theater
Of the locking of the bathroom door, hiccup
Click, and how he stayed in bed
For the rest of his life.

He remembers something else.
That he did get up. He stood
Outside the door.
He went back to a bed

Even more terrible than the loyal eyes
Of a dog about to be euthanized.
Than the efforts of a racehorse
Who will have to be shot to rise.

FROM *The Cosmos Trilogy*

69. DOWNTOWN

Think of the most disgusting thing you can think of.
It is beautiful in its way.
It has two legs.
It has a head of hair.

It goes downtown.
It goes into an art gallery.
It pulls out a gun.
It kills its friend.

Never mind how much money they made.
Start thinking about what matters.
The MV Agusta motorcycle
Is the most beautiful.

I Do was one.
The Bathroom Door was another.
I Do was one.
Pulled out a gun and fired.

It was point-blank.
It died instantly.
The fragment was Sappho.
You can imagine how beautiful.

The person is walking
Ahead of you on the sidewalk.
You see its back but its face
Is facing you as it walks away.

As if the neck were
Broken, but the face is calm.
The name of the face you
Face is the United Nations.

It is a lovely Picasso walking away
On a broken neck and looking straight ahead back.
First came the seen, then thus the palpable
Elysium, though it were in the halls of hell.

70. THE SERPENT

Who is this face as little
As a leaf,
The neck a stem?
The furnace waits.

Someone is happening
To someone. Someone is
Alive and enters
Defiantly.

Her lips are full.
The mouth is open.
The living room is full
Of mahogany and art.

The serpent concentrates its gaze until the serpent is
A sumo wrestler agile as a dragonfly,
A furnace eating only good
To stay big.

The girl is a delicate
Drop.
The beautiful face
Is a leaf.

The dragonfly
Practices touch-and-go landings
At the little airport, landing to take off,
See-through with heartbeats.

The serpent is not a serpent
But a lyre.
It asks to play.
It asks the girl to let a dragon fly.

Someone is sailing clay pigeons
And blowing them apart perfectly.
Someone is kissing
The other.

FROM *The Cosmos Trilogy*

71. GETAWAY

I think you do
But it frightens you.
I have the guns
In the car.

I wanted to save
Someone and
The rest. It will happen.
I will take you hostage.

Also I wasn't
Going to fall in love
But when you're fleeing
You're flying.

Someone had to take
My blindfold off for me to
Just take off. I turn the key in your ignition.
Contact! The propeller flickers.

We are taking off to
Elope.
Have another
One

For the road. Burn the birth certificates.
Run the roadblock.
All the whirling lights
On the roofs of their cars.

They're going to check
The trunk and find our bodies.
I won't.
We jump out firing.

I am already in you.
I am rafting down your bloodstream.
That is already over.
I have entered.

72. NOTHING WILL

Root canal is talking
To the opposite—
Twenty-three years old,
With eyes like very dilated

Dewdrops sideways.
Age is visiting
The other side of the moon,
When the moon was young.

Wow, to see the side
That never faces the earth is cool,
And kiss newborn skin
That you could eat off of.

A clean twenty-three-year-old
Heart is tourism
For the senator
Visiting the strange.

You fly there, then get out and walk.
The space shot lands
And he gets out and flies and then on foot.
He is looking at her tits.

The future will not last.
It is coming toward her
On safari
To watch the ancient king of the savannah roar and mate

Despite a root
Canal spang in the middle.
Nothing will.
Not even root canal. Revive his satrapy.

He is rowing down a canal
Of royal palms on either side
And the ocean is near. The oil spill is near
Enough for her to hear it greasing the shore.

FROM *The Cosmos Trilogy*

73. PH

Phineas has turned
To face the quiet Phoebe to
Touch her cheek.
Phineas, who is tender but not meek,

And certainly is not weak,
Is also not named Phineas.
The name is art.
Phineas turns to touch her tenderly,

But the cab runs over a
Pocked-moon stretch of Brooklyn roadway
And his hand is knocked
Into being a brute.

What is the pH of New York?
PH is
Singing to PH,
Date palm to date palm.

The dunes in every
Direction tower.
Their color is octoroon
In Manhattan at dawn.

That is the color
Of the heart they share
Which is an oasis
Where one can pause

Before going out to die
In the dunes,
Strangling without water
And without a gun

To shoot at night at the stars.
For the moment, they sing.
The saddle has no camel under it.
They know.

74. VENUS

Venus is getting
Smaller.
Finally, she is
The size of a mouse.

A fully developed young woman
That size
Makes it difficult
To caress her breasts.

The curly wire
To a Secret Service agent's ear
Ends in a plug actually bigger
Than her derrière.

What a magnificent goddess!
And enormous—when
She stands on the back of your hand
With her glorious assets!

Her steatopygous ass
Sticks straight out—a Hottentot harvest moon!
Her breasts are prodigious.
Her ass is steatopygous.

Her head is
Classically small.
Her eyes and her mouth
Are equally oceans and drops from a dropper.

Venus shrank down
To go to Harvard, and got a tiny degree.
Her Junoesque figure
Is the size of a sea horse.

Mr. Universe
Is in love,
But how will he get in?
Venus, goddess, tell him how!

FROM *The Cosmos Trilogy*

75. NIGRA SUM

I'm having a certain amount of difficulty
Because I am finding it hard.
It is all uphill.
I wake up tired.

It is downhill from here.
The Emancipation Proclamation won't change that.
Evidently there have been irregularities apparently.
It is time to get out.

I am going to go public with this
Beautiful big breasts and a penis
Military-industrial complex.
I live in the infield with other connoisseurs

Behind the bars of the gate to the circuit,
Sniffing burning racing oil till I'm high.
On the other side of the gate is the start/finish,
And the red meat of the racebikes raving to race.

I'm not from anywhere. I'm from my head.
That's where I didn't grow up
And went to school.
Oh, I am totally vile and beautiful!

A military-industrial complex with soul!
Nigra sum sed formosa.
I am black but comely,
O ye daughters of Jerusalem:

Therefore has the king loved me, and brought me into his
Chambers. For, lo, the winter is past,
The rain is over and gone:
Rise up, my love, my fair one,

And come away.
Tomorrow I set sail for the bottom, never to return.
The master cabin has its own head—which I'm from.
I'm from my head.

76. RAIN IN HELL

That was the song he found himself singing.
He heard a splash before he hit the concrete.
There was no water in the pool.
He couldn't stop himself in time.

One day, while he was waiting for the light to change,
And suddenly it began to rain,
And all at once the sun came out,
He saw a rainbow of blood.

He was so excited.
Splash.
That he dove off
The diving board without a thought.

There was no water in the pool.
He heard a splash
Just before he hit the concrete.
Gosh—

From good in bed
To as good as dead!
You smell the rain before it comes.
You smell the clean cool pierce the heat.

He has the air-conditioning on
But keeps the car windows open driving back to town.
It is the story of his life.
He smells the rain before it falls.

It was the middle of the night
In 212, the area code of love.
The poem he was writing put
Its arms around his neck.

Why write a poem?
There isn't any rain in hell
So why keep opening an umbrella?
That was the song he found himself singing.

FROM *The Cosmos Trilogy*

77. DIDO WITH DILDO

The cord delivers electricity
From the wall socket to my mouth
Which I drink.
I want you all to know how much

My hair stands on end.
You will leave me alive.
You will leave me and live.
I hold midnight in my hand.

The town siren sounds because it's
Noon. The sunlight throws spears
Into the waves
And the gulls scream.

You get there.
Something instantly is wrong.
It only seems it's instantly.
It always is

The case that different time zones
Produce
Different midnights.
I hold a new year in my hand.

She stood on her toes to kiss me
Like in the nineteen fifties.
I glued my mucho macho lips to destiny.
I hurl a fireball at the logjam.

I turn on the TV.
I turn the oven off.
I make a call on my cell phone
To the mirror.

I see in the mirror Aeneas
Has changed.
He is drinking vodka odorlessly.
Into Dido wearing a dildo.

78. JANUARY

I have a dream
And must be fed.
The manta rays when you wade out
Ripple toward your outstretched hand.

The answer is
The friendliness of the body.
There is no answer, but the answer is
The friendliness of the body

Is the stars above
The dock at night.
And in the afternoon lagoon flags lazily flap
Their bodies toward yours

To be fed. I landed on
An atoll in the soft
Perfume.
The airport air was sweet. The blond January breeze was young.

The windchill factor
Which is Western thought
Received an IV drip of syrup of clove.
I have a dream. I have a dream the

Background radiation is a
Warm ocean, and a pasture for
Desire, and a
Beach of royal psalms.

The IV bag is a warm ocean,
Is a body not your own feeding your body.
My body loves your body
Is the motto of Tahiti.

Two flying saucers mating,
One on top the other, flap and flow, in love.
Each is a black
Gun soft as a glove.

FROM *The Cosmos Trilogy*

79. FEBRUARY

The best way not to kill yourself
Is to ride a motorcycle very fast.
How to avoid suicide?
Get on and really ride.

Then comes Valentine's Day.
It is February, but very mild.
But the MV Agusta is in storage for the winter.
The Ducati racer is deeply asleep and not dreaming.

Put the pills back in the vial.
Put the gun back in the drawer.
Ventilate the carbon monoxide.
Back away from the railing.

You can't budge from the edge?
You can meet her in front of the museum.
It is closed today—every Monday.
If you are alive, happy Valentine's Day!

All you brave failed suicides, it is a leap year.
Every day is an extra day
To jump. It is February 29th
Deep in the red heart of February 14th.

On the steps in front of the museum,
The wind was blowing hard.
Something was coming.
Winter had been warm and weird.

Hide not thy face from me.
For I have eaten ashes like bread,
And mingled my drink with weeping,
While my motorcycles slept.

She arrives out of breath,
Without a coat, blazing health,
But actually it is a high flu fever that gives her glory.
Life is death.

80. IN CAP FERRAT

God made human beings so dogs would have companions.
Along the promenade dogs are walking women.
One is wearing fur
Although the day is warm.

The fur
Trots behind a cur.
The mongrel sparkles and smiles
Leading her by the leash.

The month of March, that leads to hell,
Is plentiful in Cap Ferrat.
There is gambling around the bend
In the bay at the Casino in creamy Monte Carlo.

White as the Taj Mahal,
White as that stove of grief,
Is the cloud
Just passing by.

The air is herbs.
The sea is blue chrome curls.
The mutt sparkles and leers
And lifts a leg.

White as the weightless Taj Mahal,
White as the grief and love it was,
The day is warm, the sea is blue.
The dog, part spitz, part spots, is zest

And piss and Groucho Marx
Dragging a lady along.
The comedy
Is raw orison.

Dogs need an owner to belong to.
Dogs almost always die before their owners do.
But one dog built a Taj Mahal for two.
I loved you.

FROM *The Cosmos Trilogy*

81. MARCH

He discovered he would have to kill.
He went to Paris to study how.
He returned home to throw out the colonial French.
He never left the United States.

He was a boy who was afraid.
He talked arrogance, secretly sick at heart.
He oozed haughty nonchalance, like a duke sitting on a shooting stick.
He grinned toughness on the playing field running behind his teeth.

He strutted in the school library, smirking
Like Charlie Chaplin twirling his cane jauntily.
He was a genius but he was afraid
He would burst into flames of fame and cry.

This Ho Chi Minh was arrogant. This Ho Chi Minh was shy.
Then he discovered poetry. It was in Florida
One March, at spring break, with his sister and parents,
Having parted for the week from his first girlfriend ever.

He wrote: *The sea pours in while my heart pours out—*
Words to that effect.
Even for age thirteen,
This was pretty dim.

This was the year of his bar mitzvah.
It was his genocidal coming of age in Cambodia.
Everyone who wore glasses was executed.
He took his off.

They killed everything in sight in a red blur.
It rained
A rainbow of the color red.
They wore black pajamas in a red bed.

They killed anyone named Fred.
This to start Utopia. Everyone was dead.
The Algerians blew up the French.
The French horribly tortured them to find out.

82. EASTER

The wind lifts off his face,
Which flutters
In the wind and snaps back and forth,
Just barely attached.

It smiles horribly—
A flag flapping on a flagpole.
Why is this idiot patriot
Smiling?

He is horribly
In love.
It is embarrassing to see
The red, white, and blue.

The field of stars
Is the universe, his mind,
Which thinks about her constantly
And dials her number. *Hello. It's me.*

It really hurts
To see it in his face.
The awful smile of a dog
Is a grimace.

You can believe
In God again—God looks like him.
The Easter koan says the gas tank must be full
But empty. The taut wind sock

Sounds the trumpet,
Summoning all
To the new.
The trumpet sounds!

Sweet is spreading salt,
But only on the ice where people walk,
Only it is rice in slow motion showering fragrant
Spring rain on the couples.

FROM *The Cosmos Trilogy*

83. APRIL

A baby elephant is running along the ledge across
The front of an apartment building ten stories up.
What must be the young woman handler desperately gives chase,
Which has a comic aspect as she hangs on by the rope.

But the baby elephant falls, yanking the young woman floatingly
To her death on a ledge lower down.
The baby elephant lies dead on Broadway.
Every year it does.

Birds bathe in the birdbath in the warm blood.
The bed upstairs is red.
The sheets are red.
The pillows are blood.

The baby elephant looks like a mouse running away
Or a cockroach scuttling away on a shelf,
Followed by the comically running sandpiper
Holding the rope.

It is everywhere when you restart your computer.
You don't see it and then you do.
A half has already fallen to the street,
And the other is falling and hits the ledge.

Now is a vase of flowers
Maniacally blooming red.
The medallion cabs seem very yellow
Today—as yellow as lymph.

Every April 1st Frank O'Hara's ghost
Stops in front of the Olivetti showroom
On Fifth Avenue—which hasn't been there for thirty years.
He's there for the Lettera 22 typewriter outside on a marble pedestal

With a supply of paper—to dash off a city poem, an April poem,
That he leaves in the typewriter for the next passerby,
On his way to work at the Museum of Modern Art, because
The baby elephant is running along the ledge, chased by its handler.

84. MAY

A man picks up a telephone to hear his messages,
Returns the handset to the cradle, looking stunned.
The pigeon on the ledge outside the window
Bobs back and forth in front of New York City, moaning.

A man takes roses to a doctor, to her office,
And gets himself buzzed in, and at the smiling front desk
Won't give his name to the receptionist, just leaves red roses.
The doctor calls the man the next day, leaves a message.

There isn't anything more emptiness than this,
But it's an emptiness that's almost estival.
The show-off-ness of living full of May
Puts everything that's empty on display.

The pigeon on the ledge outside the window
Moans, bobbing up and down, releasing whiteness.
The day releases whiteness on the city.
And May increases.

Seersucker flames of baby blue and white
Beneath a blue-eyed Caucasian sky with clouds
Fill up the emptiness of East Side life
Above a center strip that lets red flowers grow.

They call them cut flowers when they cut them.
They sell the living bodies at the shop.
A man is bringing flowers to a doctor,
But not for her to sew them up.

And May is getting happy, and the temperature is eighty.
And the heart is full of palm trees, even when it's empty.
The center strip migraine down Park Avenue sees red.
Girl with a Red Hat in the Vermeer show is what it sees.

Vermeer went in a day and a half from being healthy to being dead.
A city made of pigeons is moaning in a morgue that's a garden.
The red hat reddens the Metropolitan.
It's its harem.

FROM *The Cosmos Trilogy*

85. VENUS WANTS JESUS

Venus wants Jesus.
Jesus wants justice.
That one wants this.
This one wants that.

I want.
It means I lack.
Working men and women on
May 1st march.

They want to increase
The minimum wage and they will form a line.
My fellow glandes march
Entirely

Around the girl while
Around the world bands
Are playing.
On the White House lawn, "Hail to the Chief"

Greets the arriving helicopter slowly curtsying
On the landing pad.
They ought
To wait till the rotor stops. The president

Descends
The stairs waving. Behind him is
The uniformed aide with the attaché case carrying
The codes.

The president
Can place a lei around
A billion necks
In an hour.

They wanted to live till June.
They wanted the time.
They wanted to say goodbye.
They wanted to go to the bathroom before.

86. MV AGUSTA RALLY, CASCINA COSTA, ITALY

Each June there is a memorial Mass
For Count Corrado Agusta in the family church,
Whose factory team of overwhelming motorcycles
Won every Grand Prix championship for years.

The courtyard in front of the sinister stark house
Where Corrado was raised blazes with victory.
The charming young choir in the tiny church sings,
To the strumming of a guitar, that other glory story.

In her MV Agusta T-shirt, the reader reads aloud the lesson.
The roaring of a lion about to devour her
Is an MV 500cc GP racer getting revved up for the rally:
The caviar and flower of Grand Prix four-stroke power.

The champions have no idle, so not
To die they have to
Roar. They roar like the lions in the Colosseum.
They roar like a pride of bloodred hearts in the savannah.

Someone blips
The throttle of the three-cylinder
500, one kind of sound, then someone pushes into life
The four. Its bel canto throat catches fire.

The priest elevates the Host
And his bored theatrical eyes,
To melodramatize the text,
Roar.

It's like the Mass they hold in France
To bless the packs of hounds before a hunt.
The choir of hunting horns blares bloodcurdling fanfares
And lordly stags answer from all the forests around.

I stand in the infield with other connoisseurs near tears
Behind the bars of the gate to the track, smelling burning castor oil.
On the other side of the gate is the start/finish line,
And Monica Agusta standing with her back to me, close enough to touch.

FROM *The Cosmos Trilogy*

87. JUNE

Eternal life begins in June.
Her name is fill the name in.
My contubernalis, my tent mate,
My woman in the tent with me in Latin.

The next world is the one I'm in.
My June contubernium.
My tent mate through the whole campaign.
The June moon, burning pure champagne,

Starts foaming from its tail and rising.
One minute into launch and counting.
The afterlife lifts off like this.
The afterlife begins to blast.

The breathing of my sleeping dog
Inflates the moonlit room with silence.
The afterlife begins this way.
The universe began today.

The afterlife is here on earth.
It's what you're doing when you race
And enter each turn way too fast
And brake as late as possible always.

Of course the world does not exist.
A racebike raving down the straight
Explodes into another world,
Downshifts for the chicane, brakes hard,

And in the other world ignites
The flames of June that burn in hell.
My contubernalis, my tent mate.
My woman in the tent with me does octane.

Ducati racing red I ride,
Ride red instead of wrong or right.
The color red in hell looks cool.
In heaven it's for sex on sight.

88. JUNE ALLYSON AND MAE WEST

In the middle
Of the field of vision
Is a hole that is
Surrounded by a woman.

The hole is life.
The ones who are
About to be born
Have no choice.

The hole is life.
The ones who are
About to be born
Have no choice.

In the middle
Of the field stood
The middle of the light
Which is love, a heart of light.

I got better.
I can remember taking
A streetcar.
It was June.

The name of the movie star was June
Allyson who was with me in my hospital room.
I bet the glorious wicked star Mae
West would.

June made Mae good.
Mae made June bad.
Is it bearable?
The situation is

No one ever gets well.
People can't
Even stand up.
They pay to cry.

FROM *The Cosmos Trilogy*

89. JULY

Phineas is crossing the pont des Arts,
But he is doing it in New York.
He has made up the Phineas part.
That is not his name.

Nothing is.
Nothing is his.
He is living in Paris,
On Broadway.

Two minutes from his door
Is the pont des Arts arcing
Over the Seine.
Bateaux mouches like bugs of light

Slide by at night under his feet, fading away in English.
Shock waves vee against the quais.
Mesdames and gentlemen, soon we have Notre Dame.
The letter *P* is walking across the pont des Arts.

Back in New York,
Except he *is* in New York,
He is in Paris.
He strolls home to the rue de Seine, punches in the code and goes in.

The next morning the streets
Are bleeding under his feet.
They are cleaning themselves.
Apparently, they are not that young.

The trees are green.
In the jardin du Luxembourg he says her name.
He watches the children riding the donkeys on the red dirt.
An adult holds the halter and walks alongside.

One tree is vomiting and sobbing
Flowers.
The smell is powerful.
How quatorze July it is to be a donkey and child.

90. HUGH JEREMY CHISHOLM

With Jeremy Chisholm at the Lobster Inn on our way to Sagaponack,
Eating out on the porch in the heat, flicking cigarettes into the inlet.
We ate from the sea and washed it down with Chablis,
Punctuated by our unfiltered Camels, in our eternal July.

Billy Hitchcock landed his helicopter at a busy gas station
In Southampton July 4th weekend, descended from the sky like a god
To buy a candy bar from the vending machine outside,
Unwrapped the candy bar and flew away, rotors beating.

Chisholm found a jeweler to paint his Tank Watch black.
It had been his father's, one of the first Cartier made.
The gold case in blackface was sacrilege.
Chisholm wore it like a wrist corsage.

In a helicopter that belonged to the Farkas family,
The carpet of cemeteries seemed endless choppering out to JFK.
So much death to overfly! It could take a lifetime.
They were running out of cemeteries to be dead in.

Hovering at fifteen feet,
Waiting for instructions on where to land,
Told to go elsewhere,
We heeled over and flew very low, at the altitude of a dream.

Bessie Cuevas had introduced me to this *fin de race* exquisite
Who roared around town in his souped-up Mini-Minor,
Who poured Irish whiskey on his Irish oatmeal for breakfast,
Who was as beautiful as the young Prince Yusupov

Who had used his wife as bait to kill Rasputin and, later in Paris,
Always in makeup, was a pal of the Marquis de Cuevas, Bessie's dad.
Yusupov dressed up a pet ape in chauffeur's livery
And drove down the Champs-Elysées with the ape behind the wheel.

WASPs can't get lung cancer smoking Camels,
Chisholm said, taking the usual long deep drag—look at cowboys!
That July they found a tumor
As big as the Ritz inoperably near his heart.

FROM The Cosmos Trilogy

91. AUGUST

Sky-blue eyes,
A bolt of lightning drinking
Skyy vodka,
A demon not afraid of happiness,

Asks me about my love life here in hell.
I lunge at what I understand I belong to.
I flee, too.
It's her fate. It's too late.

I see the sky from a couch at the Carlyle.
Blond is dressed in black.
It all comes back.
The sky is black.

Thunder violently shakes
The thing it holds in its teeth
Until it snaps the neck
And rain pours down in release and relief,

Releasing paradise,
The smell of honeysuckle and of not afraid of happiness.
Lightning flashes once
To get the sky eyes used to it,

And then flashes again
To take the photograph.
The blackout startled her and started it.
Lightning flickers in Intensive Care.

I am speaking in Ecstatic.
The couch is floating on the carpet.
The waiter burns
From all the discharge and surge, and brings more drinks.

Coition is divine human
Rebirth and ruin having drinks in a monsoon,
In the upholstered gallery outside the bar, in the gold light.
The Prince of Darkness dipped in gold is God.

92. SEPTEMBER

The woman is so refined.
The idea of refinement gets redefined.
Doing it with her is absurd.
Like feeding steak to a hummingbird.

Her hair colorist colored her hair gold
To give her a look. It made her look cold.
Her face suddenly seemed see-through like a breath
In a bonnet of gold and she was in a casket and it was death.

She looked more beautiful than life.
She said she wanted to be my wife.
She comes with a psychiatrist to maintain her.
She comes with a personal trainer.

The September trees are still green in Central Park
Until they turn black after dark.
The apartments in the buildings turn their lamps on.
And then the curtains are drawn.

One person on a low floor pulls the curtain back and stares out,
But pulls the curtain closed again when there's a shout,
Audible on Fifth Avenue, from inside the park.
Somewhere a dog begins to bark.

I climb into the casket of this New York night.
I climb into the casket of the curtained light.
I climb into the casket and the satin.
I climb into the casket to do that in.

Into her roaring arms, wings of a hummingbird,
A roar of wings without a word,
A woman looking up at me and me looking down
Into the casket at the town.

I see down there His Honor the Mayor
In St. Patrick's Cathedral, head bowed in prayer.
His friend—wings roaring—hovers beside him in the pew.
Death is all there is. Death will have to do.

FROM *The Cosmos Trilogy*

93. THE TENTH MONTH

Someone is wagging a finger in her face—*Charlotte!*
Down here in hell we don't do that!
As if she were a child. Charlotte has arrived
To test the torture.

This is a test. This is only a test. Charlotte
Is yelling at Charlotte for a violation.
Charlotte, as a Human Rights Watch
Observer of sorts, has descended from heaven to an early fall.

Oh dear, is it really October?
Is Charlotte really nearly over?
She still says actress—most actresses today would call themselves
An actor. A star walks down upper Broadway being beautiful

With her famous eyes. *Hello from hell,*
She tells her cell phone.
She's ready to hand
Down the indictments and waves her wand.

The crimes sparkle in the moonlight.
Actually, it's rather wonderful to stalk
The Upper West Side midday,
Between the Hudson River and Central Park,

Looking for a self to put the handcuffs on.
It's lovely if there's been a human rights violation.
There's also cruelty to animals,
The child pornography of do-gooders.

The animal is strapped down for the vivisection, conscious,
Buying a book in Barnes & Noble, pursued by fans
Telling her they love her movies here in hell,
And would she do it to herself for them again.

A man comes to the tenth month of the year and calls it Charlotte—
I don't believe in anything, I do
Believe in you. You always play
A garter-belted corpse of someone young.

94. FALL

It is
A hole surrounded
By a voluptuous
Migraine.

It was a universe that could
Burst out
And start
Without a trace

Of where it came from.
The background radiation
Is what's
Left of

The outburst at the start.
The background radiation
Is the delicious
Migraine. The hole of life

Is about to
Start.
Don't make sense.
It is about to start again.

Umbrellas pop open.
Mushroom caps approach a newsstand.
The trees wear truth and rouge.
The trees start to sing

In the soft.
The old penis smells food
And salivates.
One hundred ninety horsepower at

The crank
Going two hundred miles an hour down the straight
Is another motorcycle death
From Viagra in October.

FROM *The Cosmos Trilogy*

95. OCTOBER

It is time to lose your life,
Even if it isn't over.
It is time to say goodbye and try to die.
It is October.

The mellow cello
Allée of trees is almost lost in sweetness and mist
When you take off your watch at sunrise
To lose your life.

You catch the plane.
You land again.
You arrive in the place.
You speak the language.

You will live in a new house,
Even if it is old.
You will live with a new wife,
Even if she is too young.

Your slender new husband will love you.
He will walk the dog in the cold.
He will cook a meal on the stove.
He will bring you your medications in bed.

Dawn at the city flower market downtown.
The vendors have just opened.
The flowers are so fresh.
The restaurants are there to decorate their tables.

Your husband rollerblades past, whizzing,
Making a whirring sound, winged like an angel—
But stops and spins around and skates back
To buy some cut flowers in the early morning frost.

I am buying them for you.
I am buying them for your blond hair at dawn.
I am buying them for your beautiful breasts.
I am buying them for your beautiful heart.

96. NOVEMBER

I've never been older.
It doesn't.
I can't explain.
Every November is one more.

I've used up my amount.
I've nearly run out.
I'm out of penis.
I've run out.

I look out the spaceship's vast
Expense of greenhouse glass
At the stars.
It will take a million years.

You open your head.
You look in the dictionary.
You look it up.
You look at the opposite.

You open the violin case.
You take it out.
Actually, it is a viola.
Actually, it is November.

You grab the handrails with the
Treadmill speeding up.
Oh my God. Don't stop.
It is possible that

The president traveling in an open limousine
Has been shot.
My fellow Americans, ask not
What your country can do for you in

November. The doorman
Holds the door.
The taxi
Without a driver pulls up.

FROM *The Cosmos Trilogy*

97. GOD EXPLODING

They all claim responsibility for inventing God,
Including the ruthless suicides who call themselves God Exploding.
All the rival groups, of course, immediately take credit
For terrorist atrocities they did not commit.

One of the terrorist acts they did not commit
Was inventing rock 'n' roll, but, hey,
The birth of Elvis/Jesus is as absolute as the temperature
Of the background radiation, 4°K.

1, 2, 3, 4—I sing of a maiden that is makeles.
King of alle kinges to here sone che ches.
He cam also stille
Ther his moder was,

As dew in Aprille that fallith on the gras.
He cam also stille to his moderes bowr
As dew in Aprille that fallith on the flowr.
He cam also stille

There his moder lay,
As dew in Aprille that fallith on the spray.
Moder and maiden
Was never non but che;

Wel may swich a lady Godes moder be.
I hate seeing the anus of a beautiful woman.
I should not be looking. It should not be there.
It started in darkness and ended up a star.

Jewish stars on the L.A. freeway in Jewish cars
Take the off-ramp to the manger
Somewhere in the fields of Harlem,
Bearing gifts of gold and frankincense and myrrh.

Rock 'n' roll in front of the Wailing Wall and weep.
With the stump where your hand was blown off beat your chest.
Hutu rebel soldiers crucify the mountain gorillas.
Hodie Christus natus est.

98. THE WAR OF THE WORLDS

The child stands at the window, after his birthday party,
Gray flannel little boy shorts, shirt with an Eton collar,
St. Louis, Missouri, sixty years ago,
And sees the World Trade Center towers falling.

The window is the wall
The wide world presents to prepubescence.
People on fire are jumping from the eightieth floor
To flee the fireball.

In the airplane blind-dating the south tower,
People are screaming with horror.
The airplane meeting the north tower
Erupts with ketchup.

The window is a wall
Through which the aquarium visitors can see.
Airplanes are swimming
Up to the towers of steel.

Up to the Twin Towers to feed.
People rather than die prefer to leap
From the eightieth floor to their death.
The man stands at his childhood window saving them.

Old enough to undress himself,
Gray flannel little boy shorts, shirt with an Eton collar,
He stands at the worldwide window, after the birthday party,
And sees the mountains collapsing and collapsing.

On the other side of the aquarium glass is September 11th.
Under his birthday party clothes is his underwear and the underwater.
Why bother to wash your clothes, or your skin, why bother to wash,
When you will only get dirty again?

Why bother to live when you will die?
Visitors are peering through the thick glass and taking photographs
Of ground zero—of Allah akbar in formaldehyde in a jar.
God is great. Love is hate.

FROM *The Cosmos Trilogy*

99. DECEMBER

I don't believe in anything, I do
Believe in you.
Down here in hell we do don't.
I can't think of anything I won't.

I amputate your feet and I walk.
I excise your tongue and I talk.
You make me fly through the black sky.
I will kill you until I die.

Thank God for you, God.
I do.
My God, it is almost always Christmas Eve this time of year, too.
Then I began to pray.

I don't believe in anything anyway.
I did what I do. I do believe in you.
Down here in hell they do don't.
I can't think of anything we won't.

How beautiful thy feet with shoes.
Struggling barefoot over dunes of snow forever, more falling, forever, Jews
Imagine mounds of breasts stretching to the horizon.
We send them to their breast, mouthful of orison.

I like the color of the smell. I like the odor of spoiled meat.
I like how gangrene transubstantiates warm firm flesh into rotten sleet.
When the blue blackens and they amputate, I fly.
I am flying a Concorde of modern passengers to gangrene in the sky.

I am flying to area code 212
To stab a Concorde into you,
To plunge a sword into the gangrene.
This is a poem about a sword of kerosene.

This is my 21st century in hell.
I stab the sword into the smell.
I am the sword of sunrise flying into area code 212
To flense the people in the buildings, and the buildings, into dew.

100. ONE HUNDRED

There was a door because I opened it.
It was the muse. It had a human face.
It had to have to make the three parts fit.
The Cosmos Poems was fire that filled the space

With fire in *Life on Earth*. The sky
Became a blue lake I was bathing in,
But it was fire. The sun was burning. Fly
Me to the bottom where I've been. I've been

Completing *Area Code 212*.
I've been in heaven in Manhattan on
The bottom. Hell is what to live can do.
One day I went downtown but it was gone.

The World Trade Center towers still return
In dreams and fall again and fall again
And rise again and people scream and burn
And jump to certain death again and then

They rise back to the hundredth floor and turn
Their cell phones on and call to say goodbye.
The firemen coming up the stairs will burn
Their way to heaven. Everyone will die

And perish, die and live. The people on
The top floors use their cell phones to call out.
Death follows birth as sunrise follows dawn.
High pressure sends a sky-high waterspout

Fire balances on top of. It begins,
The universe begins, and death begins,
And every living being burns and thins
Down to a flame that burns away and grins.

I heard them singing and set fire to it.
I hear their screams. Their corpses run in place.
They burst in flames to make the three parts fit.
My trilogy is fire that fills the space.

FROM *The Cosmos Trilogy*

The muse now raised the laurel crown above
My corpse, and, praising me with what was fire
To hear, which I breathed in, which burned like love,
Now set ablaze the funerary pyre.

Dead white males greeted the arrival of
My ghost by praising me with what was fire
To hear, which I breathed in, which burned like love.
I wore the crown of laurel they require.

Beneath a crown of laurel lived a liar.
White man speak with forked tongue with his lyre.
They scream like gulls, beseeching. They scream higher
And dive down, crying, corpses on a pyre,

And rise back to the hundredth floor and turn
Their cell phones on. We call to say goodbye.
We firemen-coming-up-the-stairs will burn
Our way to heaven. Everyone will die.

You fling yourself into the arms of art.
You drool to sleep on consolation's shoulder.
A living donor offers you a heart.
The muse does. Yours got broken getting older.

The UFO that offers you the heart
Replacement is returning from out there,
Deep space, but beaming brain waves saying, Start
Down there, unsheathe the sword inside the ploughshare,

And cut the kindness from your chest, and stick
The Cosmos Poems in the cavity.
A hummingbird of flame sips from a wick.
My tinder drinks the lightning striking me.

Exploding fireballs vaporize the gore.
The runners-on-your-mark can't live this way.
They have to make the deal so they ignore
Their death and now the flames have come to stay.

They open windows. Now the brave begin
To lead the others to the stairs to die.
The money is the cosmic insulin
The partners in the firms must make. I fly

The UFO that offers you the heart
Replacement that's arriving from out there,
Its home, while down here the red mist is art
Exploding on the sidewalk from the air.

And some jump holding hands, but most alone,
But some jump holding hands with my warm hand.
They wait inside their offices. They phone
This poem. They stay and while they do they stand.

When I consider how my days are spent,
I'd have to say I spend a lot of time
Not being dead. I know what Garbo meant.
My life is life emerging from the slime

And writing poems. Virgil took my hand.
We started up the steep path to the crest.
He turned to warn me. Did I understand
I would be meeting Dante? I confessed

I hated cold. To flee the urban light
Pollution in the night sky and see stars
Meant getting to a crest of freezing blight
And human nature inhumane as Mars,

And things far stranger that I can't describe.
I greeted Dante. *Maestro!* Dawn neared. I
Was looking in the mirror at a tribe
In tribal costumes worshipping the sky.

It made no sense on Easter morning to
Parade in feathers down Fifth Avenue,
Except the natives worship what is true,
And firemen in white gloves passed in review.

The Jewish boy had done it once again.
Wood water tanks on top of downtown flamed.
The Resurrection has returned dead men
And women to the New York sky untamed.

GOING FAST (1998)

For a New Planetarium

MIDNIGHT

God begins. The universe will soon.
The intensity of the baseball bat
Meets the ball. Is the fireball
When he speaks and then in the silence
The cobra head rises regally and turns to look at you.
The angel burns through the air.
The flower turns to look.

The cover of the book opens on its own.
You do not want to see what is on this page.
It looks up at you,
Only it is a mirror you are looking into.
The truth is there, and all around the truth fire
Makes a frame.
Listen. An angel. These sounds you hear are his.

A dog is barking in a field.
A car starts in the parking lot on the other side.
The ocean heaves back and forth three blocks away.
The fire in the wood stove eases
The inflamed cast-iron door
Open, steps out into the room across the freezing floor
To your perfumed bed where as it happens you kneel and pray.

FROM *Going Fast*

PRAYER

But we are someone else. We're born that way.
The other one we are lives in a distant city.
People are walking down a street.
They pop umbrellas open when it starts to rain.
Some stand under an apartment building awning.
A doorman dashes out into the spring shower for
A taxi with its off-duty light on that hisses right past.
The daffodils are out on the avenue center strip.
The yellow cabs are yellow as the daffodils.
One exhausted driver, at the end of his ten-hour shift headed in,
Stops for the other one
We are who hides among the poor
And looks like the homeless out on the wet street corner.
Dear friend, get in.
I will take you where you're going for free.
Only a child's Crayola
Could color a taxi cab this yellow
In a distant city full of yellow flowers.

THE NIGHT SKY

At night, when she is fast asleep,
The comet, which appears not to move at all,
Crosses the sky above her bed,
But stays there looking down.

She rises from her sleeping body.
Her body stays behind asleep.
She climbs the lowered ladder.
She enters through the opened hatch.

Inside is everyone.
Everyone is there.
Someone smiling is made of silk.
Someone else was made with milk.

Her mother still alive.
Her brothers and sisters and father
And aunts and uncles and grandparents
And husband never died.

Hold the glass with both hands,
My darling, that way you won't spill.
On her little dress, her cloth yellow star
Comet travels through space.

FROM *Going Fast*

STARS

None of the Above
Stays down here below.
My going very fast
Describes the atmosphere.
Heady.

And when I die,
We orbit way
Above the sky of
And return
From stars.

We fall from stars
In all the colors of Brazil,
Of Africa, Iran.
We stir a black hole swirl, star
Figure skaters twirling on the black, galaxies

Unspooling on the surface tension
Of the morning coffee
In the cup.
The little bubble prickles
Are a house, a dog, a car.

One day an asteroid will come,
A mountain coming from the sky,
And from a long way off at last
The truth will see
Nothing can be done and nothing can remain.

THE STARS ABOVE
THE EMPTY QUARTER

A cat has caught a mouse and is playing
At letting it go is the sun
Over the desert letting the traveler reach the oasis.
The sink vomits all over itself
Is the sand boiling down from the blond sky in a storm.
A pre-Islamic Golden Ode lists
The hundred qualities of a camel.
Suavity, power, the beauty of its eyes.
Its horn, its tires, its perfect bumpers, its perfect fenders.
The way it turns left, the way it turns right.
The great poet Labīd sings
His Song of Songs about the one he loves.
How long it can go without water and without God.
Sings the nomad life of hardship, calls it ease.
He stares at the far-off stars.
He mounts the kneeling camel at dawn.
He lowers himself and rises.
I sing above the sand under the sun.

FROM *Going Fast*

CONTENTS UNDER PRESSURE

His space suit is his respirator breathing him
From its own limited supply of oxygen.
The hand-controlled jet nozzles squirted him away
On a space walk in short bursts that have gone haywire.
But will stop when there is no fuel seconds from now. Now.
The long tether back to the mother spaceship sticks
Straight out from his back weightlessly
In the zero gravity of space.
It has sheared off at the other end.
Absolutely nothing can be done.
The spacecraft is under orders not to try and to return and does.
He urinates and defecates
And looks out at the universe.
He is looking out at it through his helmet mask.

New York

AT GRACIE MANSION

I like motorcycles, the city, the telephone.
TV but not to watch, just to turn it on.
The women and their legs, the movies and the streets.
At dawn when it's so hot the sky is almost red.
The smell of both the rivers is the underworld exhumed.

I remember the vanished days of the great steakhouses.
Before the miniaturization in electronics.
When Robert Wagner was mayor and men ate meat.
I like air-conditioning, leather booths, linen,
Heat, Milan, Thomas Jefferson.

The woman got red in the face touching her girlfriend live
On one of the cable public access shows you do yourself.
Part of the redundancy built into servo systems
That can fail was when she started to spank the girl.
I took her heat straight to my heart.

I never watch TV.
But sometimes late at night. My friend
The junior senator from Nebraska, the only
Medal of Honor winner in Congress, reads Mandelstam,
Reads Joseph Roth. What happens next?

When Wagner's first wife died of cancer,
And Bennett Cerf died of cancer,
Phyllis Cerf and Bob got married—and then Bob died of cancer.
Bobby, Jr., restored by Giuliani, dropped dead on a plane to L.A.
At the age of forty-nine.

How's that again?
Bobby died suddenly in a hotel room in San Antonio.
Bennett expired from Parkinson's.
It ought to matter what battlefield you died on.
A deputy mayor under Koch and the founder of Random House.

I like it when the long line of headlights on behind the hearse
Is stuck in backed-up traffic on the Drive.
A tug tows a barge slowly by
The closed smoked-glass windows of the limousines.
I read Olmsted. I kiss the parks commissioner.

I like anything worth dying for.
I like the brave. I like the Type A personality which is hot.
I like the hideous embarrassment of Nelson Rockefeller
Dying inside somebody young.
He had an attack heart.

I watch a floater in my eye cross Jimmy Walker on the wall.
I like the bead curtains of hot rain outside on the street.
I hold a "see-through on a stem," an ice-cold martini.
Take the heat in your hand. It is cold.
Take the heat. Drink.

THE PIERRE HOTEL, NEW YORK, 1946

The bowl of a silver spoon held candlelight,
A glistening oyster of gold.
The linen between us was snowblind, blinding white.
I felt a weight too light to weigh
Which was my wings.

I heard the quiet of his eyes.
I heard the candle flame stand still.
I saw the long line of her jaw become
Too beautiful to bear. I was a child.
I lifted my empty spoon and licked the light.

FROM *Going Fast*

HOTEL CARLYLE, NEW YORK

Inside the dining room it was snowing.
Men and linen stayed warmly candlelit.
The gay waiters returned from the heat of the kitchen
Unsmilingly cold as Lenin.
Women were vast white estates
Measured in versts.
The chandeliers were Fabergé sleighs
Flying behind powerful invisible horses,
Powerful invisible forces,
On runners of serfs over
The foam of snowdrifts of fine linen.
Take us
Home from the ball
Through the dark, in the deepening snow!
Through an onion-domed metropolis,
Down the ghosts of avenues,
Furs covered us as we raced through the silence
Of the candlelight of the Carlyle.
Our corner table in the back room was
The last White Russian winter of the Czar
Across from a robed Black African
Ambassador to the UN and his entourage
At the height (in the depth) of the 1991 recession.
It was 1917.
I couldn't overthrow anything.
You were my height and depth.
We were a perfect fit.
You were my destiny if only
I would overthrow myself and take over!
Your grave dignity looked at me until I saw
The long line of your jaw become
Too beautiful to bear.
Life achingly said, *Do* something!
And I didn't dare.

DAS KAPITAL

The without blinds or curtains and incapable of being opened
That let the light in after dawn to mop the blood up into day
Are lighted up tonight because people are working late.
Some of the office towers are lighted up empty
So they can be cleaned overnight,
Hours the undertaker needs
To prepare the corpse to last.
The Gross Anatomy class debris
Becomes the Puerto Rican Day parade.
And the cleanup after becomes
Bare clean stainless steel tables with drains.

CHRISTMAS

A man comes in from the whirl
To a room where he does yoga
High above the homeless. He runs smack
Into still space.
He sits in the air.
He hangs upside down to the floor.

A forest of severed trees,
A million needles on sale,
Christ has fragrant breath.
He faints into heightened awareness.
He levitates to the Cross.
He comes to in his own arms.

MOOD INDIGO

One was blacker.
The other one was frightened.
They cut the phone wires.
They used my neckties.
They had me on my stomach.
They tied a hangman's noose around my neck
And stretched the rope of neckties down my back
To my wrists and ankles.
The slightest movement choked me.
He grabbed a carving knife I had
And stabbed me in the temple over and over,
While his partner looked on in horror,
And never even broke the skin,
A technique used in Vietnam.
He find the biggest knife he can
An stab this white boy pretty good
An never even break the skin,
A torture used in Vietnam.
A war there is
And stuck it in a sideburn hard
And didn't even scratch the surface.

FROM *Going Fast*

NOON

A shallow, brutal flood of energy
With high cheekbones and almond eyes.
Cow-eyed bull with a vagina seeing red everywhere.
The *muleta* in the mirror between her thighs.
She sits down naked in front of herself.
Arouses her. Her fury
Flattens Holland and then floods it.

The shallow, brutal flood of energy
Has the bones and Hera's eyes.
The cow-eyed bull with a vagina seeing red everywhere
On fire in a room of Rubenses.
A little girl in the Rubens Room
Is feminism, sword in hand.
The *muleta* trembles in the mirrored hand teasingly. ¡*Toro!*

Her fantasy is to have said to a god deeply
Asleep beside her in bed, in a normal voice, "How did you sleep?"
Waking the bastard up. ¡*Olé!*
7:00. The sun is in heaven.
9:00. The blue is nude.
Noon. The Sag Harbor noon
Siren goes off. The garden flows

Back and forth. There's a breeze
To help with and fan the gross.
The mirrored suit of lights goes rigid
Shaking the trembling *muleta*. The raw sword asks the hairy hump,
The battered, beaten, victimized and sweetened,
Wounded, weakened, tenderized, and moaning to die, to charge. The stadium
Of right-thinking women roars. Bleeds, bellows and roars.

Vive l'amour! Vive la mort!

SPRING

I want to date-rape life. I kiss the cactus spines.
Running a fever in the cold keeps me alive.
My twin, the garbage truck seducing Key Food, whines
And dines and crushes, just like me, and wants to drive.
I want to drive into a drive-in bank and kiss
And kill you, life. Sag Harbor, I'm your lover. I'm
Yours, Sagaponack, too. This shark of bliss
I input generates a desert slick as slime.

DUNE ROAD, SOUTHAMPTON

The murderer has been injecting her remorselessly
With succinylcholine, which he mixes in her daily insulin.
She's too weak to give herself her shots. By the time she has figured it out,
She is helpless.

She can't move any part of her face.
She can't write a note.
She can't speak
To say she hasn't had a stroke.

It's terrifying that she's aware
That something terrible is being done to her.
One day he ups the dose. And gets scared.
She has to be rushed to the local hospital and intubated.

They know at the hospital who she is,
One of the richest women in the world.
The murderer hands the attending a faked M.R.I.
It flaunts the name of a world authority. Showing she has had a stroke.

The neurologist on call introduces herself to the murderer and concurs.
Locked-in syndrome, just about the worst.
Alive, with staring eyes.
The mind is unaffected.

And with the patient looking on expressionlessly,
Screaming don't let him take me home, without a sign or sound,
The doctor tells the murderer he can take her home,
If that's their wish.

Their little beach house has forty rooms.
Her elevator is carved mahogany.
The Great Gatsby swimming pool upstairs is kept full and never used.
Her tower bedroom flies out over the winter ocean, spreading its wings.

Mother, you're going to die,
He tells her, once they're alone.
You have the right to remain silent.
I'm making a joke.

I'll read you your rights.
He takes a syringe.
A woman has the right to bare arms. I particularly like them bare.
I might as well be talking to cement.

London

IN MEMORIAM

Great-grandson of George Boole as in Boolean algebra.
First in his class at Cambridge till he received an inheritance.
Spent it all brilliantly in a flash flood of champagne.
Loved girls and genius. Loved Lord Rothschild his friend.

After a gentleman's Third fled to Paris.
Out of money but life was sweet.
Whisky and style and car-running across borders.
Imprisoned in Spain terrifying.

Meanwhile his father with whom he'd almost had a rapprochement died.
Rothschild visited him in prison once.
How can a boy renounce himself? He began.
But years later he was wonderfully still the same.

Letting rooms to pretty lodgers.
Selling off the Georgian silver piece by piece.
Fired as the engineering consultant for refusing to lie to England.
British Steel tried hard to ruin him but he won.

Stuttered and lisped and wouldn't look you in the eye
In a lofty gwandly Edwardian way.
Jimmy, in America it'll make you seem shifty.
Laughter and delight and he looks you in the eye for a second.

THE GREAT DEPRESSION

Noël Coward sweeps into a party late in 1928
In evening clothes, London.
Spotting the other divinity
In the room, twenty-year-old Tallulah Bankhead standing on her head,
Her dress down over her head,
No underpants, no face,
Too lovely, her whole life ahead of her—
Time for a Coward mot.
Hair slick, svelte in black and white, in tails,
Coward sublimely drawls,
Ah, Tallulah—
Always standing there with her mouth hanging open.

Paris & Tahiti

THE BALLAD OF LA PALETTE

I fly to Paris with the English language
To write a script set in Tahiti.

This will be translated into French for the cast
By a son of the Hollywood blacklist.

The wife of the Hollywood blacklist son has cancer,
Only it will turn out she doesn't.

The Cajun singer on a CD
The movie director plays for me

We meet with an hour later
Outside in the light at La Palette.

We discuss a score,
A young Rimbaud good ole boy.

His week of concerts has sold out.
He brings the bayou to the Seine.

The overloaded sound system howls.
Testing, un, deux, trois.

With kids, has cancer,
Only doesn't.

Down in the bayou,
They hunt in the middle of the night with flashlights.

The spotted Catahoula hound, pink as a pig,
With the strangest voice you ever heard,

Trees the trembling prey
Without a word.

FROM *Going Fast*

ANYONE WITH THE WISH

The lagoon of the biggest atoll in the world,
So wide across you can't see the other shore,
Is soft as dew.
Water is love
In Rangiroa.

Fish move away from you without fear,
Like buffalo on the plains before they disappeared.
The boat far above you on the surface waits,
The pale hull,
The motor as gonads.

You haven't come here only for the shark show.
Their fixed smiles glide.
Their blank eyes go along for the ride.
They bury their face in life explosively,
And shake their head back and forth to tear some off.

Every day a guide sets out a bait
So anyone with the wish can swim with the sharks,
And circle the meat,
And feel close to the teeth.
Sharks swim in the love.

THE RESUMPTION OF NUCLEAR TESTING
IN THE SOUTH PACIFIC

People in their love affairs.
People in their loneliness.

People in their beds alone.
People in each other's arms.

I woke up this morning.
I went to sleep last night.

I woke up this morning.
I went to sleep last night.

The beauty of Tahiti.
That lagoon in Huahiné.

Manta rays were mating.
One on top the other.

Venus, with Chinese eyes,
On the motu at Maupiti.

I wish I was a head of state.
I'd wave away my bodyguards.

I'd never been unhappy.
Now, I would never be.

A *force de frappe* is Gaston Flosse.
Tahitians always call him Gaston.

Gaston did this. Gaston said that.
Nobody better mess with Gaston!

The president of French Polynesia,
Gaston Flosse, has flown in to Paris.

FROM *Going Fast*

Their Kingfish, their Huey Long,
Is very close to Jacques Chirac.

They're strolling down the rue de Seine.
Chirac is France's president.

Faster

A GALLOP TO FAREWELL

Three unrelated establishments named Caraceni in Milan
On streets not far apart make custom suits for men.
They are the best,
Autistically isolated in the pure,
Some might say in the pure
Pursuit of gracefully clothing manure.
Superb, discreet, threading their way to God,
The suits curve with beauty and precision,
Perfection on the order of Huntsman in Savile Row
And their jacket cutter, Mr. Hall.

The attitude to take to shoes is there is Lobb.
The one in Paris, not the one in London.
No one has surpassed
The late George Cleverley's lasts,
The angle in of the heel, the slightly squared-off toe, the line,
Though Suire at Lobb is getting there.
His shoes fit like paradise by the third pair.
Like they were Eve. The well-dressed man,
The vein of gold that seems inexhaustible,
Is a sunstream of urine on its way to the toilet bowl.

A rich American sadist had handcuffs made at Hermès
To torture with beauty the duchesse d'Uzès.
A cow looking at the understated elegance would know
Simplicity as calm as this was art.
A briefcase from Hermès
Is ravishing and stark.
Flawless leather luxury made for horses out of cows
Is what the horsy cows grazing daily in the Faubourg St-Honoré store
Want to buy. Tour group cows in a feeding frenzy
Devour everything like locusts.

FROM *Going Fast*

There are travelers who prefer the British Concorde to the French
For the interior in beige and gray.
Hermès has created a carry-on in water buffalo
For them called the Gallop.
Their seat is in the first cabin.
Three kinds of Caraceni suits chose the aisle.
The most underrated pleasure in the world is the takeoff
Of the Concorde and putting off the crash
Of the world's most beautiful old supersonic plane, with no survivors,
In an explosion of champagne.

A VAMPIRE IN THE AGE OF AIDS

He moves carefully away from the extremely small pieces
Of human beings spread around for miles, still in his leather seat.
He looks like a hunchback walking in the Concorde chair,
Bent over, strapped in, eyes on the ground
To avoid stepping on the soft.
He will use his influence to get
The cockpit voice recorder when it is recovered copied.
He loves the pilot in the last ninety seconds'
Matter-of-factness turning into weeping screams,
Undead in the double-breasted red velvet smoking jacket Huntsman made.

FROM *Going Fast*

ANOTHER MUSE

Another muse appeared, but dressed in black,
Which turned to skin the minute the light was out.
He had become a front without a back.
Arousal was a desert with a spout.

A string of women like a string of fish
Kept dangling in the water to keep them alive.
Washed down with Lynch-Bages to assuage the anguish
Of eating red meat during a muff dive.

One woman, then another, then another.
Drops of dew dropped into a flat green ocean.
They leaked purity and freshness, and mother.
The glass eye of each dewdrop magnified his lack of emotion.

You get a visa and some shots and buy
Provisions for the Amazon and fly
Instead to Africa and tell them I
Will always be your friend and then you try.

He was too busy musing to unchain them,
The women on a string inside the slave pen.
Feminists in nylons in his brain stem.
Escaped slaves recaptured. They crave men.

Women with shaved legs. Women in bondage.
Come out of the closet in their leg irons.
Hooded and gagged and garter-belted Lynch-Bages.
He hears the distant screaming of the sirens.

He lifts his glass. He bows. Testosterone,
The aviation fuel that gives him wings,
Drinks to the gods. His kamikaze starts its flight from his zone
For her zone. Redlined, on full honk, he sings.

RED GUARDS OF LOVE

The Red Guards of love rhythmically stomp their feet
In the stands as their leaders denounce themselves and beg to be retrained.
Venus is dancing a tango called *Banco!* (as in baccarat).
She's wearing donkey's ears. She's wearing an amazing necklace
Of fetus heads.
The Guards rove through the modern cities,
Stoning to death the busts they don't like in the libraries.
The hypnotic suit of rights very slowly struts.

YANKEE DOODLE

Hart Crane wrote *The Bridge*—
The Great American Hart Attack stampedes
Rush hour to a standstill in every stanza.
The John Philip Sousa outburst of trombones,
And fireworks powdering the summer night,
Are very American Charles Ives. Nowadays,
When an earring in one ear makes a pioneer,
Gender Studies find *Tender Buttons*
Is all about the sacred body
Of the rhino and author, Miss Stein,
And parts of her companion, Miss Toklas.
Leonard Bernstein pounces on the piano
To illustrate the point literally with his dick.
Now, Robert Frost is different.
Someone saw Frost
Whipping a tree. I would like to strip
You and whip you till I see Stars and Bars,
O big American Beauty.

OVID, *METAMORPHOSES* X, 298–518

A daughter loved her father so much
She accused him of sexual abuse.
But I am getting ahead of my story.
Ten years after
He had simply been being a good father
She made the charge.
But I am ruining it.
Not that the man was ever told.
And when the accused is not even advised
He has been accused,
And is therefore deprived of a chance to defend himself, society—
Shit! the teleprompter stopped—
Which camera is on?
So it goes these days
With the help of radical feminist therapy
Redressing so many obvious wrongs.
Also because the specialists
Advise against confronting the incestuous rapist
Who may of course have done nothing and be innocent,
But who if he has will deny it to the grave.
One slightly feels he must have done something for the charge
In the first place to have been made.

Muse, put your breast in my mouth
If you want me to sing.
(Fuck the muse.)

Sunlight yellow as a canary.
Perfume from the garden made the room tropical.
The maid in her uniform struggles to draw the heavy curtains.
Darkness in spasms spreads as she tugs.

Light covers the hot and humid girl on the bed
And then is yanked away
By the maid. The last light the maid sees slants across
The girl's eyes and nose like a blindfold.
One of the eyes is green as an emerald.
The fourteen-year-old nose is classical.
The eyes are open in the darkness.

FROM *Going Fast*

Darkness shrink-wraps her
And where her hands are.
The maid leaves the room adjusting herself.

Please,
The girl says to her father, Please
Let me go to Harvard, Daddy.
They are on a cruise.
The water the white ship cuts through is flowers.
The tube they lean their elbows on is warm.
The sky is black. The stars are out.
White birds fly overhead in the middle of the ocean.
Bam bam
Men are shooting skeet on a higher deck.
Her mother is up there shooting.
The girl is in the stateroom with her father
Who is panting as if he were
Having a heart attack while she undresses.
She can't stop herself.
They are doing it.

The maid comes in the room without knocking.
It is time to wake the princess from her nap.
She pulls the curtains back
And finds the girl
Standing naked on a chair.

She has a noose around
Her neck attached to nothing,
Which is a metaphor for love.

If you really love your father that much,
The maid says an hour later
To the naked girl in her arms,
I will have to do something.

It happens that
The girl's mother is off at Canyon Ranch,
Best of the Fat Farms, getting in shape.
She has been there already a week,
And the king is extremely interested when he is told

One of the women in the palace
Is obsessed with His Highness.
Oh, really, how old?
Oh, young, about your daughter's age.

The girl walks into her dream
Late that night when the maid arrives to take her
To her father.
A bird throbbily coos in the warm darkness outside.
The night air smells so sweet.
She immediately trips and knows perfectly well
What that means, but can't, won't, not.
The maid is sexually excited.
The virgin is in a delirium.

It's the familiar fear-of-heights terror
Of being irresistibly drawn
To the edge. You fall
From the other side of the edge toward the street
To get to Mars.
She feels the moisture of desire.

The man is fast asleep after a lot of drinking
So when the maid says, This is the one,
In the dark room he at first grabs the maid
Who redirects his hands and he is immediately
Inside the girl.

For the next two nights the maid
Stands outside in the corridor perspiring,
With her eyes tightly shut, clenching and unclenching her fists.

The father has hidden a flashlight next to his penis in the darkness
In the bed so he can see
Who it is the next night,
When it dawns on him he can simply turn the light on.
He does and tries to kill her,
But she is too fast.
The next thing he hears she is in Sagaponack.
She backtracks to Islip and flies
Out West and keeps going to Hawaii and Bali and on.

FROM *Going Fast*

She sees the Komodo dragons twenty feet long
And carnivorous and fast and keeps going.
Sri Lanka, southern India, Myanmar
(Where Ne Win, the senile military dictator who has tried to ruin
Rangoon and everywhere else and everyone, still keeps the daughter
Of the great patriot democrat of the country
Under house arrest, but one day that will end).
For nine months she travels, pregnant.

On the day she turns into a tree,
She gives birth to a boy.

HEART ART

A man is masturbating his heart out,
Swinging in the hammock of the Internet.
He rocks back and forth, his cursor points
And selects. He swings between repetitive extremes
Among the come-ons in the chat rooms.
But finally he clicks on one
World Wide Web woman who cares.

Each of her virtual hairs
Brings him to his knees.
Each of her breasts
Projects like a sneeze.
He hears her dawning toward him as he reads her dimensions,
Waves sailing the seas of cyberspace—
Information, zeros-and-ones, whitecaps of.

Caught in a tangle of Internet,
Swinging in the mesh to sleep,
Rocking himself awake, sailing the virtual seas,
A man travels through space to someone inside
An active-matrix screen. Snow falls.
A field of wildflowers blooms. Night falls.
Day resumes.

This is the story about humans taking over
The country. New York is outside
His study while he works. Paris is outside.
Outside the window is Bologna.
He logs on. He gets up.
He sits down. A car alarm goes off
Yoi yoi yoi yoi and yips as it suddenly stops.

Man has the takeover impact
Of an asteroid—throwing up debris, blotting out the sun—
Causing the sudden mass extinction
Of the small bookstore
At the millennium. The blood from the blast cakes
And forms the planet's new crust:
A hacker in Kinshasa getting it on with one in Nome.

FROM *Going Fast*

Their poems start
With the part about masturbating the heart—
Saber cuts whacking a heart into tartare—
Heart art worldwide,
Meaning that even in the Far East the subject is love.
Here in the eastern United States,
A man is masturbating his art out.

An Ice Age that acts hot
Only because of the greenhouse effect
Is the sort of personality.
Beneath the dome of depleted ozone, they stay cold.
Mastodons are mating on the Internet
Over the bones of dinosaur nuclear arms,
Mating with their hands.

SPIN

A dog named Spinach died today.
In her arms he died away.
Injected with what killed him.
Love is a cup that spilled him.
Spilled all the Spin that filled him.
Sunlight sealed and sent.
Received and spent.
Smiled and went.

PUBERTY

I see a first baseman's mitt identical to mine
On the right hand of the best who ever lived.

The dark deep claw of leather
Called a trapper hungrily flaps shut and open

While Stan Musial stands there glowing and magnified
In Sportsman's Park on the red dirt behind the bag,

A crab whose right claw is huge,
Costumed legs apart and knees slightly bent,

Springy on spikes, a grown man on springs,
Source of light with wings

(And when he is at bat, one of the beautiful swings).
The pitcher goes into the windup and rears back with desire.

Stan the Man pounds our glove
Broken in with neat's-foot oil.

We get a runner caught in a rundown between first and second.
I can't get the ball back out of the pocket

To throw to the pitcher covering second in time.
Then fifty years pass.

Nothing is next.

THE INFINITE

The beauty of the boy had twisted
Into a shape brain damage has.
Into the room walked a twenty-year-old
Helix with a head
Lopsidedly.

The radiant
Grimness of the Shostakovich
Fifteenth Quartet, the last,
Most austere, most beautiful solemn terror,
The most music one repeated note can make, put out green leaves.

The twentieth century was drawing
To a close with a foal caught in amber smiling
At his mother.
Whose infinite eyes as he limped
In the room smiled.

FROM *Going Fast*

TRUE STORY

A gerbil running on an exercise wheel whirs away the hours
To eternity by reciting the *Iliad*.
Just a gentle gerbil under Joseph Stalin, the eagle Osip Mandelstam.
Biting the arctic stars, black sky,
Spruce trees line his lower jaw.
Stalin flutters like a moth against his hot light.
Lightning flutters against the hot night.

St. Petersburg and Moscow are having sexual intercourse
In a slaughterhouse,
And will produce many sons.
But in the meantime there are the mixed moans.
The cockroach telephones Boris Pasternak from the Kremlin to croon
His fellow poet will be all right—but adds, "You don't really say
Much to save your friend," and hangs up.

HOT NIGHT, LIGHTNING

The United Nations is listening
Via simultaneous translation to the poet Mandelstam.
Tier after tier of the Tower of Babel tribunal being
Breast-fed by their headsets hear his starry eyes,
Marbles of melody and terror.
PowerBooks, powder of the rhinoceros horn, delegates
In every kind of suit and sari and sarong and dream
Men and women around the round world wear, rip
The ribbon from a box of chocolates
And find inside his wife and him,
And hear him begging Nadezhda not to leave the box.
A United Nations of all the languages is going
Through the air, a motorcycle going fast
Into the Nevada desert,
The joy of the original
Into a beautiful emptiness.
Through the double-parked side streets of New York
Into a tunnel, under a river,
The joy of the original goes
Into a tile hole
Which amplifies the sound.

The leading edge of the wing is your face
That comes to earth to me.
I watch you wait.

A twentieth-century
Power outage brings the darkness back
In the vicinity of Jesus Christ, a Caucasian male.
I want the General Assembly to know
How China greets the day.
They don't like blonds and they don't like blacks.
The smell won't go away.
The smell of sperm on the edge of the axe.
Among them Mandelstam, among the millions.
Into the aurora borealis cathedral he walks, filling the choir.
He and the other children weave

A rose window with the face of Shakespeare as the rose.
The tale he tells is made of Northern Lights.
Hairs of titanium are the bridge cables, of spun glass.
Horror has been hammered
Into white gold and gold gold,
Benumbed. Stalin has become sweet butter and salt
On an ear of summer butter-and-sugar corn.
The phonograph record pinned
Under the needle reaches the scratch.
Don't stop *thump* don't stop *thump* don't stop.

Snow is falling.
A candle burns.
I watch you waiting for me to wake.

THE STORM

The perfect body of the yoga teacher
Stains a timeless pose.
Her perfect tan
Is an untouchable.

The beauty of her body
Is a storm
About to hit.
The monsoon air is rank and sweet.

Lightning storms a room
Which thunder overpowers
With stun grenades
That blind and deafen.

Her skin contains the storm
Inside the pose.
Rain squalls wash
The sidewalks raw.

The bombing run unleashes
Mushrooms on a path.
The Stealth flies unseen
Inside out.

High above the homeless,
Back and forth,
Job walks inside out
Weeping storms.

The widow throws her body
On her husband's pyre.
The pose is pain
About to fall in floods.

The goal is grain
Enough to feed the world.
Bodies floating down the Ganges
Do the pose but while they do

FROM *Going Fast*

The king is entering the field.
The queen is entering a grove.
The king is singing to the troops.
The storm is starting.

LITTLE SONG

My tiny Pitts
Fifteen and a half feet long
Brightly painted so it can be seen easily
By the aerobatics judges on the ground
Is a star.

The invisible biplane
Parked on display in my living room
With an inferior roll rate cheerily
Outperforms the more powerful Sukhoi's
Loops and spins.

G's of the imagination fasten
My five-point harness
To the star upside down
The sky is my living room
A chuck behind each wheel.

EISENHOWER YEARS

Suddenly I had to eat
A slowly writhing worm
A woman warmed on a flat stone in a jungle clearing
Or starve. I had to charm a Nazi waving a Lüger
Who could help me escape from a jungle river port town or die.

I had to survive not being allowed to sit down,
For ten hours, in a Mexico City
Jail, accused of manslaughter because
My cab driver in the early morning rush hour
Had killed a pedestrian and jumped out and run.

The prostitute even younger than I was that
I had spent the night with had been
So shy I had gone home with her to meet her parents
When she asked. In the Waikiki Club
Where she worked, I'd faced her machete-faced pimp wielding a knife.

At the Mayan Temple of the Moon, "that" instead of "whom,"
Which the explorer Richard Halliburton
Has written everyone must climb on a night of the full moon
At midnight who wants to say he or she has lived,
The guard dog woke the guard up.

I heard the lyrical barking from the top.
I saw the wink of the rifle barrel far below in the moonlight and hit
The deck like a commando on the ramp along the outside of the pyramid to hide.
When at last I looked up Orson Welles stood there, doe-eyed sombrero silence
Expecting a bribe. I walked with him all innocence down the ramp.

I walked past him out the gate and he fired.
I felt invulnerable, without feelings, without pores.
A week after I got back home to St. Louis I fainted
At the wheel of a car just after I had dropped off a friend,
And for four months in the hospital with a tropical disease I nearly died.

Suddenly in the jungle there was an American professor named Bud Bivins
Who had fled from Texas to avoid the coming nuclear war.
The Nazi found passage for us both on a tramp steamer which ran
Into a violent storm in the Gulf not long after Bivins had gone mad
And taken to pacing the deck all night after the cook had demanded

On the captain's behalf that we pay him more, on top of what
We'd already paid, or swim, with his butcher knife pointing to a thin line
Of green at the horizon, the distant jungle shore.
The captain would be delighted to let us off immediately if we wished.
No one saw Bivins when we reached port.

In the middle of the night a huge wave hit
The rotten boatload of tarantulas and bananas, slam-dunking us under.
The cook and all the others, including our captain,
Kneeled at the rail holding on, loudly praying, so who was at the wheel?
Bivins was last spied on the deck. I was sixteen.

VICTORY

Nothing is pure at 36,000 feet either.
Even in First, there is only more.
The wing is streaked
By the jet engine's exhaust. Sometimes
I stand outside a toilet
Which is occupied, staring out
A window somewhere over Malaysia at dawn.
I am the wing,
The thing that should be lift,
Soiled by power.

Make no mistake about the heat.
It also has to eat.
It eats the fuel it's fed.
It eats the air.
It eats the hair.
It eats what's there.
The jungle devours me with its eyes which are
Screamed skyscrapers of plasm.
I said dismal. I meant passion.
The sky unfreezes me alive.

There is heaven the mainland. And there is heaven the island.
There is the warm water of heaven between.
The minister of defense bull's-eyes on the helicopter pad
With security all around wearing a curly wire into one ear.
Code-named Big Fish, he likes Eau Sauvage
To be there ahead of him wherever he goes.
There is heaven the novel, and heaven the movie.
Below you is the sky at 35,000 feet.
Above you is the muezzin until it ends.
I have the lift, but think I ought to land.

The blank eye of the sky muezzins the faithless to rise
And face the heat
And urinate and defecate and eat and act

Another day.
I wish I knew your name.
Powerful forces have built a road
Through the jungle. Muslim apparently
Women fully clothed are apparently allowed to expose in the lucky
Warm water with their brown kids sporting like putti flying fish.
Quiet on the set, please, thank you. The actors are rehearsing.

My penis is full of blood for you
Probably won't win her hand.
But you bet
Susanna the movie has to pull in the Elders.
She has designs.
She was designed to. She is audience response questionnaire–designed to
Get them to feast their eyes.
They're sitting in the dark and certainly
They're in the dark about
The lights will go on and the vile will be caught by a questionnaire.

Jungle covers an island in the South China Sea.
The interior is the first step in.
Perpetual summer sleeps with sixteen kinds of snakes.
My penis is full of love for you starred
In a road movie with Dorothy Lamour and
The beautiful bay
Used to be a breeding ground for sharks
Where we're swimming now. The head
Of the British fleet, here for the joint
Naval exercises, told me he remembered it well, charming man.

The Steadicam glides everywhere,
Holding its head in the air like a King Cobra.
The ecology
Of the island is fragile, but the second airport will never be built.
This isn't Acapulco 1949 about to Big Bang.
You step into the jungle and it's thick.
You step into the warm water and it's thin.
But nothing jiggles the Steadicam.
The poisonous viper is authorized to use deadly force
Only on the jungle path to the waterfall above the golf course.

FROM *Going Fast*

Someone has seen a ten-foot lizard
Near the set. Someone was seen feeding a monkey
Bananas. The set itself is a subset of itself,
A jungle set in the jungle.
Islam is aerosolized into the atmosphere,
Coating the jungle scenes with time.
St. Agatha is the martyr whose breasts got hacked off,
But in the movie they don't.
The breasts that don't get removed
Anticipate the replenishing monsoon.

God is everywhere you're not,
And you are everywhere. I wish I knew your name.
Congestion in the brain is cleared
By the tropical haze which mists the coconut palms
And by the horrible heat of heaven. Oddly sudden
Mountains rise right out of the sea, jungle-clad. Hairy
Angels are friendly, but not too friendly.
Palm trees can mean Palm Beach,
But where the monkeys are semi-tame
We are semi-saved.

I never sleep on planes, but woke
Belted in, seat upright, table stowed,
To the roar of the reverse thrust,
Semi-saved. I undressed into the ocean
Surrounded by security and businessmen talking into cellular phones.
The jungle is within. The jungle also comes down
To the heavenly warm water lapping the sand.
The jungle is the start and the jungle is the end.
The jungle is behind. The jungle is ahead.
Ahead of me is heaven.

VERMONT

The attitude of green to blue is love.
And so the day just floats itself away.
The stench of green, the drench of green, above
The ripples of sweet swimming in a bay
Of just-mowed green, intoxicates the house.
The meadow goddess squeaking like a mouse
Is stoned, inhales the grass, adores the sky.
The nostrils feed the gods until the eye
Can almost see the perfume pour the blue.
A Botticelli ladled from a well,
Your life is anything you want it to—
And loves you more than it can show or tell.

FROM *Going Fast*

Milan

RACINE

When civilization was European,
I knew every beautiful woman
In the Grand Hôtel et de Milan,
Which the Milanese called "The Millin,"
Where Verdi died, two blocks from La Scala,
And lived in every one of them
Twenty-some years ago while a motorcycle was being made
For me by the MV Agusta
Racing Department in Cascina Costa,
The best mechanics in the world
Moonlighting for me after racing hours.
One of the "Millin" women raced cars, a raving beauty.
She owned two Morandis, had met Montale.
She recited verses from the Koran
Over champagne in the salon and was only eighteen
And was too good to be true.
She smilingly recited Leopardi in Hebrew.
The most elegant thing in life is an Italian Jew.
The most astonishing thing in life to be is an Italian Jew.
It helps if you can be from Milan, too.
She knew every *tirade* in Racine
And was only eighteen.
They thought she was making a scene
When she started declaiming Racine.
Thunderbolts in the bar.
With the burning smell of Auschwitz in my ear.
With the gas hissing from the ceiling.
Racine raved on racing tires at the limit of adhesion.
With the gas hissing from the showers.
I remember the glamorous etching on the postcard
The hotel continued to reprint from the original 1942 plate.
The fantasy hotel and street
Had the haughty perfect ease of haute couture,
Chanel in stone. A tiny tailored doorman
Stood as in an architectural drawing in front of the façade and streamlined
Cars passed by.
The cars looked as if they had their headlights on in the rain,
In the suave, grave
Milanese sunshine.

FROM *Going Fast*

MILAN

This is Via Gesù.
Stone without a tree.
This is the good life.
Puritan elegance.
Severe but plentiful.
Big breasts in a business suit.
Between Via Monte Napoleone and Via della Spiga.

I draw
The bowstring of Cupid's bow,
Too powerful for anything but love to pull.

Oh the sudden green gardens glimpsed through gates and the stark
Deliciously expensive shops.
I let the pocket knives at Lorenzi,
Each a priceless jewel,
Gods of blades and hinges,
Make me late for a fitting at Caraceni.

Oh Milan, I feel myself being pulled back
To the past and released.
I hiss like an arrow
Through the air,
On my way from here to there.
I am a man I used to know.
I am the arrow and the bow.
I am a reincarnation, but
I give birth to the man
I grew out of.
I follow him down a street
Into a restaurant I don't remember
And sit and eat.

A Ducati 916 stabs through the blur.
Massimo Tamburini designed this miracle
Which ought to be in the Museum of Modern Art.

The Stradivarius
Of motorcycles lights up Via Borgospesso
As it flashes by, dumbfoundingly small.
Donatello by way of Brancusi, smoothed simplicity.
One hundred sixty-four miles an hour.
The Ducati 916 is a nightingale.
It sings to me more sweetly than Cole Porter.
Slender as a girl, aerodynamically clean.
Sudden as a shark.

The president of Cagiva Motorcycles,
Mr. Claudio Castiglioni, lifts off in his helicopter
From his ecologically sound factory by a lake.
Cagiva in Varese owns Ducati in Bologna,
Where he lands.
His instructions are Confucian:
Don't stint.

Combine a far-seeing industrialist.
With an Islamic fundamentalist.
With an Italian premier who doesn't take bribes.
With a pharmaceuticals CEO who loves to spread disease.
Put them on a 916.

And you get Fred Seidel.

Bologna

A PRETTY GIRL

Umber, somber, brick Bologna.
They could use some Miami Jews
In this city of sensible shoes.

In the city of Morandi,
The painter of the silence
Of groups of empty bottles,
Arcades of demure
Men dressed in brown pneumonia
Look for women in the fog.

Bare, thick, spare, pure,
Umber, somber, brick Bologna.
This year's fashion color is manure,
According to the windows
Of fogged-in manikins
In Piazza Cavour.
Reeking of allure,
Arcades of demure
Young women dressed in odorless brown pneumonia
Give off clouds of smoke,
Dry ice in the fog.

Bare, thick, spare, pure:
Shaved heads reading books flick
Their cigarettes away and cover their mouths with their scarfs,
Leaned against the radical Medical School,
Punks with stethoscopes, horoscopes.
They listen to the heart with the heart,
Students in the medieval streets.

Their tangerine fingernails heal
The Emergency Room in gloves
Till dawn, and still come out eager to Day-Glo Bologna.
The tangerine tirelessly sheds disposable latex
Gloves until the day glows.
Emergency path lighting
On the airplane floor has led me to the exits
Through the cold and the fog.

FROM *Going Fast*

Follow the tangerine path through the dark and the smoke.
Beneath the unisex jeans
Is cunnus soft as shatoosh.

The Communist mayor who underwrites the Morandi Museum
Takes a right-wing industrialist through the silence.

And the Ducati motorcycle factory
In Via Cavalieri Ducati breathes to life
Another piece of sculpture that goes fast.
Art and engineering meet and make
A brain wave
Of beauty suitable to ride.

The advice of my physician
Is, turn sixty.

I limit lovemaking to one position,
Mounted on a Ducati, monoposto:
Equivalent to warm sand as white as snow,
And skin as brown as brandy,
And swimming in the blue of faraway.

A well-dressed man is lying on a bed
With Leopardi in his arms.
The fog outside the window is Bologna.
He does the dead man's float
Next to the sleek hull of the sloop *A Pretty Girl*,
Stuck in a sheet of glue
Which extends for a hundred miles
Without a sip of wind,
Under a sky.
The blue is infinite.
He can see three miles down.
He free-floats in glass in his body temperature.
He does not know yet that he has dived in
Forgetting to let the ladder down,
And he does not know
He cannot climb back up.
There are no handholds.
The sloping sides are smooth.

The deck too high.
She heads for the horizon under full sail
In his flash hallucination. You never
Leave no one onboard,
But he does not know yet what has happened since
A Pretty Girl is not going anywhere.
The sailboat pond in Central Park
Is where a boy's days were a breeze.
He does the dead man's float
Next to the motionless boat,
But in art there is no hope.
Art is dope.

The fog glows,
Tangerine toward sundown.

The Communist mayor who is said
To be tough but fair
Is waiting.

Take me, silence.

FROM *Going Fast*

Going Fast

GOING FAST

I
Extra Heartbeats

Red
As a Ducati 916, I'm crazed, I speed,
I blaze, I bleed,
I sight-read
A Bach Invention.

I'm at the redline.
When I speak you hear
The exhaust note of a privateer.

I see an audience of applause.
Pairs of hands in rows.
Palestinian and Jew.
And black and brown and yellow and red.
Wedding rings wearing watches
Pound lifelines into foam.
Fate lines. Date lines. Date palms. Politics. Foam.

The air blurs with the clapping.
The sidewalks sizzle with mica.
The colors tremble and vibrate.
The colors in the garden start to shake apart
While the applause swells.

The four walls of the world pump,
Pump their chemicals.

When I give my lectures,
The tachometer reads at the redline.
When I speak you hear
The exhaust note of a privateer.

The flutter in my chest is extra heartbeats,
My ectopy.

And Rabin is calling Arafat.
And Arafat, Rabin.
The touch-tone beeps are rising
To the sky like the bubbles in champagne.

The chemo is killing the white cells.
The white cells are killing the red cells.

They'll have to kill me first.

They'll find me
Flying on the floor.

II
Candle Made from Fat

The most beautiful motorcycle ever made
Was just made.
I ride to Syria
To Assad on one.

A hundred and sixty-four miles an hour
On the 916
Makes a sound,
My friend, makes a sound.

I seek the most beautiful terror.
Massimo Tamburini designed it.
I ride to Syria
To President Assad on one.

Hafez al-Assad, a hundred and sixty-four miles an hour
On the Ducati 916
Makes a sound,
My friend, makes a certain sound.

A group that calls itself
The Other Woman,
In southern Lebanon, apparently with money
From Iran, is assembling the bomb.

It's red,
Flying through the desert
Toward the border with Israel,
As I approach my sixtieth birthday.

The school bus entering the outskirts
Of Jerusalem is full.
The motorcycle
Is screaming, God is great.

The kangaroo effect
Is boing-boing-boing as the white light bounds away,
Leaving in their blood the burning curls
Of Jewish boys and girls.

III
Lauda, Jerusalem

My violent Honda 125cc Grand Prix racer
Is the size of a bee.
It is too small to ride
Except for the joy.

My on-fire 1996 RS125R
Flies on its little wings,
A psalmist, all stinger,
On racing slicks.

It absolutely can't stop
Lifting its voice to scream.
It mounts the victory podium.
Lauda, Jerusalem, Dominum.

I am a Jew.
I am Japan.
I shift gears over and over.
I scream to victory again and again.

Fall leaves inflame the woods.
It is brilliant to live.
The sorrow that is not sorrow,
The mist of everything is over everything.

FROM *Going Fast*

IV
Poem Does

The god in the nitroglycerin
Is speedily absorbed under the tongue
Till it turns a green man red,
Which is what a poem does.
It explosively reanimates
By oxygenating the tribe.

No civilized state will execute
Someone who is ill
Till it makes the someone well
Enough to kill
In a civilized state,
As a poem does.

I run-and-bump the tiny
Honda 125cc Grand Prix racer. Only
Two steps and it screams. I
Slip the clutch to get the revs up, blipping and getting
Ready not to get deady,
Which also is what a poem does.

They dress them up in the retirement centers.
They dress them up in racing leathers.
They dress them up in war paint and feathers.
The autumn trees are in their gory glory.
The logs in the roaring fire keep passing
The peace pipe in pain, just what a poem does.

Stanza no. 5. We want to be alive.
Line 26. We pray for peace.
Line 27. The warrior and peacemaker Rabin is in heaven.
28. We don't accept his fate.
But we do. Life is going ahead as fast as it can,
Which is what a poem does.

V
Israel

An animal in the wild
Comes up to you in a clearing because it
Has rabies. It loves you. It does not know why.
It pulls out a gun.
You really will die.

The motorcycle you are riding
Is not in control of itself.
It is not up to you to.
The sky is not well.
It wants to make friends.

It stalks you to
Hold out its hand
At a hundred and sixty-four miles an hour.
It asks you to
Take down your pants.

Daphne fleeing Apollo
Into the Sinai shrinks to a bonsai.
The Jewish stars that top the crown
Prime Minister Rabin is wearing
As he ascends to heaven assassinated, twinkle.

The main tank holds the dolphins.
Land for peace is not for them.
Daphne fleeing Apollo
Across the desert of your desk becomes
In India a cow.

The icing on the cake
Is stone. The Ten Commandments
Are incised in it.
You take a bite
Of Israel and spit out teeth, señor.

FROM *Going Fast*

You throw your head back and wheelie
On the RS125R
And the Ducati,
Surrounded by security rushing you forward,
Suddenly aware you have been shot.

VI
Killing Hitler

A Ducati Supermono walks down the aisle
At a hundred and forty-one miles an hour
To kiss the Torah, trumpeting,
An elephant downsized to a gazelle that devours lions.

Red Italian bodywork
Designed by the South African
Pierre Terblanche is sensuous lavish smoothness
With mustard-yellow highlights.

Even the instrument binnacle
Is beautiful and the green
Of the top triple clamp
Means magnesium, no expense spared, very trick.

The rabbi weighs only
301 lbs. with the tank full.
It wails straight
To the Wailing Wall.

It is big but being small
The Supermono has a mania.
The double con-rod balance system is elegance.
The total motorcycle bugles petite magnificence.

How to keep killing Hitler
Is the point.
How to be a work of art and win.
How to be Supermono and marry Lois Lane in the synagogue, and love.

M Y T O K Y O (1993)

TO THE MUSE

I'd had a haircut at Molé.
I called you from the first pay phone that worked.
You were high above Park Avenue,
Having damask troubles in their library.

I saw the man approaching not see me.
I held the phone and heard the servants getting you.
I watched him squat in the street near the curb while the traffic passed,
Spreading under himself sheets of newspaper;

Which when he rose he folded neatly
And carried to the trash basket at the corner.
Across the street were Mortimer's' outside tables set for lunch.
Now the maître d' was seating an early customer,

While a woman pushing a shopping cart
Picked through the trash in the trash basket the man had used,
And the butler finally came back
To the phone to say you had gone.

FROM A HIGH FLOOR

City of neutered dogs,
How homeless can you be
In a nine-room apartment
With windows on three sides?
Waiting to be shot
At sunrise by sixteen windows!
Everything you need is
A wall to stand in front of.
With a southern exposure.
Paneling in front of
The wall you stand in front of.
The doorman calls upstairs.
Shall I send it up?
It is coming up.
Your back is to the wall
This pleasant afternoon,
This autumn afternoon,
This final afternoon.
You on all sides of you
In the mirrored bathroom.
You on all sides of you
In the walk-in closet.
In your booklined blindfold.
In the deep fatigue
The sunset warms with rouge.

The *homeless* homeless have
The center strip of Broadway.
To live where you should jump.

FROM *My Tokyo*

THE HOUR

They can't get close enough—there's no such thing.
Look. When they smile. Each rising like a tree
Inside the other, breathing quietly.
Two women start their hour by moistening.

The engine pulling them around the bend
Exposes irresistibly the train
They're on extending from them through the rain.
And then it's night. And it will never end.

They're in a limousine. The plane they're on
Is over water. Dawn reveals the two
Berlins becoming one. And now they knew
The time had come. And now the rain is gone.

Two passengers aboard their lives undress
Down to their hands. The lifelines touch. They stay
Behind their smiles. The guard comes in to say
The hour is over, and they tell her yes.

HAIR IN A NET

If you're a woman turning fifty,
You're a woman who feels cheated.
This message now will be repeated.

The bittersweetness known as Jesus
Was not some nice man saying he is
Not quite a feminist and not quite not one.

Every man's a rapist until he's done.
The bitch relieves the dog. The wound, the gun.
The Sermon on the Mount, the Son.

Was it better back in Peapack
Riding over hills to hounds,
Your consciousness not yet raised?

At Foxcroft, under Miss Charlotte,
Polishing your boots till they were bittersweet,
The fields were a girl's cantata.

Doing the rumba at the regatta,
Plato in Greek, amphetamines your stallion, were your alma mater,
And the Metropolitan, and the Modern . . . and then S/M.

Oh, the tiny furs and the red stench of the fox
Of all those white girls taking cold showers
And then lining up to jump

Hair in a net in a hat over perfectly maintained fences.
Everything male is a rapist, certainly God,
Except for Henry James.

At the Institute for Advanced Study,
Which your father helped organize,
Your father made lives,

Scientists he saved from the Nazis,
Putting his face on the cover of *Time*,
Or was that for his part in building the Atom Bomb?

FROM *My Tokyo*

And otherwise—the man made gushers in Texas rise.
He macadamized the roads of Greece.
His sword was terrible and swift.

He strode up the hill in the heat.
He dove into the ice-cold pool and burst
Instantly into death like a flame.

RACKETS

Reginald Fincke was his name,
The son of Reginald Fincke.
All his friends called him Rex.
Rex lost his eye playing rackets.
The match at the New York City Racquet Club,
In the battleship-gray rackets court,
With the lines done in red like a Mondrian,
Was stopped short,
With the light from the skylight streaming down,
And the overhead electric lights also on
(So the light in the court would be even).
A dashingly handsome young man,
Flawless brutal power.
Hot elegance of a thoroughbred being hot-walked
By George Santayana and Learned Hand through Harvard.
The slender long shaft of the rackets racket,
With its rather small head, so graceful.
The rifle shot crack of the rackets ball
When a hard forehand drive meets the faraway front wall
(And the clang if the ball hits the telltale).
And the lovely backhand backswing
Flowing back to a cocked position.

A rackets ball is a rock. A rackets ball is a *rocketing* rock.
Once the ball is served,
In between each shot,
The marker calls out *Play!*
If the path for the next shot is free,
If the other man is not in the way.
When the ball is crackling back and forth,
Picking up speed off four stone walls,
Accelerating right at you, exploding away,
In the lightning exchanges of a rally,
Over and over the marker cries *Play!*
Meaning the other man is not in your way,
Play!—Play!—Play!—Play!
Meaning the other man is not in your way,

Except when the marker yells *Time!*
The ball can do such damage!
George Santayana, what kind of insane is it
If someone has to okay each shot!

And the gasp from the gallery when the marker called *Play!*
And immediately Fincke was struck.
Fincke was his name,
Fincke went his game.
He'll never fight in a war,
Not that there'll be a war,
Now that he's lost an eye.
He'd become number one in the world earlier that year,
Crushing the previous number one in a private court near Oxford.
He answered a challenge at Tuxedo Park.
Ten thousand dollars had been put up.

Eight million men will die.
The instinct for self-preservation is real though in young men
It pulls its head in but sticks its neck out.
The enormous gun starts firing at the world,
Fires and recoils, fires and recoils.
Franz Ferdinand and his wife the duchess, the duchess,
Are dead at Sarajevo. It echoes.
Welcome to the Racquet Club, Mr. Princip.
Welcome, everyone, to the Porcellian.

Wise—he would have said simply hardworking, sane. Plain
Human magnificence, ugly as Socrates.
Fat hairy caterpillar eyebrows.
Learned Hand was America's.
My former wife's mother was Hand's daughter, one of three.
(He had always wanted a son.)
She curled her pinky in smiling imitation
Of the ancient crone she had known as a child
Who seized every opportunity to say,
Her fabulous diamonds winking away,
"I am Mrs. Reginald Fincke! Fincke with an 'e'!"

THE COMPLETE WORKS
OF ANTON WEBERN

That wasn't it.
The other wasn't either.
I woke up looking through a hole.
Love was blowing through.
It was fresh.

The clouds were clean as only
Squeezed out of a tube
In blobs can be.

The universe begins,
And look what happens. It's spring
At the event horizon.
My future former wife expands
In the ungovernable first seconds to a speck
Which will be high school age fifteen
Billion years from now.

Donna mi priegha—
A lady asks me, I speak in season,
What is the origin of the universe?
What is an event horizon?

If you put a gun to your temple and close your eyes,
And the enormous pressure builds and builds,
And slowly you squeeze the trigger . . .
Do you hear the big bang?

When you kill yourself,
Do you hear the sound?

Followed by the universe.

On the far side of the invisible,
On the inside of a black hole, is
The other universe, which is closed,
Which you can't enter or see,
Which you don't know is right there,
Without dimensions and unknowable.

FROM *My Tokyo*

Eyelet
As vast as a pore.

An entire universe in less than a dot.
The opposite of infinite.
Less than a dot that weighs more than the world.
The opposite of infinite

Is infinite.
The gravity is so great.
Light can't escape.
It weighs more than the world.

The opposite of infinite is
WNYC's signal reaches it.

Listen . . .

How an angel would sing, utterly inhuman.
The ethereal cockroach music of Anton Webern.

They're playing
All his rarefied work on
The anniversary of his death.

An entire universe in less than a dot.
Faint brief frosts of breath
Fly-cast precise and chaste.
It doesn't ask to be loved.

These briefest exhalations
In the history of music are vast.
The absolutely infinite God
Of the Cabala
In the twinkling of an eyelet, Ensof.

The future of the past was the New Music.
He believed
The atonal was eternal. He believed

Fifty years
In the future children would be whistling
It on their way to school. The irresistible
Ravisher was pure
Tunelessness.

And the angel
        Raised his hand to greet her,
At the same time bowing low.
        To the woman,
Never mind her terror,
        His hand before he spoke
Seemed to sing.
        His utterly inhuman voice,
Which suddenly she heard,
        Startled her,
Was gorgeously strange.

Sang without a melody. Sang
So grand a neatness, precision, briefness.
So unnatural and severe
Would come to seem so natural
Kids would whistle it.

Stuck at a fixation point, he sings.
Where the match scratch and hiss sweetens to flame.
Where the boy soprano's eternal voice is breaking.
And the slow caterpillar turns silently into wings.

Sing a song of sealed trains
Arriving day and night.
These trains had kept it all inside.
These trains had never let their feelings out.
These train-sick trains were just dying.
These trains couldn't hold it any longer.
These trains shat uncontrollably
All over the sidings and ramps
Jews for the camps.

This century must end.
To modern art I say—
It's been real.

FROM *My Tokyo*

He fled Vienna with his family
For the mountain village of Mittersill to escape the bombs.
　　　Now with the war over,
He was standing outside
　　　His son-in-law's house just after curfew
Enjoying the night air.
　　　An American soldier who had been drinking mistook
A great composer smoking an after-dinner cigar
　　　For a black marketeer reaching for a gun.

I am a toupee walking toward me
With no one under it.
I put the gun to my head.

THE RITZ, PARIS

A slight thinness of the ankles;
The changed shape of the calf;
A place the thigh curves in
Where it didn't used to; and when he turns
A mirror catches him by surprise
With an old man's buttocks.

FROM *My Tokyo*

UNTITLED

Brought to the surface from the floor of the ocean
And the crushing atmospheres of pressure there,
The thing had wings, a mouth, no eyes.
It started to speak when it exploded.
I see I have described a confessional poet.
Senator, I have no memory of that.

The car alarms go off day and night,
The sound of hard times, easy money. In the dream,
The crack dealer over and over hides his stash
Inside a parked car's hubcap just in time. Warbling police cars arrive
In rut, wearing on their heads an ecstatic whirling light show as antlers.
I have no memory of that.

I have no memory of that
Is what to say in court. Or when appearing
At a Senate Select Committee hearing
Under oath, and upon being asked
Tell us a bit about yourself.
I have no memory of that.

Thirty-five years ago I strolled through Harvard Yard.
The steps of Widener led one to the doom of reading.
I was a nose looking for the blush of blood—
Sharks glide for hours this way behind their smiles.
Dictionaries opened their mouths. I devoured them.
Girls lay face up behind their smiles.

Stylish Senator John F. Kennedy and I sat facing each other behind our smiles
In his former tutor's former rooms in Eliot House.
Nothing has been the same since the Zapruder film
Of the assassination was endlessly replayed
On television worldwide. Darkness lies behind the light
That makes home movies.

Nothing could ever be the same after the Zapruder film
Of the Dallas motorcade was endlessly replayed
On TV worldwide, assassinating the young president again and again.
In his wife's arms. His head explodes.
Darkness lies behind the light.
Blind people feel this way behind their smiles.

Two leaping dolphins stay behind their smiles
And catch treats tossed to them,
And delight a paying audience. Others out at sea on a beautiful day
Talk about everything they love in a language of clicks.
Others, trained by us, moan a kind of baby talk
And a few long whalesongy words, hauntingly unintelligible.

The U.S. Navy experimented with having
Them lay underwater mines in the mid-sixties when I was thirty.
Meanwhile, the civil rights movement I completely missed.
I was so busy doing nothing,
I had no time. They lynched and burned.
I played squash drunk.

GLORY

Herbert Brownell was the attorney general.
Ezra Pound was reciting some Provençal. I was seventeen
Every terrifying hungover sunrise that fall.
Thanksgiving weekend 1953 I made my pilgrimage to Pound,
Who said, Kike-sucking Pusey will destroy Harvard unless you save it.
I persuaded him two words in his translation of Confucius should change.

His pal Achilles Fang led me to the empty attic of the Yenching Institute,
In the vast gloom arranged two metal folding chairs
Under the one lightbulb hanging from the ceiling,
And hating me, knee to knee,
Unsmilingly asked, What do you know?
Pound sent a message to MacLeish. Archie, wake up.

United States of America v. Ezra Pound.
My song will seek and detonate your heat.
Pound reciting with his eyes closed filled the alcove with glory.
My art will find and detonate your heart.
I was a freshman and everywhere in Washington, D.C.
I walked, I dreamed.

THE EMPRESS RIALTO

Native Americans were still Indians
In the Saturday afternoon double features a minute ago,
War paint and feathers still bloomed from the brain stem
Of a brave. He strode from his hogan and wickiup and tepee and wigwam
Into a politically correct text
A woman riffles through crossing Harvard Yard,
What used to be called a beautiful girl a minute ago
Rushing to an hour exam in Sever Hall.

Bison and bison calfs,
Each looking rather like Toulouse-Lautrec, snowed back and forth in black
Across the plains, so many millions they could be seen from the moon,
The only visible feature on Earth beside the Great Wall of China—
Vanished, genocide, more martyrs than in Islam! His eyesight was an
        arrowhead parting the air.
His silence, immensely, tiptoed forward.
He came on an enemy praying, the chant aimed at something in the sky,
The hands held out, palms up.

Silence the size of a lunar sea,
In war paint and feathers, dressed to kill,
Gazed at the million antelope a few feet away in another world,
Gazed at the prostitute named Jean,
Her pubic hair cut in a Mohawk
By a steady customer
Who was a barber, in the Empress Rialto Hotel,
The walls splashed with brains and rainbow, a minute ago.

LORRAINE MOTEL, MEMPHIS

An angel's on his knees in front of her.
She's watching in a mirror while she moans.
The other woman, seated, spreads her legs.

Winged light is on its knees in front of her.
She watches in the mirror while she moans.
The other, head thrown back, has spread her legs.

I have a dream! is here in front of her.
She's staring in the mirror while she moans.
The other sister, still clothed, spreads her legs.

He's blazing on his knees in front of her.
She's praising in the mirror when she moans.
Her daughter has a dream and spreads her legs.

Death sits up like a little dog and begs:
The man who will kill King is eating eggs.
He pricks a yolk. The yellow spurts and groans.

THE NEW WOMAN

They can't get close enough—there's no such thing.
Look. When they smile. Each rising like a tree
Inside the other, breathing quietly.
Two women start their hour by moistening.

The engine pulling them around the bend
Exposes irresistibly the train
They're on extending from them through the rain.
And then it's night. And it will never end.

They're in a limousine. The plane they're on
Is over water. Dawn reveals the two
Berlins becoming one. And now they knew—
The time had come. And now the rain is gone.

Two passengers aboard their lives undress
Down to their hands. They're holding guns. They stay
Behind their smiles. The guard comes in to say
The hour is over, and they tell her yes.

FROM *My Tokyo*

THE FORMER GOVERNOR
OF CALIFORNIA

The beauty in his arms could kill him easily.
The busboy bending down to take his plate
Could stab him quickly fifteen times.
The woman in the store this afternoon
Walked toward him strangely, selling perfume.
The former governor of California,
The only candidate for president
Who studied Zen, is pitching woo
To eminent New Yorkers in someone's studio.
The group is small—he's close enough to kiss;
And close enough to kiss is close enough to blow away.
What a wilderness of empty voting booths
The curtain rises to reveal.
The scene is North America now.
I miss the dry-ice fire of Bobby Kennedy.
I met McGovern in your living room.
Hubert Humphrey simply lacked the lust.
It's hard to die. It's hard to live.
We got that way by being
Durable but delicate.
The body lasts and lasts and yet
Is half in love with death. The smiling
President-for-Life is love. The smiling
President-for-Life is love.
The smiling President-for-Life is love.
Idi Amin forces the gazelle to swallow a grenade.
Stalin isn't a psychosomatic disorder.

LIFE AFTER DEATH

Hundreds stand strangely
In a landscape of vast emptiness on an ocean,
In a silent black-and-white sequence:
A noon of duneless desert with a seat at the U.N.,
A tribal bloodbath nation with a raw gold flag.
A Socialist, poet, murderer king is president.
I made that up.
And when the mass execution starts, one man
Raises his human hands in front of him to block
The bullets. The central character in this serious
Bringing meat to the vegetarians
Movie in ravishing color watches real footage
Of a mass execution glumly. He's trying
The arc flown by a jet for the astronauts to give
Them a few seconds' practice weightlessness.
The existential American antihero reporter of nothing
Is impersonating an international arms dealer in a desert.
He'll have to die.
He'll find he has a cause.
He'll find exchanging identities
Is a conversion. The former foreign correspondent
On the lam from himself, floating free,
Trying to float, glares at the footage glumly.
Free will is his fate.
The twentieth century made it possible
For us more and more fictional characters to see
Real human beings being killed
And leave the theater and live.
Leave and live!
Leave yourself and live!

FROM *My Tokyo*

SONNET

The suffering in the sunlight and the smell.
And the bellowing and men weeping and screaming.
And the horses wandering aimlessly and the heat.
The living and the dead mixed, bleeding on one another.
A palm with two fingers left attached
Lying on the ground next to the hindquarters of a horse.
A dying man literally without a face
Pointed at where his face had been.
He did this without a sound.
The forty thousand dead and wounded stretched for miles
In every direction from the tower.
Not a cloud in the sky all day, the sunlight of hell.
Bodies swelled and split, erupting their insides
Like sausages on the fire.

BURKINA FASO

The first is take the innards out when you
Do Ouagadougou. Clean with a grenade.
Thus Captain Compaoré's kitchen made
From Clément Ouedraogo human stew.

The one man who might help them disappears
And reappears in bowls. You eat or are
The eaten here. French-speaking, Muslim tar
That once sold slaves and blames the French, in tears.

POL POT

Dawn. Leni Riefenstahl
And her cameras slowly inflate the immense Nuremberg Rally.
The Colorado looks up in awe at the Grand Canyon
It has made. Hitler.

European clouds. 1934. Empty
Thought-balloons high above Lascaux
Without a thought inside. The Führer
Is ice that's fire, physically small.

They all were. Stalin.
Trotsky's little glasses
Disappear behind a cloud
From which he won't emerge alive.

The small plane carrying
The Grail to Nuremberg got Wagnerian clouds
To fly through, enormous, enormous. Mine eyes have seen the glory, it
Taxis to a stop. The cabin door swings open.

Leni schussed from motion pictures
To still photography after the war. From the Aryan ideal, climbed out
In Africa to shoot the wild shy people of Kau,
Small heads, tall, the most beautiful animals in the world.

Artistically mounted them into ideal
Riefenstahl. Riefenstahl! Riefenstahl! Riefenstahl! Really,
From blonds in black-and-white to blacks in color.
Now Pol Pot came to power.

Now in London Sylvia Plath
Nailed one foot to the floor;
And with the other walked
And walked and walked through the terrible blood.

STROKE

The instrument is priceless.
You can't believe it happened.
The restoration flawless.
The voice is almost human.
The sound is almost painful.
The voice is almost human.
I close my eyes to hear it.
The restoration flawless.
The beauty is inhuman.
The terrifying journey.
O strange new final music.
The strange new place I've gone to.
The blinding light is music.
The starless warm night blinding.
The odor of a musk rose
Presents itself as secrets.
Paralysis can't stop them.
The afterburners kick in.
The visitors are going.
I dreamed that I was sleeping.
Physiatry can't say it.
I can't believe it happened.
A handshake is the human
Condition of bereavement.
A thixotropic sol is
A shaken-up false body.
I know another meaning.
A life was last seen living.
A life was last seen leaving.
The summit of Mount Sinai,
The top of their new tower,
The stark New North Pavilion,
Looks out on New York City,
The miles of aspiration,
The lonely devastation.
I listen to the music
Nine years before 2000.

FROM *My Tokyo*

CHARTRES

The takeoff of the Concorde in a cathedral.
Ninety seconds into it they cut
The afterburners and the deathly silence
Was like a large breast as we banked steeply left.

AUTUMN

A fall will come that's damp and delicate,
A geisha voice, a male ventriloquist.
The dummy on his knee will coo she'll get
The other woman ready to be kissed.

The garter belt–and-stockings one will crawl
For him, will crawl on all fours down the hall,
His voice between her teeth. She'll show him all.
He'll want to see. He'll walk behind. She'll call.

FROM *My Tokyo*

THE LIGHTING OF THE CANDLES

Her lighting all the candles late at night,
Hours after he had turned out every light,
Was her preparing to be left alone
Once she had pushed aside the heavy stone
And left the tomb and their apartment where
She'd leave herself behind to not be there.

THE LOVER

(René Char's last poem, L'Amante)

I'd been so seized by passion for this delectable lover.
I not exactly exempt from feeling, from tremblors of lust.
It meant I must, meant I absolutely must not,
Just fade away quietly, mildly changed,
Recognized only by the eyelids of my lover.
Nights of savage newness found for me again
The flaming saliva that connects, and perfumed the fevered connection.
A thousand precautions gave way thirstily
To the most voluptuous flesh there could be.
In our hands desire that transcends.
What fear on our lips tomorrow?

FOR MARIE-CLAUDE CHAR

FROM *My Tokyo*

THE

The poem as a human torch. I burn. Burns out.

THE DEATH OF META BURDEN
IN AN AVALANCHE

I don't believe in anything, I do
Believe in you, vanished particles of vapor,
Field of force,
Undressed, undimmed Invisible,
Losing muons and gaining other ones,
Counterrotations with your
Robed arms raised out straight to each side
In a dervish dance of eyes closed ecstasy,
Tireless, inhuman,
Wireless technology
Of a ghost,
Of a spinning top on its point,
Of a tornado perspiring forward a few miles an hour
Uprooting everything and smelling sweetly like a lawn.
It's that time of year.
It's that time of year a thousand times a day. A thousand times a day,
A thousand times a day,
You are reborn flying to out-ski
The first avalanche each spring,
And buried alive.

I went to sleep last night so I could see you.
I went to see the world destroyed. It was a movie.
I went to sleep that night so I could see you.
And then a drink and then to sleep.
That's Vermont.
The universe hung like a flare for a while and went out,
Leaving nothing, long ago.
Each galaxy at war exhaled
A firefly glow, a tiny quiet, far away . . .
On and off . . . worlds off and on—and then
The universe itself brightened, stared and went out.
I cannot see.
I will not wake though it's a dream.
I move my head from side to side.
I cannot move.
The nights are cold, the sun is hot,
The air is alcohol at that altitude

FROM *My Tokyo*

Three thousand miles from here—is here
Today a thousand times.
You haven't changed.

There is a room in the Acropolis Museum.
The kouroi smile silence.
The way a virus sheds. The way
A weave of wind shear
And the willingness to share is the perfect friend
Every child invents for his very own. I don't know.
The Parthenon suddenly made me cry.
I saw it and I sobbed,
And it doesn't share.
I was so out of it
You came too close. I got too near
The temple, flying low. I got too near
The power, past the ropes. I touched the restoration work.
It could mean a loss of consciousness
In the right-hand seat to be with God.
The Early Warning Ground Proximity Indicator is flashing.
Never mind. I knew it was.
The alarm ah-oooga ah-oooga and the computer-generated
Voice says
And says and says Pull Up Pull Up Pull Up Pull Up.

You say come closer.
You say come closer.
I cannot move.
You say I have to whisper this. Come closer.
I want to hear.
There also is the way a virus sheds.
I want to see. And the ground whispers
Closer. In the Littré the other day and you were there
In the Petit Robert. Grévisse—Larousse—
Ten million years from now, will there be anything?
The rain came down convulsively on the dry land,
As if it would have liked to come down even harder,
Big, kind, body temperature
Shudderings, and on the far bank of the newborn river,
The joyous drumming of the native drums,
Making a tremendous sound twelve feet beneath the snow

Without an avalanche beeper in those days. It's true—
I don't believe in anything I *do*
Believe in, but I do believe in you
Moving your face from side to side to make a space to breathe.

I think I am crying on all my legs
From a dark place to a dark place like a roach.
I am running on the ground with my wings folded—
But now I am extending them,
Running across my kitchen floor and
Running down the rue Barbet-de-Jouy,
Trying historically before it's too late to get into the air.
I have on my ten Huntsman suits,
And many shining shoes made to my last.
I believe in one Lobb.
Faites sur mesure. Everything
Fits my body perfectly now that I'm about to disappear.
I don't believe in anything.
Lightning touches intimately the sable starless. Thunder.
It starts to rain, in your intoxication.
Communism and capitalism go up in flames
And come back down as rain—I'm coming now—
But Greece stays parched.
I'm coming now.

I'm being thrown violently at the sky,
The deck of the carrier shrinking to a dot,
Thirty-some years ago
Suddenly catching sight of Chartres Cathedral miles away;
Horizon to horizon, a molten ocean
The beautiful urine color of vermeil,
Color and undercolor as with a fur;
Soaring stock-still above the windblown waves of wheat,
Dialing on the seemingly inexhaustible power.
Break it.
I swim over to the sealed
Aquarium window of the TV screen to try.
President of the United States descending the stairs
Of his helicopter pixels snap a salute at the American flag

FROM *My Tokyo*

Pixels. I turn the sound off
And the Marine band explodes.
I'm coming now.
I can't breathe.
I'm coming now to the conclusion that
Without a God. I'm coming now to the conclusion.

THE SECOND COMING

Half Japanese, half Jewish.
Hemispheres of a one-night stand in Cambridge, Massachusetts.
God instantly appeared.
Nine months later born in Rome.
Put up for adoption after four days.
Half Jewish, half Japanese.
Imagine the solitude that is.
Imagine how beautiful she is.
How powerful and pale.
The courier arrives.
The millennium begins.

FROM *My Tokyo*

MY TOKYO

Moshi-moshi. (Hello.)
Money is being made.
Money was being made.
Make more make more make more consumer goods.

But the shelves were empty.
The snow was deep.
At Lenin's Tomb the Honor Guard
Stood there actually asleep.

Red Square was white.
Snow was falling dreamily on Beijing.
This was global warming.
Twenty-four hours passed and it was still snowing.

In New York the homeless
Reify the rich.
The homeless in the streets.
The car alarms go off.

The cherry blossoms burst
Into Imperial bloom. The handheld fax machine has something
Coming in. This spring our Western eyes are starting to slant.
They caution you composites can't.

O O O Ochanomizu,
You are my station.
The polished businessman warrior bowed
Cool as a mountain forest of pine.

And the adolescent schoolgirls like clouds of butterflies
On the subway in their black school uniforms
At all hours of the day going somewhere,
Daughters of the Rising Sun.

New York is an electrical fire.
People are trapped on the top floor, smoking
With high-rise desire
And becoming Calcutta.

Tokyo is low
And manic as a hive.
For the middle of the night they have silent jackhammers.
Elizabethan London with the sound off. Racially pure with no poor.

Mishima himself designed the stark far-out uniform
His private army wore, madly haute couture. He stabbed the blade in wrong
And was still alive while his aide tried in vain
To cut his head off as required.

Moshi-moshi I can't hear you. I'm going blind.
Don't let me abandon you, you're all I have.
Hello, hello. My Tokyo, hello.
Hang up and I'll call you back.

You say to the recyclable person of your dreams *Je t'aime*,
And the voice recognition system,
Housed in a heart made from seaweed,
Murmurs in Japanese *Moi aussi*.

FROM *My Tokyo*

RECESSIONAL

How many breasts a woman has depends.
But not on how much need for them you have.
A woman with no breasts applied the salve.
The modem won't receive, it only sends.

What hasn't happened isn't everything
Until in middle age it starts to be.
I woke up wrinkled underneath a tree.
The breasts above me swayed, not listening.

Drought. Ethiopia. We circle low.
Each parachute a breast. Blind mouths look up.
Each breast is liquid living in a cup,
A nippled Nobel Peace Prize Stockholm snow.

The famine's everywhere there's UNICEF.
The Red Cross carpet-bombs the dead with food.
We hear, Zaire, you're in a bitter mood.
(We do have better hearing than the deaf!)

I had a radical mastectomy.
Crack troops flew in at once with extra breasts.
Big Bang of AIDS in Africa invests
The dark with vaster stars than I can see.

It is the role of government to rule
The Congo crocodile who likes blond curls.
The lab discovered undigested girls
Inside the humid darkness of his stool.

I swing from tree to tree and beat my chest.
I beat my breast and cling from tree to tree.
I'm going back. I start to squat to pee.
You were my partner and I liked you best.

THESE DAYS (1989)

SCOTLAND

A stag lifts his nostrils to the morning
In the crosshairs of the scope of love,
And smells what the gun calls Scotland and falls.
The meat of geology raw is Scotland: Stone
Age hours of stalking, passionate aim for the heart,
Bleak dazzling weather of the bare and green.
Old men in kilts, their beards are lobster red.
Red pubic hair of virgins white as cows.
Omega under Alpha, rock hymen, fog penis—
The unshaved glow of her underarms is the sky
Of prehistory or after the sun expands.

The sun will expand a billion years from now
And burn away the mist of Caithness—till then,
There in the Thurso phone book is Robin Thurso.
But he is leaving for his other castle.
"Yes, I'm just leaving—what a pity! I can't
Remember, do you shoot?" Dukes hunt stags,
While Scotsmen hunt for jobs and emigrate,
Or else start seeing red spots on a moor
That flows to the horizon like a migraine.
Sheep dot the moor, bubblebaths of unshorn
Curls somehow red, unshepherded, unshorn.

Gone are the student mobs chanting the *Little Red
Book* of Mao at their Marxist dons.
The universities in the south woke,
Now they are going back to the land of dreams—
Tour buses clog the roads that take them there.
Gone, the rebel psychoanalysts.
Scotland trained more than its share of brilliant ones.
Pocked faces, lean as wolves, they really ran
To untrain and be famous in London, doing wild
Analysis, vegetarians brewing
Herbal tea for anorexic girls.

Let them eat haggis. The heart, lungs, and liver
Of a sheep minced with cereal and suet,
Seasoned with onions, and boiled in the sheep's stomach.
That's what the gillie eats, not venison,
Or salmon, or grouse served rare, not for the gillie
That privilege, or the other one which is
Mushed vegetables molded to resemble a steak.
Let them come to Scotland and eat blood
Pud from a food stall out in the open air,
In the square in Portree. Though there is nothing
Better in the world than a grouse cooked right.

They make a malt in Wick that tastes as smooth
As Mouton when you drink enough of it.
McEwen adored both, suffered a partial stroke,
Switched to champagne and died. A single piper
Drones a file of mourners through a moor,
The sweet prodigal being piped to his early grave.
A friend of his arriving by helicopter
Spies the procession from a mile away,
The black speck of the coffin trailing a thread,
Lost in the savage green, an ocean of thawed
Endlessness and a spermatozoon.

A vehement bullet comes from the gun of love.
On the island of Raasay across from Skye,
The dead walk with the living hand in hand
Over to Hallaig in the evening light.
Girls and boys of every generation,
MacLeans and MacLeods, as they were before they were
Mothers and clansmen, still in their innocence,
Walk beside the islanders, their descendants.
They hold their small hands up to be held by the living.
Their love is too much, the freezing shock-alive
Of rubbing alcohol that leads to sleep.

FLAME

The honey, the humming of a million bees,
In the middle of Florence pining for Paris;
The whining trembling the cars and trucks hum
Crossing the metal matting of Brooklyn Bridge
When you stand below it on the Brooklyn side—
High above you, the harp, the cathedral, the hive—
In the middle of Florence. Florence in flames.

Like waking from a fever . . . it is evening.
Fireflies breathe in the gardens on Bellosguardo.
And then the moon steps from the cypresses and
A wave of feeling breaks, phosphorescent—
Moonlight, a wave hushing on a beach.
In the dark, a flame goes out. And then
The afterimage of a flame goes out.

OUR GODS

Older than us, but not by that much, men
Just old enough to be uncircumcised,
Episcopalians from the Golden Age
Of schools who loved to lose gracefully and lead—
Always there before us like a mirage,
Until we tried to get closer, when they vanished,
Always there until they disappeared.

They were the last of a race, that was their cover—
The baggy tweeds. Exposed in the Racquet Club
Dressing room, they were invisible,
Present purely in outline like the head
And torso targets at the police firing
Range, hairless bodies and full heads of hair,
Painted neatly combed, of the last WASPs.

They walked like boys, talked like their grandfathers—
Public servants in secret, and the last
Generation of men to prefer baths.
These were the CIA boys with EYES
ONLY clearance and profiles like arrowheads.
A fireside frost bloomed on the silver martini
Shaker the magic evenings they could be home.

They were never home, even when they were there.
Public servants in secret are not servants,
Either. They were our gods working all night
To make Achilles' beard fall out and prop up
The House of Priam, who by just pointing sent
A shark fin gliding down a corridor,
Almost transparent, like a watermark.

FROM *These Days*

EMPIRE

The endangered bald eagle is soaring
Away from extinction, according to the evening news—
Good news after the news, after
The stocking masks and the blindfolds,
Contorted and disfigured nature in the dying days of oil.
What a surprise happy ending for the half hour.
Eagles airlift above the timberline—*cut to*
Their chicks nesting in the rocks.

The TV anchorman who predigests it all,
Himself has a great American carnivore prow,
But he is more an oak than an eagle.
According to polls, our father image comforts like the breast,
Is more trusted than the president by far.
Oh so honestly Carter's eyes widen and glitter
For emphasis—the expression of a very sober child
Who is showing you he can wiggle his ears.

Flags fly at half-mast all over the nation
For the fallen, each flagpole a pinprick,
So many pinpricks it becomes pain—
Three thousand continental miles from sea to sea
Reforested with half-flying flags. How unsuitable
For being on its knees Old Glory is,
Bomb burst and cheer on its knees under
Incomparable American skies, the famous North American light.

The famous humidity. Condensation frosts the bottom inch
Of the windshield, the first air conditioner day.
A rainbow of stainless steel, the Gateway Arch,
Takes off and lands, takes off and lands, takes off
And rises sixty stories, and swoops back and lands
A little way down the levee. A railroad bridge
Filigrees across the brown sumptuous river.
Humid flags sog at half-mast.

Bitter bitter bitter bitter
Cries a bird somewhere out over the river
At dusk, as darkness filters down through the soft evening
On Ste. Genevieve, near St. Louis. Remember,
The creek out there somewhere in the dark
Burbles, remember. You cannot see:
But close your eyes anyway, and smell.
The houses when you open your eyes are watching the news.

Unshaved men in suits walk ahead of others in masks.
It might be the men one sees strolling
Together outside Claridge's in London followed
At a submissive distance by their veiled wives,
But in Central America—hostages and their slaves
By relay satellite. Rank as the odor in urine
Of asparagus from the night before,
This is empire waking drunk, and remembering in the dark.

THE NEW COSMOLOGY

Above the Third World, looking down on a fourth:
Life's aerial photograph of a new radio telescope
Discoloring an inch of mountainside in Chile,
A Martian invasion of dish receivers.
The tribes of Israel in their tents
Must have looked like this to God—
A naive stain of wildflowers on a hill,
A field of ear trumpets listening for Him,
Stuck listening to space like someone blind . . .

If there was a God.
There never is.
Almond-eyed shepherd warriors
Softly pluck their harps and stare off into space,
And close their eyes and dream.
In one tent, the Ark;
The chip of kryptonite.
They dream a recurring dream
About themselves as superpowers, and their origin.

Man is the only animal that dreams of outer space,
Epitome of life on earth,
The divine mammal which can dream
It is the chosen people of the universe
No more. But once you have got up high enough to look down,
Once you have got out far enough to look back,
The earth seems to magnify itself
In intensely sharp focus against the black,
Beautiful blind eye milky blue.

That we are alone, that we are not, are unimaginable.
We turn a page of *Life*,
Lying open in the grass,
To a pink earthworm slowly crossing the Milky Way
At nearly the speed of light—red-shifted protein!
The rest is unimaginable,
Like the silence before the universe.
The last nanosecond of silence twenty billion years ago
Before the big bang is endless.

A ROW OF FEDERAL HOUSES

A row of Federal houses with one missing,
The radicals' bomb factory, now blue sky,
An elegantly preserved "landmark block"
Address the last quake of the sixties' underground leveled;
Leaving a prize street with an empty lot
Worth its weight in caviar, stripped naked
Between the wound-pale windowless raw side walls
Of the neighbors, left homeless in a flash
Whose value grows and grows. The years roll by,
Gray as big grains of butter-sweet beluga,
Real estate booms. The lot is still empty.
The purchaser still waits for permission to build.
No yellow ribbons yet for the hostages, tied
To the door knockers, sashed around the trees,
Which will become the symbol of support
For them, the Americans held in Iran. Surreal,
The Shah's dying of cancer in Cairo; his body
Escaped the revolution only to find
His insides turning into caviar,
The peacock and his court of torturers.
Marvelous, how time takes care of things;
Shad are running in the river with their
Delicious roe after years of none,
And seemingly hopeless pollution. There is hope.
The Landmarks Commission tells the community
The latest compromise design succeeds,
Protects the past, the unity of the block,
Your wishes went into it, etc.,
The way the mind negotiates a dream.
Gradually, Versailles bricks up the hole;
A million-dollar Bastille seals it off;
Till fountains rise from the swimming pool that fills
The garden space and the vast moment when
The daughter whose parents were gone for the summer heard
A thud while shopping, knew her friends were dead,
Smiled at the cashier, blankly turned
And walked away in the silence before the sirens.

FROM *These Days*

THAT FALL

The body on the bed is made of china,
Shiny china vagina and pubic hair.
The glassy smoothness of a woman's body!
I stand outside the open door and stare.

I watch the shark glide by . . . it comes and goes—
Must constantly keep moving or it will drown.
The mouth slit in the formless fetal nose
Gives it that empty look—it looks unborn;

It comes into the room up to the bed
Just like a dog. The smell of burning leaves,
Rose bittersweetness rising from the red,
Is what I see. I must be twelve. That fall.

A DIMPLED CLOUD

Cold drool on his chin, warm drool in his lap, a sigh,
The bitterness of too many cigarettes
On his breath: portrait of the autist
Asleep in the arms of his armchair, age thirteen,
Dizzily starting to wake just as the sun
Is setting. The room is already dark while outside
Rosewater streams from a broken yolk of blood.

All he has to do to sleep is open
A book; but the wet dream is new, as if
The pressure of *De bello Gallico*
And Willa Cather face down on his fly,
Spread wide, one clasping the other from behind,
Had added confusion to confusion, like looking
For your glasses with your glasses on.

A mystically clear, unknowing trance of being . . .
And then you feel them—like that, his first wet dream
Seated in a chair, though not his first.
Mr. Hobbs, the Latin master with
A Roman nose he's always blowing, who keeps
His gooey handkerchief tucked in his jacket sleeve,
Pulls his hanky out, and fades away.

French, English, math, history: masters one
By one arrive, start to do what they do
In life, some oddity, some thing they do,
Then vanish. The darkness of the room grows brighter
The darker it gets outside, because of the moonlight.
O adolescence! darkness of a hole
The silver moonlight fills to overflowing!

If only he could be von Schrader or
Deloges, a beautiful athlete or a complete
Shit. God, von Schrader lazily shagging flies,
The beautiful flat trajectory of his throw.
Instead of seeking power, being it!
Tomorrow Deloges will lead the school in prayer,
Not that the autist would want to take his place.

FROM *These Days*

Naked boys are yelling and snapping wet towels
At each other in the locker room,
Like a big swordfighting scene from *The Three Musketeers*,
Parry and thrust, roars of laughter and rage,
Lush Turkish steam billowing from the showers.
The showers hiss, the air is silver fox.
Hot breath, flashes of swords, the ravishing fur!—

Swashbuckling boys brandishing their towels!
Depression, aggression, elation—and acne cream—
The ecosystem of a boy his age.
He combs his wet hair straight, he hates his curls,
He checks his pimples. Only the biggest ones show,
Or rather the ointment on them caked like mud,
Supposedly skin-color, invisible; dabs

Of peanut butter that have dried to fossils,
That even a shower won't wash away, like flaws
Of character expressed by their concealment—
Secrets holding up signs—O adolescence!
O silence not really hidden by the words,
Which are not true, the words, the words, the words—
Unless you scrub, will not wash away.

But how sweetly they strive to outreach these shortcomings,
These boys who call each other by their last names,
Copying older boys and masters—it's why
He isn't wearing his glasses, though he can't see.
That fiend Deloges notices but says nothing.
Butting rams, each looks at the other sincerely,
And doesn't look away, blue eyes that lie.

He follows his astigmatism toward
The schoolbuses lined up to take everyone home,
But which are empty still, which have that smiling,
Sweet-natured blur of the retarded, oafs
In clothes too small, too wrong, too red and white,
And *painfully* eager to please a sadist so cruel
He wouldn't even hurt a masochist.

The sadistic eye of the autist shapes the world
Into a sort of, call it innocence,
Ready to be wronged, ready to
Be tortured into power and beauty, into
Words his phonographic memory
Will store on silence like particles of oil
On water—the rainbow of polarity

Which made this poem. I put my glasses on,
And shut my eyes. O adolescence, sing!
All the bus windows are open because it's warm.
I blindly face a breeze almost too sweet
To bear. I hear a hazy drone and float—
A dimpled cloud—above the poor white and poorer
Black neighborhoods which surround the small airfield.

THE BLUE-EYED DOE

I look at Broadway in the bitter cold,
The center strip benches empty like today,
And see St. Louis. I am often old
Enough to leave my childhood, but I stay.

A winter sky as total as repression
Above a street the color of the sky;
A sky the same gray as a deep depression;
A boulevard the color of a sigh:

Where Waterman and Union met was the
Apartment building I'm regressing to.
My key is in the door; I am the key;
I'm opening the door. I think it's true

Childhood is your mother even if
Your mother is in hospitals for years
And then lobotomized, like mine. A whiff
Of her perfume; behind her veil, her tears.

She wasn't crying anymore. Oh try.
No afterward she wasn't anymore.
But yes she will, she is. Oh try to cry.
I'm here—right now I'm walking through the door.

The pond was quite wide, but the happy dog
Swam back and forth called by the boy, then by
His sister on the other side, a log
Of love putt-putting back and forth from fry

To freeze, from freeze to fry, a normal pair
Of the extremes of normal, on and on.
The dog was getting tired; the children stare—
Their childhood's over. Everyone is gone,

Forest Park's deserted; still they call.
It's very cold. Soprano puffs of breath,
Small voices calling in the dusk is all
We ever are, pale speech balloons. One death,

Two ghosts . . . white children playing in a park
At dusk forever—but we must get home.
The mica sidewalk sparkles in the dark
And starts to freeze—or fry—and turns to foam.

At once the streetlights in the park go on.
Gas hisses from the trees—but it's the wind.
The real world vanishes behind the fawn
That leaps to safety while the doe is skinned.

The statue of Saint Louis on Art Hill,
In front of the museum, turns into
A blue-eyed doe. Next it will breathe. Soon will
Be sighing, dripping tears as thick as glue.

Stags do that when the hunt has cornered them.
The horn is blown. Bah-ooo. Her mind a doe
Which will be crying soon at bay. The stem
Between the autumn leaf and branch lets go.

My mother suddenly began to sob.
If only she could do that now. Oh try.
I feel the lock unlock. Now try the knob.
Sobbed uncontrollably. Oh try to cry.

How easily I can erase an error,
The typos my recalling this will cause,
But no correcting key erases terror.
One ambulance attendant flashed his claws,

The other plunged the needle in. They squeeze
The plunger down, the brainwash out. Bah-ooo.
Calm deepened in her slowly. There, they ease
Her to her feet. White Goddess, blond, eyes blue—

Even from two rooms away I see
The blue, if that is possible! Bright white
Of the attendants; and the mystery
And calm of the madonna; and my fright.

FROM *These Days*

I flee, but to a mirror. In it, they
Are rooms behind me in our entrance hall
About to leave—the image that will stay
With me. My future was behind me. All

The future is a mirror in which they
Are still behind me in the entrance hall,
About to leave—and if I look away
She'll vanish. Once upon a time, a fall

So long ago that they were burning leaves,
Which wasn't yet against the law, I looked
Away. I watched the slowly flowing sleeves
Of smoke, the blood-raw leaf piles being cooked,

Sweet-smelling scenes of mellow preparation
Around a bloodstained altar, but instead
Of human sacrifice, a separation.
My blue-eyed doe! The severed blue-eyed head!

The windows were wide-open through which I
Could flee to nowhere—nowhere meaning how
The past is portable, and therefore why
The future of the past was always now

A treeless Art Hill gleaming in the snow,
The statue of Saint Louis at the top
On horseback, blessing everything below,
Tobogganing the bald pate into slop.

Warm sun, blue sky; blond hair, blue eyes; of course
They'll shave her head for the lobotomy,
They'll cut her brain, they'll kill her at the source.
When she's wheeled out, blue eyes are all I see.

The bandages—down to her eyes—give her
A turbaned twenties look, but I'm confused.
There were no bandages. I saw a blur.
They didn't touch a hair—but I'm confused.

I breathe mist on the mirror . . . I am here—
Blond hair I pray will darken till it does,
Blue eyes that will need glasses in a year—
I'm here and disappear, the boy I was . . .

The son who lifts his sword above Art Hill;
Who holds it almost like a dagger but
In blessing, handle up, and not to kill;
Who holds it by the blade that cannot cut.

ON WINGS OF SONG

I could only dream, I could never draw,
In Art with the terrifying Mrs. Jaspar
Whom I would have done anything to please.
Aquiline and aloof in the land of the button nose, her smile
Made her seem a witch, my goddess,
Too cool, too cold. She was my muse
Because she hardly spoke a word.

We used to pronounce her name to rhyme with Casbah,
Mimicking her fahncy Locust Valley lockjaw.
Say Christ through your nose!
Part of her allure and majesty and
Wonderful strange music for St. Louis certainly,
Though not as musical as her silence was. Casbah,
White flannels on a summer evening, Jasbah,

Endless lawn down to the sea. The accent
Was preposterous, the voice beautiful
Green running down to the sea nine hundred miles inland,
Preposterous. The accent
Was preposterous, her beautiful voice a
Bassoon, slow velvet cadence of the sound,
Shy but deep. Shy but deep. Clangs / The bell. Eliot.

The lips are drawn back slightly;
As if it had been hinged that way, the jaw doesn't quite close—
Actually, the opposite of lockjaw since it
Moves, and it doesn't close.
The very back of the throat without the use of the lips
Produces the bloated drawl of the upper class.
You hear it in a certain set, you see it in a certain scene,

Which has equivalents abroad who sound incredibly the same,
And bong the same aristocrat gong in their own languages.
The stag hunting gang in France who hunt on horseback.
Most aquiline being the honorary hunt servants
In livery and wearing tricorns, always
Dukes and such and others who
The very back of the throat without using the lips much.

It is an accent you can *see*—
That you could hear through soundproof glass from what you saw.
It is a sound you see in the Sologne when
The huntsman blows his haunting horn.
The hounds open their mouths. Silence. The servants in their
White breeches and long blue coats dismount. The
Stag stands in the water dropping tears of terror and exhaustion.

They do that when the hunt has them at bay.
The king is in his counting-house counting out his money.
His head will be hacked off and saved;
The carcass goes to the dogs—after the servants drink the blood
And defecate. There is another accent, that goes to Harvard,
That anyone who does can have. My babysitter
Harold Brodkey will. One day I, too, I will.

The servants dip their fingers in
The blood and paint themselves, and smear each other's blouses,
With all the time in the world apparently until it's time. It's time
To pass the chalice and drink. They defecate
In their breeches, but their coats are quite long,
The flecks on their boots are only mud,
Everything I've written here is lies.

The flecks could be flecks of blood,
But the coattails completely hide the other. There's a smell.
Though there's the smell rising in silence
From the page, but that's a lie. Brodkey knows. Lies that rise.
Now my unseen neighbor in New York four blocks away.
He is finishing the novel, he knows
Il miglior fabbro means a bigger liar. Lies that rise.

Ab lo dolchor qu'al cor mi vai
Pound catches the thermals in every language, and soars.
Eliot rises in the pew to kneel.
When he opens his mouth it is a choir.
Les souvenirs sont cors de chasse
Dont meurt le bruit parmi les vents.
The cockpit voice recorder in its crashproof case remembers and sings.

Flesh and juice of the refreshing and delicious.
Inside a crashproof housing. But I don't recognize the voice.
This is your captain. In the unisex soprano of children his age.
We are trying to restart the engines
On wings of song. The pilot giggles posthumously—
"You may kiss my hond," he drawls, for the last time
Holding a hond out to be kissed from this page. (Sound of crash.)

MORPHINE

What hasn't happened isn't everything
Until in middle age it starts to be.
Night-blooming jasmine, dreams—and when they bring
You out on stage there's silence. Now I see,
You tell the darkness which is watching you.
Applause. Then instantly a hush, a cough.
It was another darkness once you knew
You had a blindfold on. You took it off,
But this is darker—down an unlit street,
An unmarked street, the three blocks to the shore.
They call it Banyan Street, night air so sweet.
Too much increasingly turns into more—
This is the martyr's grove on Banyan Street.
You breathe a perfumed darkness, numberless
Perfumes. The glistening as wet as meat
Deliciousness of sinking in. The S
OS of it. But it's too late. You reach
The can't stop trembling yes oh yes of it—
Already when you're two blocks from the beach
You start to drown. Love ruled your White House. Sit,
You named your dog. Come, Sit; *sit*, Sit; was love.
Your head explodes although you hear a shot.
Then archaeology . . . below above—
Beneath amnesia, Troy. But you forgot.

ELMS

It sang without a sound: music that
The naive elm trees loved. They were alive.
Oh silky music no elm tree could survive.
The head low slither of a stalking cat,
Black panther darkness pouring to the kill,
Entered every elm—they drank it in.
Drank silence. Then the silence drank. Wet chin,
Hot, whiskered darkness. Every elm was ill.
What else is there to give but joy? Disease.
And trauma. Lightning, or as slow as lava.
Darkness drinking from a pool in Java,
Black panther drinking from a dream. The trees
Around the edge are elms. Below, above,
Man-eater drinking its reflection: love.

THE FINAL HOUR

Another perfect hour of emptiness.
The final hour, calm as a candle flame.
The evening, enlarging as it neared, became
A sudden freshness, stillness, then the yes,
The fragrant falling yes of summer rain.
The huge grew larger as it neared, the smile,
The smell of rain, and waited for a while,
And went away. Time spilled. It left no stain.

FROM *These Days*

JANE CANFIELD (1897–1984)

"The speed of light is not the limit. We
Are free. We glide. Our superluminous
Velocity will take us far. For us,
The superluminous is only the
Beginning of our birth. How born we are.
Compared to how we started. Vast, oh vast.
A lifetime as the measure couldn't last,
The nearest destinations were too far:
A billion years to reach the one inside
You if you could—who holds you, whom you hold.
You kick the covers off asleep, are cold,
And someone covers you, is all. And glide
Off into space. Is all. Space curved by speed—
We really leave the light behind. But hark.
The infinite beginning in the dark
To sigh the universe out of its seed.
The speck that weighs more than the world. Before
The universe—which has no meaning—was
Before the singularity which does.
Invisible nonzero, and we soar.
We sigh from the beginning, and we soar.
We leave the light behind and soar. And soar."

THE LITTLE WHITE DOG

The way the rain won't fall
Applies a velvet pressure, voice-off.
The held-back heaviness too sweet, the redolence,
Brings back the memory.

Life watches, watches,
From the control room, through the soundproof window,
With the sound turned off,
The orchestra warming up, playing scales.

It listens to the glistening.
The humidity reels, headier than methanol.
Treelined sidestreets, prick up your leaves.
The oboe is giving the *la* to the orchestra.

Someone shoots his cuffs to show his cufflinks,
Yellow gold to match his eyes, and pays the check.
Someone else is eight years old.
Her humility is volatile.

And when they kiss, he can't quite breathe.
The electric clouds perspire.
It's meteorology, it's her little dress, it's her violin,
It's unafraid. It's about to.

A sudden freshness stirs then stills the air, the century.
The new jet-black conductor raises her baton.
The melody of a little white dog,
Dead long ago, starts the soft spring rain.

FROM *These Days*

AIDS DAYS

I
"Perfection Eludes Us"

The most beautiful power in the world has buttocks.
It is always a dream come true.
They are big. They are too big.
Kiss them and spank them till they are scalding.
Till she can't breathe saying oh.
Till your hand is in love.
Till your eyes are raw.
Stockings and garter belt without underpants are
The secret ceremony but who would imagine
She is wearing a business suit. She is in her office. She merely touches
The high-tech phone. Without a word,
She lies down across the hassock and eases her skirt up.
How big it is.
Her eyes are closed . . . She has the votes.
They know she does. They're waiting for her now next door.
The number is ringing.
She squeezes them together. She squeezes them together.
She presses herself against the hassock.
She starts to spank herself.

II
The American Sonnet

She has the votes; they know she does;
They're waiting for her now next door.
Her eyes are closed.
We were discussing the arms race when the moderator died,
Presumably a performance piece, was
What it's called. He said it is.
It actually wasn't so political was only
Broadcast without a live audience.
The telephone is warbling.
The secretary has allowed the call through which means the president
Herself is on the line.
Her dreams are calling her. The press will be there.
Her skirt is all the way up.
I am the epopt. Thou art the secret ceremony.

III
Aleph, Beth, Gimel, Daleth . . .

A man sits memorizing a naked woman—
A slot cut in a wall
Which has a metal slide which opens
When he puts a quarter in
Lets him look for hours.
It seems like hours.
He keeps forgetting what he sees.
He pays and stares
Into the brightly lit beyond
Dancing on a stage just beyond the wall, bare feet
On a level with his chin.
He looks up at it,
Without the benefit of music
Just standing there.
And then the music starts again.
The wall in which the slot is cut is curved.
So when the slot is open, besides a dance he sees
Curving away from him to either side an ocean liner row
Of little windows.
Prisoners in solitary confinement
Might get their meals through one of these—
Presumably behind each one a booth like his.
The open slots are dark.
A slot of darkness in the wall
Is someone.
Someone hidden is hunching there.
From some slots money waves.
The woman ripples over and squats
In front of it, her knees spread wide.
She takes the bill—
Sometimes she presses herself against the slot.
A man stays in a booth.
The door stays locked. The slot stays open.
He can't remember what he memorized.
It seems like hours.
It is too late.

FROM *These Days*

IV
L'Hallali

Serve me the ice cream bitterer than vinegar
Beneath a royal palm covered with needles.
Tell me a love story that ends with acyclovir
Five times a day for five days.

You never had it so good.
He made me my dog which He took.
Houseflies and herpes He brings.
Buttery ice cream smooth as Vaseline.

Florida. Dawn. Five hundred clouds.
Anal chocolate turning pink.
Oxygen-rich, from an opened artery
In the warm water

In the claw-footed tub. Dawn
Spreads from Gorbachev these arms talks AIDS days.
Will it spread?
Venus on the half-shell, moist and pink rose of salt—

Belons 000 when they're freshest are as sweet.
Chincoteagues from the bay are as plump.
Freshly squeezed is as sweet.
This is your life. You live in France,

Klaus Barbie, in 1983, and '84, and '85, and '86, and '87.
And every day is the bissextus.
And every dawn is Hiroshima.
Hallali!

GETHSEMANE

My life.
I live with it.
I look at it.
My spied on, with malice.

It's my wife. It's my husband.
It sleeps with me.
I wake with it.
It doesn't matter.

If I'm unfaithful—if I drank too much—
It's me. It's mine. It's all legal.
I smell the back of my hand,
And like the smell.

Twenty-five years ago when I was still alive.
I was twenty-five.
My penis pants. My penis
Rises, hearing its name, like a dog.

I ought to cut it off
And feed it to itself.
Like the young bride in the Babel story
Forced to eat her husband's penis

By the peasant who has cut it off.
A railroad telegrapher and a peasant
On the White Army side have found some Jews.
Russia 1918.

Interior railroad boxcar.
The boxcar door is slid open from the outside
Like a slowly lifted guillotine blade.
There they are.

FROM *These Days*

I am fifty today. I hold the little cape and sword.
I dedicate this bull
That I'm about to kill
To the crowd.

To the crowd.
To the crowd.
To the crowd.
To the crowd. To the crowd. To the.

STANZAS

I don't want to remember the Holocaust.
I'm *thick* of remembering the Holocaust.
To the best of my ability, I wasn't there anyway.
And then I woke.

My hands were showing me how they wash themselves.
They're clean. The heart is too. The hands are too.
They flush in unison like a row of urinals
Every few hours automatically. Two minutes Cockfosters.
My heart was pure. And stood on a subway platform in London
Staring at the sign. One minute Cockfosters.

I wasn't there anyway.
I don't believe in anything.
I was somewhere else
Screaming beneath an avalanche.

Skiers wearing miners' headlamps were not
Skiing down the mountain in the dark,
It would be beautiful. Seeds of light floating slowly on the dark
Downward without a prayer
Of finding any elephants to save because
The International Red Cross and the Roman Catholic Church had not.

I cannot move.
I move my face from side to side
To make a space to breathe. I cannot breathe.
The screaming stops.

FROM *These Days*

EARLY SUNDAY MORNING
IN THE CHER

The solemn radiance
On the radio is Poulenc.

The boy soprano seems to dream
He doesn't breathe.
And then the much shyer wings,
Of new materials, that add enormous range.
Oh, the power of the perfume!

The boys choir glides high above
The airborne orchestra.
Sweetness poured calmly and with innocent
Translucency blown
Into a glass.

While it's still warm it cools.

The glass is warped
On purpose, beautifully.
Poulenc, Auric, Milhaud, et cetera. Les Six.
A champagne flute contains the tears of Christ.

For this is France.

The radio predicts the weather for the region with such charm.
Charm followed by more rain will crucify the harvest.

And it is cold. So far,
The summer day is pure
Boy soprano blue without a cloud.

The naive fields of sunflowers don't know they suffer.
Suffer the little sunflowers to come unto me.
Their childish big faces gaze at everyone with love.

They sing so sweetly in the cold. They sing completely.

Shy wings repeat the
Seven last words of Christ,
I don't feel anything but it hurts.
I'm typing this with fingers of cold wax.
I can see my breath in the salon.

In August,
With green leaves warbling liquids of birdsong,
We have reached the Pole.

The Poulenc ripples chastely as an eel
Off the shores of silence, immaculately
To the place where they press olives.

Jesus prostrates himself on the ground.
Jesus jaywalks through the perfumed night air
Back and forth. How sweet it smells.
He is davening and stops.
Abba, Father.
He looks for them and finds them
Fast asleep, Peter especially. Could
You not watch with me one hour? They couldn't
Even stay awake.
They sleep in the dark.

Who when I thought my son was dying slept.
My son was dying slept.

There she was.

Who when I thought my son was dying slept
And slept while I paced,
While they performed the emergency operation.
For hours. But then I too.
Could you not watch with me one hour?
Can't wake from my life either.
I too must wake.

FROM *These Days*

The sun streams in and makes
Sunbeams of my solid house.
Blond air is my igloo.
The houseflies cryogenically unfreeze
And regain consciousness in order to be flies.
Before they fly, they jitter-walk around and pause
To rub their two front legs together.

Androgynous Akhenaten is singing his hymn to the Aten.
The awed wide-eyed words rise
On the wings of my houseflies,
Franciscan in their intimacy which shook the earth.

The radio is singing Christ is risen.
The sunflowers are singing to the sun.

These words I say to you are sunflowers singing to the sun.

There was a God
With human chromosomes, nearly human . . . I fly
Across the inland flatness of the Cher
In my old car, in love. I give you God. I fly my car.
I'm bringing God back to God.

It doesn't matter what happens.

And when I said my car was me, instantly
My dingy bronze Simca's alternator was broken, yesterday.

We overheat up to the red.
We'll try to float to a garage.

I'm going nowhere fast. The
Same old 66.
Same difference.
Shades of the past. It doesn't matter what happens.

Just outside the door,
The dear cur snores on its tires. It sleeps in la France profonde.
The centerlines are silver, the roads are gold, en Berry today.
Shed a joyous tear for me
And my bronze-colored pal.

I made a clearing. I meditated. I made a temple.
To meet you in.

Carved the everywhere of Buddha out
Of polished quiet.

And Krishna's smile. And Krishna's
Heavenly hands pressed together in candent greeting.

Introibo ad altare Dei.
You've put my eyes out so I will see.

The heat-seeking missile desires the faraway sun.
Thy pheromones invite thy suitor.

The radio announcer on France Musique
Is speaking so melodiously his words perspire,
That professional sugar sound I abhor, but I can't hear.
I am listening to the rustle of your long black dress
On the telephone last night as you pulled it up
A thousand miles away.
Someone could have walked in.
The husky hush of your voice.
Raise your evening gown for me forever.

THE LAST POEM IN THE BOOK

I don't believe in anything, I do
Believe in you, vanished particles of vapor,
Field of force,
Undressed, undimmed Invisible,
Losing muons and gaining other ones,
Counterrotations with your
Robed arms raised out straight to each side
In a dervish dance of eyes closed ecstasy,
Tireless, inhuman,
Wireless technology
Of a ghost,
Of a spinning top on its point,
Of a tornado perspiring forward a few miles an hour
Uprooting everything and smelling sweetly like a lawn.
It's that time of year.
It's that time of year a thousand times a day. A thousand times a day,
A thousand times a day,
You are reborn flying to out-ski
The first avalanche each spring,
And buried alive.

I went to sleep last night so I could see you.
I went to see the world destroyed. It was a movie.
I went to sleep that night so I could see you.
And then a drink and then to sleep.
That's Vermont.
The universe hung like a flare for a while and went out,
Leaving nothing, long ago.
Each galaxy at war exhaled
A firefly glow, a tiny quiet, far away . . .
On and off . . . worlds off and on—and then
The universe itself brightened, stared and went out.
I cannot see.
I will not wake though it's a dream.
I move my head from side to side.
I cannot move.
The nights are cold, the sun is hot,
The air is alcohol at that altitude

Three thousand miles from here—is here
Today a thousand times.
You haven't changed.

There is a room in the Acropolis Museum.
The kouroi smile silence.
The way a virus sheds. The way
A weave of wind shear
And the willingness to share is the perfect friend
Every child invents for his very own. I don't know.
The Parthenon suddenly made me cry.
I saw it and I sobbed,
And it doesn't share.
I was so out of it
You came too close. I got too near
The temple, flying low. I got too near
The power, past the ropes. I touched the restoration work.
It could mean a loss of consciousness
In the right-hand seat to be with God.
The Early Warning Ground Proximity Indicator is flashing.
Never mind. I knew it was.
The alarm ah-ooga ah-ooga and the computer-generated
Voice says
And says and says Pull Up Pull Up Pull Up Pull Up.

You say come closer.
You say come closer.
I cannot move.
You say I have to whisper this. Come closer.
I want to hear.
There also is the way a virus sheds.
I want to see. And the ground whispers
Closer. In the Littré the other day and you were there
In the Petit Robert. Grévisse—Larousse—
Ten million years from now, will there be anything?
The rain came down convulsively on the dry land,
As if it would have liked to come down even harder,
Big, kind, body temperature
Shudderings, and on the far bank of the newborn river,
The joyous drumming of the native drums,
Making a tremendous sound twelve feet beneath the snow

FROM *These Days*

Without an avalanche beeper in those days. It's true—
I don't believe in anything I *do*
Believe in, but I do believe in you
Moving your face from side to side to make a space to breathe.

I think I am crying on all my legs
From a dark place to a dark place like a roach.
I am running on the ground with my wings folded—
But now I am extending them,
Running across my kitchen floor and
Running down the rue Barbet-de-Jouy,
Trying historically before it's too late to get into the air.
I have on my ten Huntsman suits,
And many shining shoes made to my last.
I believe in one Lobb.
Faites sur mesure. Everything
Fits my body perfectly now that I'm about to disappear.
I don't believe in anything.
Lightning touches intimately the sable starless. Thunder.
You start to breathe too much.
It starts to rain, in your intoxication.
Communism and capitalism go up in flames
And come back down as rain—I'm coming now—
But Greece stays parched.
I'm coming now.

I'm being thrown violently at the sky,
The deck of the carrier shrinking to a dot,
Thirty-some years ago
Suddenly catching sight of Chartres Cathedral miles away;
Horizon to horizon, a molten ocean
The beautiful urine color of vermeil,
Color and undercolor as with a fur;
Soaring stock-still above the windblown waves of wheat,
Dialing on the seemingly inexhaustible power.
Break it.
I swim over to the sealed
Aquarium window of the TV screen to try.
President of the United States descending the stairs

Of his helicopter pixels snap a salute at the American flag
Pixels. I turn the sound off
And the Marine band explodes.
I'm coming now.
I can't breathe.
I'm coming now to the conclusion that
Without a God. I'm coming now to the conclusion.

SUNRISE (1980)

1968

A football spirals through the oyster glow
Of dawn dope and fog in L.A.'s
Bel Air, punted perfectly. The foot
That punted it is absolutely stoned.

A rising starlet leans her head against the tire
Of a replica Cord,
A bonfire of red hair out of
Focus in the fog. Serenading her,
A boy plucks "God Bless America" from a guitar.
Vascular spasm has made the boy's hands blue
Even after hours of opium.

Fifty or so of the original
Four hundred
At the fundraiser,
Robert Kennedy for President, the remnants, lie
Exposed as snails around the swimming pool, stretched
Out on the paths, and in the gardens, and the drive.
Many dreams their famous bodies have filled.

The host, a rock superstar, has
A huge cake of opium,
Which he refers to as "King Kong,"
And which he serves on a silver salver
Under a glass bell to his close friends,
So called,
Which means all mankind apparently,
Except the fuzz,
Sticky as tar, the color of coffee,
A quarter of a million dollars going up in smoke.

This is Paradise painted
On the inside of an eggshell
With the light outside showing through,
Subtropical trees and flowers and lawns,
Clammy as albumen in the fog,
And smelling of fog. Backlit
And diffuse, the murdered

Voityck Frokowski, Abigail Folger and Sharon Tate
Sit together without faces.

This is the future.
Their future is the future. The future
Has been born,
The present is the afterbirth,
These bloodshot and blue acres of flowerbeds and stars.
Robert Kennedy will be killed.
It is '68, the campaign year—
And the beginning of a new day.

People are waiting.
When the chauffeur-bodyguard arrives
For work and walks
Into the ballroom, now recording studio, herds
Of breasts turn round, it seems in silence,
Like cattle turning to face a sound.
Like cattle lined up to face the dawn.
Shining eyes seeing all or nothing,
In the silence.

A stranger, and wearing a suit,
Has to be John the Baptist,
At least, come
To say someone else is coming.
He hikes up his shoulder holster
Self-consciously, meeting their gaze.
That is as sensitive as the future gets.

FROM *Sunrise*

DEATH VALLEY

Antonioni walks in the desert shooting
Zabriskie Point. He does not perspire
Because it is dry. His twill trousers stay pressed,
He wears desert boots and a viewfinder,
He has a profile he could shave with, sharp
And meek, like the eyesight of the deaf,
With which he is trying to find America,
A pick for prospecting passive as a dowser.
He has followed his nose into the desert.

Crew and cast mush over the burning lake
Shivering and floaty like a mirage.
The light makes it hard to see. Four million dollars
And cameras ripple over the alkali
Waiting for the director to breathe on them.
How even and epic his wingbeats are for a small fellow.
He sips cigarette after cigarette
And turns in Italian to consult his English
Girlfriend and screenwriter, who is beautiful.

In Arizona only the saguaros
And everybody else were taller than he was.
Selah. He draws in the gypsum dust selah
He squats on his heels for the love scene, finally
The technicians are spray-dyeing the dust darker.
It looks unreal, but it will dry lighter,
Puffs of quadroon smoke back out of the spray guns.
The Open Theater are naked and made up.
Between his name and néant are his eyes.

THE TRIP

Nothing is human or alien at this altitude,
Almost a drug high, one mile in the blue,
I am flying over what I will have to live through:
So this is love, four curving jet trails of flock.
How different it was to look up and see
The train you rode on curving away from you
On a long bend—like your child body, part
Of you, apart from you. It felt so odd,
How hauntingly it straightened and disappeared.

This is love reflected in the window
Tippling a complimentary cup of broth,
Myself and Magritte, the desert takes a drink.
I gaze through my forehead at the rising desert,
Dots and dashes like meanings, pain-points of green,
Cactus crucifying the beautiful emptiness.
I hold my own hand while I slowly find
The horizon on the other side of my eyes.
It I feel close to, it cannot come near:

There and beyond one like heaven, as Che is. Once,
On the new Metroliner fleeing New York,
Fleeing the same girl I am flying to . . .
The experimental train dreamed of flight,
Eupeptic sleek plastic, Muzak, its steel skin twinkled.
We rose on music from under Park Avenue
To the fourth floors of Harlem where only the bricked-up
Windows didn't reflect us. I saw them, the slightly
Lighter bricks within the brick window frames.

FROM *Sunrise*

THE ROOM AND THE CLOUD

The tan table of the desert is an empty
Sunlit plaza by de Chirico
That has no meaning, that is like the desert
Rising in the windows of an Astrojet
As it so coldly dips to right itself.
A rich man in Arizona drives a tan
Mercedes, bulbous and weightless as an astronaut.
It barely moves, it walks through space the way Mao does,
Tan freezing silence like a freeze frame.

Across a desk top, in his fuselage,
The rudimentary tail brain of his two
Propels the largest living dinosaur,
Schizophrenia. And when he tilts
His head Tucson turns, a slow veronica,
The horizon lifts to one side like a drawbridge.
Years float by, cold novocaine nirvana
Aloft in a holding pattern as if forever.
They bring the stairs up, First Class ducks out first.

Step one is to be rich. The two men are beaming:
My host with the Mercedes and his guest
Fly in on the freeway through a desert noon.
Their conversation seems to them an oasis,
Air-conditioning sanitizes the air.
The giant saguaros stand up, without hearts or hair,
Autoplastic adaption that can't fail.
I see a desert. I look down at the typed page:
We are the room and the cloud on its painted ceiling.

THE SOUL MATE

Your eyes gazed
Sparkling and dark as hooves,
They had seen you through languor and error.
They were so still. They were a child.
They were wet like hours
And hours of cold rain.

Sixty-seven flesh inches
Utterly removed, of spirit
For the sake of nobody,
That one could love but not know—
Like death if you are God.
So close to me, my soul mate, like a projection.

I'd loved you gliding through St. Paul's sniffing
The torch of yellow flowers,
The torch had not lit the way.
Winter flowers, yourself a flame
In winter. In the cold
Like a moth in a flame.

I seemed to speak,
I seemed never to stop.
You tossed your head back and a cloud
Of hair from your eyes,
You listened with the beautiful
Waiting look of someone

Waiting to be introduced,
Without wings but without weight, oh light!
As the fist which has learned how
Waving goodbye, opening and closing up to the air
To breathe. The child
Stares past his hand. The blank stares at the child.

Goodbye.

FROM *Sunrise*

SUNRISE

FOR BLAIR FOX

The gold watch that retired free will was constant dawn.
Constant sunrise. But then it was dawn. Christ rose,
White-faced gold bulging the horizon
Like too much honey in a spoon, an instant
Stretching forever that would not spill; constant
Sunrise blocked by the buildings opposite;
Constant sunrise before it was light. Then it
Was dawn. A shoe shined dully like liquorice.
A hand flowed toward the silent clock radio.

Bicentennial April, the two hundredth
Lash of the revolving lighthouse wink,
Spread out on the ceiling like a groundcloth.
Whole dream: *a child stood up*. Dream 2: *yearning,*
Supine, head downhill on a hill. Dream: *turning*
And turning, a swan patrols his empty nest,
Loops of an eighteenth-century signature, swan crest,
Mother and cygnet have been devoured by the dogs.
The dogs the dogs. *A shadow shivered with leaves.*

Perth, Denpasar, Djakarta, Bangkok, Bom
Bombom bay. Dogs are man's greatest invention. Dogs.
They were nice dogs. Find a bottle of Dom
Pérignon in Western Australia.
Find life on Mars. Find Jesus. "You are a failya,"
The president of the United States said.
He was killed, and she became Bob's. His head,
Robert Kennedy's, lay as if removed
In the lap of a Puerto Rican boy praying.

Ladies and gentlemen, the president
Of the United States, fall in the air,
A dim streetlight past dawn not living to repent,
Ghostwalks by the canal, the blood still dry
Inside soaked street shoes, hands washed clean that try
To cup the rain that ends the drought. No one
Spoke. Blindfolds, plus the huge curtains had been drawn.
Because of his back he had to be on his back.
Neither woman dreamed a friend was the other.

Innocence. Water particles and rainbow
Above the sweet smell of gasoline—hiss of a hose
Drumming the suds off the town car's whitewalls, which glow!
Pink-soled gum boots, pink gums of the ebony chauffeur,
Pink summer evenings of strontium 90, remember?
Vestal black panther tar stills the street.
The coolness of the enormous lawns. Repeat.
O innocent water particles and rainbow
Above the sweet smell of gas, hiss of the hose!

When you are little, a knee of your knickers torn,
The freshness of rain about to fall is what
It would be like not to have been born.
Believe. Believed they were lined up to take showers
Dies illa, that April, which brought May flowers.
Safer than the time before the baby
Crawls is the time before he smiles, maybe.
Stalin's merry moustache, magnetic, malignant,
Crawls slowly over a leaf which cannot move.

If the words sound queer and funny to your ear,
A little bit jumbled and jivey, it must be
Someone in 1943 you hear:
Who like a dog looking at a doorknob
Does not know why. Slats of daylight bob
On the wall softly, a gentle knocking, a breeze.
A caterpillar fills the bed which is
Covered with blood. 1943.
The stools in the toilet bowl, are they alive?

Harlem on fire rouged the uptown sky.
But the shot squeezed off in tears splashes short.
But bullets whizzing through hell need no alibi
Before they melt away. Intake. Compression,
Ignition, explosion. Expansion. Exhaust. Depression
Reddens the toilet paper. That black it feels.
Endomorphic round-fendered automobiles
Slow, startle each other, and bolt in herds across
Spuyten Duyvil for the fifties and Westchester.

FROM *Sunrise*

The cob stayed on the pond, perfect for Westchester,
Circling a nonexistent pen. Polly
Urethane sat on his face, Polly Esther
Sat on his penis. Protecting the non-cygnet.
Walking one day through the Piney Woods, he met
Three dogs in that peculiar light, strays. Two
Were shitting, looking off in that way dogs do,
Hunchbacked, sensitive, aloof, and neither
Male nor female. The third sat licking its teeth.

At the Institute they are singing *On Human*
Symbiosis and the Vicissitudes
of Individuation. Light of the One—
A summer sidewalk, a shadow shivered with leaves.
The mother smiles, *fa, so,* the mother grieves,
Beams down on the special bed for spinal
Injuries love that is primary and final,
Clear crystal a finger flicked that will ring a lifetime.
Plastic wrap refuse in the bare trees means spring.

And clouds blowing across empty sky.
A gay couple drags a shivering fist-sized
Dog down Broadway, their parachute brake. "Why
Robert Frost?" the wife one pleads, nearly
In tears; the other sniffs, "Because he
Believed in Nature and I believe in Nature."
Pacing his study past a book-lined blur,
A city dweller saw breasts, breast; their sour
And bitter smell is his own smoker's saliva.

The call had finally arrived from Perth:
He would live. C-4, a very high cervical
Lesion, but breathing on his own—rebirth
Into a new, another world, just seeing,
Without losing consciousness, and being,
Like being on the moon and seeing Earth,
If you could breathe unaided. God, in Perth,
Twelve hours' time difference, thus day for night,
It was almost winter and almost Easter.

So accepting life is of the incredible.
2 a.m., the reeking silky monsoon
Air at Bombay Airport is edible,
Fertile, fecal, fetal—thunder—divine
Warm food for Krishna on which Krishna will dine.
The service personnel vacuum barefooted,
Surely Untouchables. Thunder. The booted
Back down the aisles spraying disinfectant,
By law, before disembarkation in Perth.

Down Under thunder thunder in formation
Delta wing Mach 2 dots time-warp to dust
Motes, climb and dissolve high above the one
Couple on the beach not looking up,
In the direction of Arabia, Europe,
Thunder, thunder, military jets,
Mars. The man smokes many cigarettes.
The man was saying to the woman, "Your son
Has simply been reborn," but can't be heard.

All is new behind their backs, or vast.
House lots link up like cells and become house,
Shade tree and lawn, the frontier hypoblast
Of capitalism develops streets in minutes
Like a Polaroid. The infinite's
Sublime indifference to the mile—Mao
On nuclear war. Inches; dust motes; they go bow wow
At the heels of history. The dust
Imitates the thunder that will bring rain.

By the Indian Ocean, he sat down
And wept. Snarl suck-suck-suck waaah. It was the Grand
Hôtel et de Milan. It was a gown
Of moonlight, moving, stirring a faint breeze,
Gauze curtains hissing softly like nylons please
Please crossing and uncrossing. Who—how had
The shutters opened? and the heavy brocade
Curtain? How far away the ceiling was.
The bedlamp. One floor below, Verdi died.

How far away Australia was, years.
A man asleep listened while his throat
Tried to cry for help. He almost hears
The brayed, longing, haunting whale song the deaf speak,
Almost words. Out of silence, sounds leak
Into silence, years. He lay there without
Love, in comfort, straining to do without,
And dreamed. A spaceship could reach the ceiling, the special
Theory of relativity says.

Leave love, comfort, not even masturbate,
Not even love justice, not even want to kill,
O to be sterile, and to rise and wait
On the ceiling at sunrise, for dawn! stainless blond
Ceiling, the beginning of the beyond!
But the TV showed outstretched hands—a revolver
Blocked the open door of the last chopper,
Struggling to get airborne. The ditto sheet served
With espresso began: *Good morning! Here are the news.*

Phosphorescent napkins don't make a bomb;
Under the parasols of Bicè's, Via
Manzoni, chitchat chased the firefly of Vietnam.
The courtyard flickered; the tablecloth glowed like lime.
Corrado Agusta's chow chow took its time
Turning its head to look at one, very
Refined and inhuman and dark as a mulberry,
Not a dog. Its blue tongue was not on view.
It had a mane and wore a harness, unsmiling.

Being walked and warmed up, they roared like lions on leashes.
The smell of castor oil. Snarl suck-suck-suck waaah
A racing motorcycle running through
The gears, on song; the ithyphallic faired
Shape of speed waaah an Italian's glans-bared
Rosso di competizione. The Counts
Agusta raced these Stradivarius grunts
As genteelly as horse farms race horses—helicopter
Gunships, Agusta Aeronautiche.

The communists organized. Domenico
Agusta reigned. Of course the one who knew
Kennedys was the cold white rose Corrado.
The boss nailed each picket by name with a nod,
While Ciudad Trujillo and Riyadh
Kept unrolling more terror dollars for Corrado.
The iron and pious brother saw God go;
The salesman brother settled for everything:
Small arms fire, new nations; splits of brut, dry tears.

Domenico Agusta saw God go
Backwards like a helicopter in
A film he saw in Rome—i.e., in tow
With a helicopter. Sunbathers on Rome's
Roofs looked sideways from their cradled arms.
Just outside the window Jesus appears.
He faces us and steadily disappears.
The audience applauded. So odd to be
Agusta lifting off in your Agusta.

Goodbye. Goodbye. The stuck door was freed
And thrown open, and then closed and sealed.
The moviegoers of the world recede,
The White House and the tiny Marine band
Were wheeled away. A bulbously gloved hand
Frees the faulty door. Thrown open. Into
The countdown, and counting. −9. When you
Are no longer what you were. Thrown open.
−8. O let me out nor in.

Forty stories stock still like a boy
Whose height is being measured stands on smoke
As they withdraw the gantry, wheeled awoy,
Away. Perth Denpasar Djakarta Bangkok
Bombay in the capsule at the extreme tock,
La la, in the minute head above
The rest, eye movement peck peck like a dove,
A man sits on his back strapped down reading
Off numbers and getting younger, counting, cooing.

FROM *Sunrise*

Millions of pounds of propellants make one dream,
Even more than psychoanalysis,
Of getting somewhere. Eyes glow in the gleam
Of the fuel gauges. Liquid oxygen
And kerosene. Check. Liquid oxygen
And liquid hydrogen—liquid in a freeze
Of $-420°$
F. Smoke boils off the ice that sheathes
The stainless steel building beneath him, forty floors.

Blue as the winder sapphire of the Cartier
Watch he has no use for now, goodbye,
The diodes of the digital display—
Information the color of his eyes,
As if his life were passing before his eyes,
−7. *Fin de race* face Louis
Cartier designed, inside a chewy
Candy of gold; face in a diver's helmet
Glassed in, prickles of the gold rivets and screws.

For everyday use, but by a Tutankhamen.
It would look feminine on a girl. The first
Wristwatch amused the sports of 1907.
The sport who commissioned the original,
The Brazilian Santos-Dumont, for a while
In 1906 believed he was the first man
To fly. Who says he did? None other than
The National Air and Space Museum says
Fernando Hippolyto da Costa does—

Believes Santos *was*. How could—but then
Who cares? Santos did not. Santos was not.
The watch was 1908, some say seven.
−6. What is there to believe in?
−6. What kind of god is not even
Immortal! −6. Nothing lasts.
A block of hieroglyphics trumpets, blasts
A golden long upended riff of silence,
It says for whom, whose name has been effaced.

To speak the name of the dead is to make them live
Again. O pilgrim, restore the breath of life
To him who has vanished. But the names they give.
No one can pronounce the hieroglyphs.
Then they had vowels to breathe with their bare midriffs,
Yes which? No one's known how to vocalize
The consonants. The kings don't recognize
Their names, don't recognize our names for them;
The soft parts that could not be embalmed are life.

One simply stares at the autistic face,
Charred rock-hard paper, a god. Stares at the stared-at.
Ramesses II in an exhibit case.
The Mummy Room is packed with Japanese
And German tours there to take in Ramesses.
The guides call in their languages, "This way please."
It seems one stares until one hardly sees.
It seems the room is empty. Like a dog
Looking at a doorknob, one stares at the stared-at.

As at a beetle rolling a ball of dung.
As at a large breast, with its nipple erect.
—5, soft and hard together among
The million things that go together one
Will lift away from, everything under the sun,
Everything—dog and doorknob—combustion to vapor
Lock—scissors cut paper, rock breaks scissors, paper
Covers rock. Everything is looking
For something softer than itself to eat.

Think of the energy required to get
Away from this hunt and peck for energy
That's running out. This need to look! O let
Your spirit rise above the engines below you.
Prepare for launch. O let a new way know you
Helmeted and on your back strapped down.
The moisture of the viscera, the blown
Coral rose of the brain on its stem—in this
Container, soft will never be exposed.

And leave behind the ancient recipes,
That cookbook for cannibals the Old Testament,
Bloody contemporary of course of Ramesses.
Cuisine minceur, urging one to eat less
But well. O Egypt! O Israel's salt sweetness!
From going soft and hard, from going up
And down, deliver us: struggling up
The steep path as Abraham with fire and knife,
And struggling down as Moses bent under the Law.

O let me go. O Israel! O Egypt!
The enemy's godless campfire at night, meat roasting
As you breathed near, sword drawn. *Cut.* Juice that dripped—
Later—from the dates from the hand of your daughter
Placed on your tongue in joy. Salute the slaughter.
O let me go. Salute the screenwriter,
DNA. Salute the freedom fighter
Kalishnikov machine pistol. A spider
Oiling the weapon spreads its legs and sighs.

TERROR OUR PLEASURE. O let me go. Logo
Of the age of ass—this age of movements—
Members and dismembers is our motto.
Oiling her weapon while in the mirror eyeing
Herself, turbaned in a black howli, sighing,
Is our muse *It feels good*, the spider. Mothers,
The children must die with dignity. Brothers,
Die. Mothers, calm the children. Squirt the poison
Far back in your child's throat. Stanza thirty-five.

Seated on your back strapped tight, tighter,
Feeling the contoured chair's formfitting
Love—no more hunt and peck on the typewriter
For energy that's running out. Stable
Fireproof love ideally comfortable!
You stare up at the gauges' radiance.
The mummy priest stares back in a trance,
And places beside you the silent clock radio,
And on the floor shoes for the long journey.

To lie on the horizon unable to rise—
How terrible to be the horizon! be
The expression in the quadriplegic's eyes,
Constant sunrise of feelings but no feeling.
The patient on the couch cow-eyes the ceiling.
Under his broken armor is a flower
Pinned down, that cannot reach its dagger, a flower.
Tongs in his skull, and dreams, not every man
Will wake. Can stand to look down at his penis and urine.

I am less than a man and less than a woman,
Wave after wave of moonlight breaks
On the trembling beach, dogs howl everywhere. One
Heave, and the water of the swimming pool
Sprang up, turning on its side like a pole-
Vaulter as it rose −4
In impossible slow motion. Whisper. Roar.
Because the stirred-up air only smells sweeter.
Because on Bali the earthquake toll is this sweet.

The Ketjak dancers roar and whisper *ketjak*
In ecstasy, the monkey dancers, k-*tchuck*.
They sway, but stayed seated, *ketjak, ketjak*.
−3, C-4, we have ignition.
Lit up, the streets of Cairo are singing of urine,
The streets of Bombay are quiring human faeces.
−2 is the sea anemones
Which elsewhere are galaxies. Time-space is the amoeba's
Pouring motion into itself to move.

Organizations of gravity and light,
Supremely mass disappears and reappears
In an incomprehensible −1 of might.
Sat up at last, the quadriplegic boy
Feels beyond pain, feels beyond joy—
Still, stately as the Christ of Resurrection.
I wake beneath my hypnopompic erection,
Forty stanzas, forty Easters of life,
And smile, eyes full of tears, shaking with rage.

"NOT TO BE BORN IS OBVIOUSLY
BEST OF ALL"

Your face swims to my window, beautiful
Translucence, a pearl, the fetal teardrop, little
Sea horse unswaying as time flows by. You nose
The glass, forever about to have a soul.
New York flows by, not now flows by, not now,
The traffic flows by. Moonlit dunes of amnesia
Flow by, flow by. In the rearview mirror dawn
The messenger sent back without a reply
Turning back into the Sahara.

O idea swimming on the blue,
Your face swims to the window, beautiful
Translucence against the blinding id of blue,
A leaf, the afterimage of a leaf,
Almost enough shade. I breathe in
Your breath and breathe a million miles away.
A mirror is backing through a blinding desert,
Autoroute to the end. Already there—
Still waiting! It is too late to be yourself.

TO ROBERT LOWELL AND
OSIP MANDELSTAM

I look out the window: spring is coming.
I look out the window: spring is here.
The shuffle and click of the slide projector
Changing slides takes longer.

I like the dandelion—
How it sticks to the business of briefly being.
Shuffle and click, shuffle and click—
Life, more life, more life.

The train that carried the sparkling crystal saxophone
Osip Mandelstam into exile clicketyclicked
Through suds of spring flowers,
Cool furrowed-earth smells, sunshine like freshly baked bread.

The earth was so black it looked wet,
So rich it had produced Mandelstam.
He was last seen alive
In 1938 at a transit camp near Vladivostok

Eating from a garbage pile,
When I was two, and Robert Lowell was twenty-one,
Who much later would translate Mandelstam,
And now has been dead two years himself.

I sometimes feel I hurry to them both,
Stand staring at the careworn spines
Of their books in my bookshelf,
Only in order to walk away.

The wish to live is as unintentional as love.
Of course the future always is,
Like someone just back from England
Stepping off a curb, I'll look the wrong way and be nothing.

Heartbeat, heartbeat, the heart stops—
But shuffle and click, it's spring!
The arterial branches disappearing in the leaves,
Swallowed like a tailor's chalk marks in the finished suit.

FROM *Sunrise*

We are born.
We grow old until we're all the same age.
They are as young as Homer whom they loved.
They are writing a letter, not in a language I know.

I read: "It is one of those spring days with a sky
That makes it worthwhile being here.
The mailbox in which we'll mail·this
Is slightly lighter than the sky."

FINALS

A fat girl bows gravely like a samurai
On a bank of the Charles touching her toes,
Her tights in time with a sunrise sculler's stroke,
Then stroke, then stroke, dipped in pink, until
He crabs an oar, a burst of sudden white.

Four winters of grinding away then freaking on this
Soft-focus air not quite body temperature!
It feels pristine as the sweet-smelling world
Near a lawn sprinkler felt to a child.
Expulsion into Paradise for finals!

A red dome, and a green, a blue, a gold,
Veritas just above the leafiness.
The locked iron gates on Memorial Drive—
The eyes of a bachelor waiting for water to boil.

FROM *Sunrise*

MEN AND WOMAN

Her name I may or may not have made up,
But not the memory,
Sandy Moon with her lion's mane astride
A powerful motorcycle waiting to roar away, blipping
The throttle, a roar, years before such a sight
Was a commonplace,
And women had won,

And before a helmet law, or
Wearing their hair long, had made all riders one
Sex till you looked again; not that her chest
Wasn't decisive—breasts of Ajanta, big blue-sky clouds
Of marble, springing free of her unhooked bra
Unreal as a butterfly-strewn sweet-smelling mountainside
Of opium poppies in bloom.

It was Union Square. I remember. Turn a corner
And in a light-year
She'd have arrived
At the nearby inky, thinky offices of *Partisan Review*.
Was she off to see my rival Lief,
Boyfriend of girls and men, who cruised
In a Rolls convertible?

The car was the *caca* color a certain
Very grand envoy of Franco favored for daytime wear—
But one shouldn't mock the innocent machinery
Of life, nor the machines we treasure. For instance,
Motorcycles. What definition of beauty can exclude
The MV Agusta racing 500-3,
From the land of Donatello, with blatting megaphones?

To see Giacomo Agostini lay the MV over
Smoothly as a swan curves its neck down to feed,
At ninety miles an hour—entering a turn with Hailwood
On the Honda, wheel to wheel, a foot apart—
The tromboning furor of the exhaust notes as they
Downshifted, heard even in the photographs!
Heroes glittering on the summit before extinction

Of the air-cooled four-strokes in GP.
Agostini—Agusta! Hailwood—Honda!
I saw Agostini, in the Finnish Grand Prix at Imatra,
When Hailwood was already a legend who'd moved on
To cars. How small and pretty Ago was,
But heavily muscled like an acrobat. He smiled
And posed, enjoying his own charming looks,

While a jumpsuited mechanic pushed his silent
Racer out of the garage, and with a graceful
Sidesaddle run-and-bump started its engine.
A lion on a leash being walked in neutral
Back and forth to warm it up, it roared and roared;
Then was shut off; releasing a rather heady perfume
Of hot castor oil, as it docilely returned to the garage.

Before a race, how would Hailwood behave?
Racers get killed racing.
The roped-off crowd hushed outside the open door.
I stood in awe of Ago's ease—
In his leathers, like an animal in nature—
Inhumanly unintrospective, now smiling less
Brilliantly, but by far the brightest being in the room.

I feared finding his fear,
And looked for it,
And looked away so as not to mar the perfect.
There was an extraordinary girl there to study
Instead; and the altar piece, the lily
Painted the dried blood MV racing red,
Slender and pure—one hundred eighty miles an hour.

A lion which is a lily,
From the land of Donatello: where else could they design
Streamlined severe elegance in a toy color?
A phallus which was musical when it roared? By contrast,
Hailwood's Honda had been an unsteerable monster,
Only a genius could have won on it,
All engine and no art.

A lily that's a lion: handmade with love
By the largest helicopter manufacturer in Europe,
Whose troop carriers shielded junta and emir from harm,
And cicatriced presidents clutching
A golden ceremonial fly whisk and CIA dollars.
How storybook that a poor country boy
Should ride the Stradivarius of a count—

The aristocrat industrialist Agusta—against
The middle-class son of a nicely well-off businessman;
English; and weekly wallowing near death
On the nearly ungovernable Japanese horsepower.
A clone of Detroit, Honda Company, in going for power,
Empire-building
In peacetime displaced to motorcycle sales.

Honda raced no more. No need to to
Sell Hondas now. The empire flourished elsewhere
Than glory. I swooned in the gray even indoor air
Of a garage in Finland, as racetime neared.
Daylight blinded the doorway—the day beyond,
The crowd outside, were far away. I studied
The amazing beauty, whom Ago seemed determined to ignore.

Seated like Agostini in skintight racing leathers.
Her suit looked sweet, like Dr. Denton's on a child;
Until—as she stood up—the infant's-wear blue-innocence
Swelled violently to express
The breasts and buttocks of a totem, Magna Mater,
Overwhelming and almost ridiculous,
Venus in a racing suit,

Built big as Juno—out of place but filling up
The room, if you looked at her, which no one else did;
Though I still couldn't tell
Who she was, whose friend she was, if she was anyone's;
Whose girl, the one woman in the room.
The meaning of the enormous quiet split
Into men and woman around the motorcycle.

I thought of Sandy Moon,
Advancing toward me through the years to find me there,
Moving toward me through the years across the room
I'd rented, to hide and work,
Near Foley Square; where I wrote, and didn't write—
Through the sky-filled tall windows
Staring out for hours

At the State Supreme Court building with its steps
And columns, and the Federal Courthouse with its,
And that implacably unadorned low solid, the Department
Of Motor Vehicles. I'd leaf
Through one of my old motorcycle mags
And think of Sandy Moon—and here she was,
Naked and without a word walking slowly toward me.

Women have won. The theme is
Only for a cello, is the lurking glow
Pooled in the folds of a rich velvet, darkly phosphorescent.
Summer thunder rumbled over Brooklyn, a far-off sadness.
Naked power and a mane of glory
Shall inherit the earth. Outside the garage,
The engine caught and roared—time to go.

FUCKING

I wake because the phone is really ringing.
A singsong West Indian voice
In the dark, possibly a man's,
Blandly says, "Good morning, Mr. Seidel;
How are you feeling, God?"
And hangs up after my silence.

This is New York—
Some mornings five women call within a half hour.

In a restaurant, a woman I had just met, a Swede,
Three inches taller
Than I was among other things, and immensely
Impassive, cold,
Started to groan, very softly and husky voiced.
She said,
"You have utter control over me, and you know it.
I can't do anything about it."
I had been asking her about her job.

One can spend a lifetime trying to believe
These things.

I think of A.,
Before she became Lady Q.,
Of her lovely voice, and her lovely name.
What an extraordinary new one she took
With her marriage vows,
Even as titles go, extra fictitious. And ah—
And years later, at her request, paying a call on the husband
To ask if I could take her out
Once more, once, m'lord, for auld lang syne. She still wanted
To run away;
And had,
Our snowed-in week in the Chelsea
Years before.
How had her plane managed to land?

How will my plane manage to land?

How wilt thy plane manage to land?

Our room went out sledding for hours
And only returned when we slept,
Finally, with it still snowing, near dawn.

I can remember her sex,
And how the clitoris was set.

Now on to London where the play resumes—
The scene when I call on the husband. But first,

In Francis Bacon's queer after-hours club,
Which one went to after
An Old Compton Street Wheeler's lunch,
A gentleman at the bar, while Francis was off pissing,
Looking straight at me, shouted
"Champagne for the Norm'!"
Meaning normal, heterosexual.

The place where I stayed,
The genteel crowded gloom of Jimmy's place,
Was England—coiled in the bars of an electric fire
In Edith Grove.
Piece by piece Jimmy sold off the Georgian silver.
Three pretty working girls were his lodgers.

Walking out in one direction, you were in
Brick and brown oppidan Fulham.
Walking a few steps the other way, you heard
Augustus John's many mistresses
Twittering in the local Finch's,
And a few steps further on, in the smart restaurants,
The young grandees who still said "gels."

There was a man named Pericles Belleville,
There is a man named Pericles Belleville,
Half American.

FROM *Sunrise*

At a very formal dinner party,
At which I met the woman I have loved the most
In my life, Belleville
Pulled out a sterling silver–plated revolver
And waved it around, pointing it at people, who smiled.
One didn't know if the thing could be fired.

That is the poem.

PRESSED DUCK

Caneton à la presse at the now extinct Café Chauveron.
Chauveron himself cooking, fussed
And approved
Behind Elaine, whose party it was;
Whose own restaurant would be famous soon.

Poised and hard, but dreaming and innocent—
Like the last Romanovs—spring buds at thirty, at thirty-two,
We were green as grapes,
A cluster of February birthdays,
All "Elaine's" regulars.

Donald, Elaine's then-partner,
His then-wife, a lovely girl; Johnny
Greco, Richardson, Elaine, my former wife, myself:
With one exception, born within a few days and years
Of one another.

Not too long before thirty had been old,
But we were young—still slender, with one exception,
Heads and necks delicate
As a sea horse,
Elegant and guileless

Above our English clothes
And Cartier watches, which ten years later shopgirls
And Bloomingdale's fairies would wear,
And the people who pronounce chic *chick.*
Chauveron cut

The wine-red meat off the carcasses.
His duck press was the only one in New York.
He stirred brandy into the blood
While we watched. Elaine said, "Why do we need anybody else?
We're the world."

FROM *Sunrise*

WHAT ONE MUST CONTEND WITH

There was a man without ability.
He talked arrogance, secretly sick at heart.
Imagine law school with his terrible stutter!—
He gagged to be smooth. But it wasn't good.
Hadn't he always planned to move on to writing?
Which of course failed, how would it not? He called
Himself a writer but it didn't work,
He chose middling friends he could rise above
But it made no difference, with no ability.

He talked grand, the terrible endearing stutter.
Batting his eyes as if it felt lovely.
He batted and winced his self-hate, like near a sneeze.
He wrote and wrote, still he could not write,
He even published, but he could not write:
The stories one story of honey and abuse—
Love and the law—he was the boy . . . de Sade
Scratching his quill raw just once to get it off.
His pen leaked in *Redbook* the preseminal drool.

He must do something, do *something*. Boy you can
Reminisce forever about Harvard,
The motorboat won't run on your perfume,
Endless warm anecdotes about past girls
Aren't a wax your cross-country skis will ride on.
He took an office just like Norman Mailer.
He married a writer just like—yes exactly.
He shaved his beard off just like—et cetera.
It is a problem in America.

You never know who's dreaming about you.
They must do *something* to try to shift the weight
They wear—painted and smiling like gold the lead!
No wonder he walked staidly. They've time to dream.
Oh hypocrites in hell dying to catch up!
Oh in etterno faticoso manto!
And if you hail one and stop—he's coming—he'll stutter,
"Costui par vivo all'atto della gola,"
"This man seems alive, by the working of his throat."

The dreaming envying third-rate writhe in America.
He sucked his pipe. He skied he fished he published.
He fucked his wife's friends. Touching himself he murmured
He was not fit to touch his wife's hem.
He dreamed of running away with his sister-in-law!
Of doing a screenplay. Him the guest on a talk show—
Wonderful—who has read and vilifies Freud!
How he'd have liked to put Freud in his place,
So really clever Freud was, but he was lies.

It was autumn. It rained. *His* lies drooped down.
It was a Year of the Pig in Vietnam,
In Vietnam our year the nth, the Nixonth,
Sometimes one wants to cut oneself in two
At the neck. The smell. The gore. To kill! There was
The child batting her head against the wall,
Beating back and forth like a gaffed fish.
There was the wife who suspected they were nothing.
There's the head face-up in the glabrous slop.

You feel for him, the man was miserable.
It's mad t-*tooh* be so ad hominem!
And *avid*, when the fellow was in Vermont,
For Southeast Asia. Was he miserable?
Another creative couple in Vermont,
The wife toasts the husband's trip to New York,
The little evening he's planning. In less than a day
He will enter my poem. He picks at her daube.
There's the head face-up in the glabrous slop.

Voilà donc quelqu'un de bien quelconque!
Ah Vermont! The artists aggregate,
A suburb of the Iowa Writers' Workshop
Except no blacks with no ability.
I am looking down at you, at you and yours,
Your stories and friends, your banal ludicrous dreams,
Dear boy, the horror, mouth uncreating,
Horror, horror, I hear it, head chopped off,
The stuttering head face-up in a pile of slop.

FROM *Sunrise*

Just stay down there dear boy it is your home.
The unsharpened knives stuck to the wall
Magnet-bar dully. The rain let off the hush
Of a kettle that doesn't sing. Each leaf was touched,
Each leaf drooped down, a dry palm and thin wrist.
His beautifully battered sweet schoolboy satchel walked
With him out the door into scrutiny,
The ears for eyes of a bat on the wings of a dove.
Art won't forgive life, no more than life will.

HOMAGE TO CICERO

Anything and everyone is life when two
Radios tune to the news on different stations while
A bass recorder pulses familiar sequences of sound waves,
An old sad sweet song, live. A computer
On stage listens to it all and does a printout
Of it in Fortran, after a microsecond lag, and adds its own
Noise. The printout piles up in folds
On the stage, in a not quite random way.
"Plaisir d'Amour" was the song.

Balls of cement shaped by a Vassar
Person, "majored in art at Vassar,"
Each must weigh a hundred pounds, fill a gallery.
They are enough alike to be perhaps
The look of what? The weight the person was
When she first was no longer a child—
Her planet lifeless after the Bomb—an anorexic image.
The hideous and ridiculous are obsessed
By the beautiful which they replace.

It is an age we may not survive.
The sciences know. We do believe in art
But ask the computer to hear and preserve our cry.
O computer, hear and preserve our cry.
Mortem mihi cur consciscerem
Causa non visa est, cur optarem multae causae.
Vetus est enim, "ubi non sis qui fueris,
Non esse cur velis vivere." Or, in English:
We are no longer what we were.

DESCENT INTO THE UNDERWORLD

A woman watches the sunrise in her martini,
And drinks—and drinks darkness.
She is in a dark room,
Tubes in her nostrils and arms.

She is in her childhood bed.
Suddenly she is awake. Orpheus,
A big person, is about to do
Something to a little.

Floating in darkness, connected
To tubes like a diver . . . Eurydice.
Her breath-bubbles rise. Backing out of her throat
One by one, the Valiums rise.

Sweets to the sweet, yellow pills for a princess—
Orpheus holds out a bouquet
Of yellow tulips like a torch,
And shines it on her, and stares down at her.

She drinks his syrup, drooling in her sleep.
She lisps in a happy little girl's voice:
"The man is bad—I hate him.
The little girl is bad. She loves him."

A BEAUTIFUL DAY OUTSIDE

I still lived, and sat there in the sun,
Too depressed to savor my melancholia.
I wore a cardboard crown. I held
A sceptre with a star on top.

I was on a hill, looking over at a mountain.
The sky was bald blue above.
Pine needles made
Something softer than a breast beneath the fits-all royal hose.

I was like an inmate of Charenton
Dully propped up on a throne outdoors, playing
"Fatigue of the Brave"—fatigue such as of a fireman holding
A still warm baby, waiting for the body bag.

Professional depression,
In an age of revolutionary fire
And having to grow up. This king did not wish to—
Still declined to be beheaded at forty-three.

But that I was depressed,
I had diagnosed the depression thus:
Ambivalence at a standstill—
Party-favor crown, real-life guillotine.

I still lived. I sat there in the sun:
Just water and salt conducting a weak current
Between the scent of pine and the foot smell
Of weeds reeking in the hot sun.

The children's party crown I wore
Dazzled my thinning hair like a halo.
The crown was crenellated like a castle wall.
A leper begged outside the wall.

In an upper gallery of the castle,
A young woman curtsied to the king and said: "Sire,
You are a beautiful day outside."
The king stuck his stick down her throat to shut her up.

FROM *Sunrise*

Children, of all things bad, the best is to kill a king.
Next best: to kill yourself out of fear of death.
Next best: to grovel and beg. I took for my own motto
I rot before I ripen.

YEARS HAVE PASSED

Seeing you again.
Your glide, your gaze.
Your very quiet voice.
Your terror. Your quiet eyes.

FROM *Sunrise*

THE GIRL IN THE MIRROR

Oh never to be yourself,
Never to let be
And simply be there.

The same
Morning ink blot in the mirror
Making a face up,

Making up a face. You need
All your strength
Never to be yourself.

Skirt, boots, and sweater
Green as a stem.
I'll wear them.

Take me down from the shelf.
Oh never to be yourself
And always to be the same.

Like the air and the wind,
The wind and the air.
I hear a very quiet voice,

Emphatic like a flower,
Saying
It is I.

FEVER

The soft street canyon was silent. In silence the new snow
Layered a rolling swell. The greatest evening
Tilted and rose against the tiny window:
Like her juggled soaking fishbowl swinging
A wave that burst into suds. A feeler of ice,
See-through and frail, scaled the whitening lace
Of the window guard, now more visible,
As if a vine were growing its own trellis.
The warm room watched it whiten, counting the minutes.

Think fast! (Still dreaming?) The boy had caught his friend
Flush with a lobbed cannonball of snow.
But then they crossed the closed street hand in hand.
Their dog sprinted in zigzags like a minnow,
Or wallowing in too deep, leapt out like a deer,
Folded forepaws leaping, then his rear.
From two floors up, two floors below is deep.
They don't know it, but sometime someone will come
And take her hand and feed her to the moon.

ERATO

Suddenly the pace
Quickens, chill air dusts the air.
The leaves shrink
To a fawn color, held by their tails like mice,
The color of twine.

The fifty o'clock moon
Laid its cheek against the window,
Lay like snow on the carpet.
Outside the window,
Harlem in moonlight.

You walked outside.
Everyone knows
About the would-be suicide: you walk—
A step, a heartbeat—
Heartbeats. Sobsob, in the noon park,

The nannies were white,
Seated like napkins on the benches,
Starched and folded to sit up.
The babies did not choose the carriages,
Limousine coffers, blackly London;

They did not choose the rayless Tartar sun,
Sterile as the infected
Industrial steppes of Calvin—of
Bayonne. The reservoir banks were a purple socket
Like a black tulip.

Anything would do now
That inspired you
Below the Ninth Sphere, below the fixed stars
With fall, the electric cattle prod,
The cold juice that shocked you from your sleep

Lovelorn: slight,
Frizzy, sweating animal with feelings.
For fall, dawn rises in combers
Above the radiator shield's metal caning,
The sill flows like a pennant.

You smell the back-to-school,
Steam and rain on wool,
The tears not learning
And learning to write
With the sharp new chalk

Jacobean black and white,
The fantastic wrong and right, now dissolving
In Jamesian gray. You want to be a child—
You want to find the way
To either more or less than you are.

If you could choose.
Everywhere changes or fades.
Her hair streams like a willow's
As it leans to the river
When she leans toward you

Her anodyne, her healing face,
Eurasian, gypsy ease
(You have your memories),
Lovely lost love;
Erato's dark hair.

DE SADE

So now you've fettered that sweet bride,
The boy you've toyed with awhile and gelded,
And still not come, wretched sod.
Suck yourself off, like in your dream.

Innocents, white and fresh, bless 'em,
They belonged down in your love grotto;
They hiccup and honk on the slick flags
Looped with turds and the squashed-flat intestine.

Nothing helps, Marquis. Oh try
The scaffold again, with your bald pregnant nun.
The hired child caresses the ripped breasts;
She fingers herself, and releases the pretend-drop—

Nothing helps! At least, at least—
Sade save our republican mistress, France.
Kiss the Courrèges boot, de Sade,
The stockingful up to the stocking top.

Beyond you lies the shrine, between
The slopes of Zion, past the alehouse.
Refresh yourself, drink deep. The brine!
The salt and gall, your honey and wine!

THE NEW FRONTIER

Never again to wake up in the blond
Hush and gauze of that Hyannis sunrise.
Bliss was it
In that dawn to be alive

With our Kool as breakfast,
Make-do pioneers. Like politicians
Headed for a back room,
Each minute lived when it arrived,

And was the future. To be our age
Was very heaven. The fresh print
On the leaves dabbed
The windowscreen leaf-green;

A nestling's wing of a breeze that
Could not have stirred a cobweb
Eased through the air
And swept the room clean.

We could love politics for its mind!
All seemed possible,
Though it was barely a breeze.
The spirey steel-wool tuft in the map

Spreading apart, the city's
Wild wire and grease-rot,
Must be redeemed. When we returned
We would begin.

The city was our faith—
Ah we knew now the world need not end.
The flagpole out on the common actually
Seemed to tense,

Attentive as a compass needle,
Seemed caught in the open
Sniffing the breeze,
The little flag quivering like a sprig.

FROM *Sunrise*

Alas. We could almost see
Cloth milk flying in place of blood and stars:
A nationless white flag colorlessly
Compounded of all colors, for peace.

But the pitcher and turned-down tumbler
On their doily summed up
The trim smell of dill,
We would begin.

It was new Eden.
And there was the young light,
There the feathery sapling—our tree priest,
Let us say, stuck with glued leaves.

Eden's one anthill bred
A commune honey pallor on the lawn
Uncurbed, yet innocent
Of any metaphor.

A pipe snaking around the baseboard rose
And stood silent in the corner like a birch.
Perhaps only innocence was keeping
The common still asleep

While we overreached, and touched so easily
What we were. We were
Awake while the world slept.
We overweened. Yes, yes,

We opened the patched screen
And plucked a leaf and stem,
And chewed the stem,
And tasted its green.

NOVEMBER 24, 1963

The trees breathe in like show dogs, stiffening
Under the silver leashes of light rain
To spines. A Cyclone fence that guards the moire
Embankment of the shrunken reservoir
Bristles with rain barbs, each a milk tooth, sting
Of stings, where fall began. The park's a stain,
The black paths shimmer under cellophane.

It is so real. Shy ghosts of taxis sniff
And worry in the empty park streets, lost
And misted lights, and down Fifth Avenue:
The flags soak at half-staff, bloodshed and blue;
Bloodletting stripes repeating their mute riff;
Gray stars, wet Union sky of stars, crisscrossed
With petrifying folds and sparks of frost.

The rain points prick the lake and touch the drought,
The dusk blue of a sterile needletip.
The brightness and the light has been struck down.

FROM *Sunrise*

FREEDOM BOMBS FOR VIETNAM (1967)

The bald still head is filled with that grayish milk—
It's a dentist's glass door. It turns heavily—
There may be a weight in it. It weighs one ton.

Very even light diffuses through the globe.
But this surprise: life-squiggles, fishhooks,
Minnowhooks, surround the mineral eyes.

Someone like Muzak is burbling slant rhymes—
-*om* and -*am*, -*om* and -*am*—and holds up a telltale map
Of rice swimming in blood like white flies.

Ears almost as large as the president's
And more eloquent than lips,
That swallow toothlessly like polyps.

A spit glob and naked flashbulbs pop in Rusk's ear
And go down with whole heads, whole fields of heads
Of human hair, jagged necks attached.

Tangled unwashed bangs lengthening and cut, lengthening and cut,
The civilian population knows no more
Than a cellar of pocked Georgia potatoes.

This Press Talk is like a ham discussing pigs—
They need our help. He's a cracker showing the kids
The funny human shapes his potatoes have.

They must be scrubbed and eaten in their skins.
That's the nourishment. Rusk sets no other condition.
Rusk's private smile that looks like incest.

ROBERT KENNEDY

I turn from Yeats to sleep, and dream of Robert Kennedy,
Assassinated ten years ago tomorrow.
Ten years ago he was alive—
Asleep and dreaming at this hour, dreaming
His wish-fulfilling dreams.
He reaches from the grave.

Shirtsleeves rolled up, a boy's brown hair, ice eyes
Softened by the suffering of others, and doomed;
Younger brother of a murdered president,
Senator and candidate for president;
Shy, compassionate and fierce
Like a figure out of Yeats;
The only politician I have loved says *You're dreaming* and says
The gun is mightier than the word.

FROM *Sunrise*

THE DRILL

"Have the bristles at an angle and gently
Work them in between the tooth and gum
Back and forth," a woman says.
Her breast is next to my ear.
She moves a set of teeth four inches high
And a foot-long toothbrush.

Breast; and then the teeth; and then
The window without a shade or curtains—then the day,
Twelve floors above the street;
And the empty lighted office windows always
On the other side of a street
From the drill,
Since childhood,
The obsolete slow drill that now only polishes.

HAMLET

Alive. Yes and awake. Flowers
Fall through his mind, in one slant, like snow.
The electric toothbrush flames in his hand.
Mozart sweetens the small room.

LSD tears he wept all night,
One hundred for a dead father.
LSD tears, they roll heavy
And burn like molten metal drops.

Now as the drug wears off he waits.
For a mother has remarried.
Oh the man swelled, supple bitch,
And smiled as if he might give birth.

Completely to be shut of both,
Purged pure and bare to all in one's fate,
The drug makes possible at last
[*The curtain stirs*], out of the shell,

The old self, new and neat as a chick.
This dew, haze softness on waking has opened
His window on the street a crack.
Midnight tolls. The curtain stirs.

THE FUTURE

Fifth Avenue has the flickers, heat
Lightning lit. A voodoo doll's
Whey little bursts of breath stare,
And fits of fluttering like an eye;

A Haitian nurse at her window altar
Tutoyers the hatpin. The terrified trees'
Bursts of breath stare, as though Fifth
Were lined with dandelion clocks.

Scree in the void, Sinai is snuffed,
Half re-created. Parting the black:
Arrow one-way signs plunged through,
The twitched buildings dancing and chalk-white.

It is too late for people but
A rag barfs on a curb. But it's
A sandwich board mouldering there
Draws the nose of his tetchy chow:

Seen in a sheet-flap of sight just now
And gone now. In the blinded dark;
Streetlights, stars sapped—repeated blows
That leave unstirred the humid silence.

Silence . . . Even Harlem is still—
Harlem is near. The galaxies,
The brainstorms of zero, gasp the fainter
And fainter last breaths of the future.

This time we may go out for good.
Blacked out after the zillionth stroke.
This may be a good time not to wake.
Fifth Ave. The white man's night-light, the future.

WANTING TO LIVE IN HARLEM

Pictures of violins in the Wurlitzer collection
Were my bedroom's one decoration,
Besides a blue horse and childish tan maiden by Gauguin—
Backs, bellies, and scrolls,
Stradivarius, Guarnerius, Amati,
Colored like a calabash-and-meerschaum pipe bowl's
Warmed, matured body—

The color of the young light-skinned colored girl we had then.
I used to dream about her often,
In sheets she'd have to change the day after.
I was thirteen, had just been bar mitzvah.
My hero, once I'd read about him,
Was the emperor Hadrian; my villain, Bar Kokhba,
The Jew Hadrian had crushed out at Jerusalem:

Both in the *Cambridge Ancient History*'s Hadrian chapter (1936
Edition), by some German. (The Olympics
Year of my birth and Jesse Owens's *putsch* it had appeared.)
Even then, in '49, my mother was dying.
Dressed in her fresh-air blue starched uniform,
The maid would come from Mother's room crying
With my mother's tears shining on her arm,

And run to grab her beads and crucifix and missal,
I to find my violin and tuning whistle
To practice my lessons. Mendelssohn. Or Bach,
Whose Lutheran fingering had helped pluck
The tonsured monks like toadstools from their lawns,
And now riddled the armor I would have to shuck:
His were life-sized hands behind his puppet Mendelssohn's.

One night, by the blue of her nitelite, I watched the maid
Weaving before her mirror in the dark, naked.
Her eyes rolled, whiskey-bright; the glass was black, dead.
"Will you come true? It's me, it's me," she said.
Her hands and her hips clung to her rolling pelvis.
Her lips smacked and I saw her smile, pure lead
And silver, like a child, and shape a kiss.

FROM *Sunrise*

All night I tossed. I saw the face,
The shoulders and the slight breasts—but a boy's face,
A soft thing tangled, singing, in his arms,
Singing and foaming, while his blinding pelvis,
Scooped out, streamed. His white eyes dreamed,
While the black face pounded with syncope and madness.
And then, in clear soprano, we both screamed.

What a world of mirrored darkness! Agonized, elated,
Again years later I would see it with my naked
Eye—see Harlem: doped up and heartless,
Loved up by heroin, running out of veins
And out of money and out of arms to hold it—where
I saw dead saplings wired to stakes in lanes
Of ice, like hair out cold in hair straightener.

And that wintry morning, trudging through Harlem
Looking for furnished rooms, I heard the solemn
Pedal-toned bowing of the Bach Chaconne.
I'd played it once! How many tears
Had shined on Mother's maids since then?
Ten years! I had been trying to find a room ten years,
It seemed that day, and been turned down again and again.

No violin could thaw
The rickety and raw
Purple window I shivered below, stamping my shoes.
Two boys in galoshes came goose-stepping down
The sheer-ice long white center line of Lenox Avenue.
A blue-stormcoated Negro patrolman,
With a yellowing badge star, bawled at them. I left too.

I had given up violin and left St. Louis,
I had given up being Jewish,
To be at Harvard just another
Greek nose in street clothes in Harvard Yard.
Mother went on half dying.
I wanted to live in Harlem. I was almost unarmored . . .
Almost alone—like Hadrian crying

As his death came on, "Your Hadrianus
Misses you, Antinous,
Misses your ankles slender as your wrists,
Dear child. We want to be alone.
His back was the city gates of Rome.
And now Jerusalem is dust in the sun,
His skies are blue. He's coming, child, I come."

THE LAST ENTRIES
IN MAYAKOVSKY'S NOTEBOOK

She loves me? She loves me not?

I wring
My hands and scatter the broken-off fingers.
Like petals you pluck from some
White little flower along your way.
You hold them up to the breeze,
They've told your fortune,
They drift off into May.

Though
Now a haircut
Lays bare thorns of gray,
Though my morning shave shows me
On the bib the salt of age,
I hope, I believe

I will never weaken.

Never be caught
Showing good sense.

•

Past one o'clock. You must have gone to sleep.
Or do

You feel, perhaps you feel the same as I?
I'm in no hurry.

Is
There no point

In a telegram that would only
Wake you? And disturb you.

•

The tide ebbs.
The sea too
Is going to sleep.
The incident as they say
Is closed.
Love's skiff
Has stove
In on the daily grind.
It would be useless
Making a list
Of who did what to whom.
We shared
Weapons
And wounds.

•

Past one. Like a

Silent moonlit Oka', the Milky Way
Streams into the night. I'm in no hurry.

As they say: the incident is closed.
A telegram would wake you.

How still it is.
Night, night sky, and stars.

What stillness there is in the world!
What stillness we are capable of!

In hours like these one rises
To address the Ages—History—the Universe!

•

I know
The power of words.

(Not the gas
The loges applaud.)

That make
Coffins rear up and break loose

And clomp off
Robotlike, rocked forward like a crate.

So we are rejected,
So we go unpublished

But the word gallops on, cinching the saddle tighter,
The word rings for centuries—a tocsin!

And steam engines creep up to lick
Poetry's calloused hands.

I know
The power of words.

It is nothing!
A fallen

Petal under
A dancer's heel.

But man
In his soul, his lips, in his bones . . .

HART CRANE NEAR THE END

1

The woman in love with him
Pleads with him, "Why
Must there be such misery?
What is there in you that wants this?"
And still he does not feel it,
Feels nothing, sealed in his self.

The beach house is filled up.
The guests drift in and out
Talking in wafts, sozzled,
Sunburns moonlit; dappled fluttering
Shirts at summery games. But
Now near dawn it's cold. He sees
The clock ticks swimming through the air,
Swimming eyelashed eyelets tiny as rotifers.
A warped smile is everywhere,
Half in, half out of water.

In youth more delicate than the boy Rimbaud's,
The sunset nose, lips like blood sausages.
Course of the day's
Lost, unsought breaths, uncounted,
Each separate as a life, a guest.
His life had purposes!
The hall clock ticks.
Oh the heresies, Oh each distinct,
Blue and bright and trite and evil, each,
Those efforts to see the light
Chasing each other's tails—
Whirled into moral butter like Black Sambo's tigers,
As the phonograph spins Ravel's "Bolero."

2

A glance—a snipe's beak—
Opens, he sees
The scorched

Tobacco-y nerve ends.
They are wandering through the sumac,
Wondering if it is poisonous,
Blondes and brunettes.
"Who belongs to you?" she whispers.

His life is falling.
His butched unruly hair boils
Through her fingers like the ocean.
The sun beats lightning on the waves,
The waves fold thunder on the sand.
She is afraid.

3

Raising his cigar and drink,
He gives a toast: "To the dying
Wildlife of Mexico—myself!
Ah, to Lorenzo,
Of course, too.

At forty-five, at his noon eclipsed—
Our former neighbor, up there
In heaven with Beiderbecke.
The famous style was just the life,
He handed you the books blade first,
Keen as a castaway's thirst.
His spirit,
Like a little straight stick,
A little straight stick,
So set and separate, so free,
Wrestled verse by verse
Favorite flowers, birds and beasts."

He barely finishes.
With a roar the surf razes
Last night's sand castle
And seizes her sailor's cap
As she gasps for breath,

Fighting back tears.
The white dot wags on the water
Like candlelight in a draft,
Flickers, dips, and reappears—
As if, someone says, on an altar offered to
The anchored white United Fruit ship,
A hospital ship,
Which it seems to want to draw near.

"Why, it reverences United Fruit"
(Up goes his glass),
"Our brilliantined
Hustler queen, our Muse.
But our Muse keeps his pitch to himself now,
From me anyway—that white lie,
Inspirer of my verse, my
Sermon on San Juan Hill *The Bridge*,
That hemorrhaged,
Flowing out under the Morgan boardroom doors
Like a ray stalking, a gliding
Opera cape of blood.

"Sweetheart, don't cry. Let's see.
Tolstoy is like the sea.
Shakespeare is like the sea. Or let's say
Whitman is like a spar
Off the *America*,
Wooed by the *Pequod*, the *Patna*, the *Lusitania*,
The *Titanic*, the maniacs,
The siren idealists—America
Weltering in her element
Like ambergris. Slick sightless mass,
Clung to by a sweet smell.
The old fag as he drowns still acting
The little girl
Who can come to no harm."

He still has his charm.
Her childless troubled soul quiets,
Glows like a flame in Vermeer;
Her startled little vices
Twinkle off like swallows.

FROM *Sunrise*

"Don't cry, sweetheart.
Keep my kisses in your pocket
Till I get back. Oh, wouldn't you like to see
Ohio with me
On my trip!
But if I come back,
Who will put up with me?
Who will put me up?
Sunshine, I've no place to go,
And no place to go
Is easy enough to find."

4

On the desk
The paper is blank,
Freezing to sleep
In the snowfield cast by the lamp.
He tries to think;
Tries to remember the evening.
Faceless
Spondee and iamb couples kick by
In a conga line.
The baker, the breadline,
The Communist and Capitalist,
To them poetry is
A saint's temptation
And his desert, both.
The wide dry heartland sky,
The teetotaling Sahara
Over Chagrin Falls,
When he was last there,
Ideally white as Moby-Dick,
Devoured him like a drop.

5

From the bed,
Through her jiggling cigarette
She recites: "Then you downed
The other bottle of tequila.
You said you were Baudelaire—
Or was it Marlowe?—
You said you were Blake
Talking English with the angels,
And said you were Christ, of course,
But *never* would say
You were yourself. And the voice!
The steady inhuman horror
Making my heart contract!
You cursed me, my makeup,
Cursed the moon, its light,
Cursed that boyfriend,
All your other friends, all the guests.
My God, you cursed the elements!
And separately, by name,
The heliotrope, the heaven-tree,
The star jessamine, the sweet-by-night;
And even the spring pool
With the small ducks, the lily pad;
And even the air we breathed together,
Because I breathed it and the flowers.
You wept. You said,
'There *is* goodness,
That from bayberry made modest candles
And rose jam from hips and haws.
And Blake talked English with the angels.'
And you wanted to make love to me,
Though I can't imagine how."

FROM *Sunrise*

6

When morning breaks, he takes
His first drink of water in a day.
Petite veille d'ivresse, sainte!
His orange fireball eye sees,
Dried yolk yellow like a slicker,
The faded fire hydrant
Pop from the grass like a bird's note,
And its black beak tweets
Me! Me!

FINAL SOLUTIONS (1963)

WANTING TO LIVE IN HARLEM

Pictures of violins in the Wurlitzer collection
Were my bedroom's one decoration,
Besides a blue horse and childish tan maiden by Gauguin—
Backs, bellies, and scrolls,
Stradivarius, Guarnerius, Amati,
Colored like a calabash-and-meerschaum pipe bowl's
Warmed, matured body—

The color of the young light-skinned colored girl we had then.
I used to dream about her often,
In sheets she'd have to change the day after.
I was thirteen, had just been bar mitzvah.
My hero, once I'd read about him,
Was the emperor Hadrian; my villain, Bar Kokhba,
The Jew Hadrian had crushed out at Jerusalem:

Both in the *Cambridge Ancient History*'s Hadrian chapter (1936
Edition), by some German. (The Olympics
Year of my birth and Jesse Owens's *putsch* it had appeared.)
Even then, in '49, my mother was dying.
Dressed in her fresh-air blue starched uniform,
The maid would come from Mother's room crying
With my mother's tears shining on her arm,

And run to grab her beads and crucifix and missal,
I to find my violin and tuning whistle
To practice my lessons. Mendelssohn. Or Bach,
Whose Lutheran fingering had helped pluck
The tonsured monks like toadstools from their lawns,
And now riddled the armor I would have to shuck:
His were life-sized hands behind his puppet Mendelssohn's.

One night, by the blue of her nitelite, I watched the maid
Weaving before her mirror in the dark, naked.
Her eyes rolled, whiskey-bright; the glass was black, dead.
"Will you come true? It's me, it's me," she said.
Her hands and her hips clung to her rolling pelvis.
Her lips smacked and I saw her smile, pure lead
And silver, like a child, and shape a kiss.

All night I tossed. I saw the face,
The shoulders and the slight breasts—but a boy's face,
A soft thing tangled, singing, in his arms,
Singing and foaming, while his blinding pelvis,
Scooped out, streamed. His white eyes dreamed,
While the black face pounded with syncope and madness.
And then, in clear soprano, we both screamed.

What a world of mirrored darkness! Agonized, elated,
Again years later I would see it with my naked
Eye—see Harlem: doped up and heartless,
Loved up by heroin, running out of veins
And out of money and out of arms to hold it—where
I saw dead saplings wired to stakes in lanes
Of ice, like hair out cold in hair straightener.

And that wintry morning, trudging through Harlem
Looking for furnished rooms, I heard the solemn
Pedal-toned bowing of the Bach Chaconne.
I'd played it once! How many tears
Had shined on Mother's maids since then?
Ten years! I had been trying to find a room ten years,
It seemed that day, and been turned down again and again.

No violin could thaw
The rickety and raw
Purple window I shivered below, stamping my shoes.
Two boys in galoshes came goose-stepping down
The sheer-ice long white center line of Lenox Avenue.
A blue-stormcoated Negro patrolman,
With a yellowing badge star, bawled at them. I left too.

I had given up violin and left St. Louis,
I had given up being Jewish,
To be at Harvard just another
Greek nose in street clothes in Harvard Yard.
Mother went on half dying.
I wanted to live in Harlem. I was almost unarmored . . .
Almost alone—like Hadrian crying

As his death came on, "Your Hadrianus
Misses you, Antinous,
Misses your ankles slender as your wrists,
Dear child. We want to be alone.
His back was the city gates of Rome.
And now Jerusalem is dust in the sun,
His skies are blue. He's coming, child, I come."

A WIDOWER

He still reads his paper in there; the john's what he comes home for.
The door kept locked the way some men keep a whore
Was his whore while his wife lived. Still up at eight,
In bed by ten. But now sometimes he's up late,
Biting his tongue to tears, to masturbate.

And now always his angina schreis like a boiling kettle.
His breath shrieks when he reaches to wash the newsprint away,
Still seated, from his cigar-stained fingers. Like rusted metal
The white and gray tiles: a veined, brownish light gray.

When he tries to think of her face,
He sees the drops clinging to the faucet droop and ache.
He sees his shadow on the pebbled glass,
Covered with the tears he's held back.

Outside the door, his visiting granddaughter barks at the dog,
Asleep there, gassing and grumbling. One foot must be bare—
The other in what must be her grandmother's beach clog,
She slops down the hall rug. *She* should care?

The bathroom cares for him like a wife.
But his little legs, swastika-like
In black sharkskin, still run his coalyards and his life,
He has no say. His dry throat stabs him, like a spike

Of unpaid bills, counting the white tiles, then again the gray.
He'd like a cigar for every time that kvetch killed
Him in her dreams every day
And *knew* he knew it—and was thrilled!

Except—the almost odorless warm sand and the smell of salt—
Where?—where they were happy. Atlantic City? L.A.?
The waves gush in fizzing, halt,
Trailing seaweed and sunlight, and flush away.

On its back, opened up, his billfold sweats on the damp tiles,
As if helpless, where it was dropped. His wife's snapshot smiles
Up from the floor—he opens the door. Turning gold-
Rimmed silver cartwheels on the hall rug, the blond child . . .
Shocked by the static in his kisses, she starts to scold.

THE COALMAN

Past nine and still snowing.
It will stop and go below zero.
The next-to-last truck disappears,
And the hiss of its tires as they unspool
Their usage, like miles of adhesive.
The last truck goes, it's time to go.

Still there, into the New Year,
The Mine Workers' huge Santa Claus
Made of coal derivatives beams
His head-lamp on their new all-glass office—
My eyes burn; my headlights swallow snow
Block after block down the soft street.

And already it's colder now.
When the small streets crack like sticks,
If they snap a gas pipe,
We'll reroute our light trucks.
We'll go nowhere.
The world is getting warmer.

I always bicker with last year—
And the cold cut as dull as garden shears
Last year. Even when
We're filling up half-full bins,
Outdistancing the need, delays set in,
Some driver cocks his empty head for spring.

Once winter was the dragon, revered,
Because we were poor. Its carborundum heels
Wore inches off my uncles and my father
Before their iron-wheeled coal carts
Sliced it into water—and a Santa Claus now.
My boy still calls tire chains sleigh bells.

FROM *Final Solutions*

The trucks and the drivers will be back
By midnight, unless they stop for a bite.
The pipe layers, tomorrow,
Have their third raise in three years.
The ice wind has flattened the river.
It tears the skin from my lips like Bible paper.

I see me and the miners, the drivers,
And some poor nigger customers
Who can't buy the smokeless fuel
Eating our soft coal whole,
And vomiting and vomiting slick eels
Of blackness. I can see this.

A NEGRO JUDGE

The juice glass throbs against his lips,
He rubs it across his brow, while a draft sips
At the bare grate and palpitates in the chimney.
His cigarette fingers are the color of whiskey.

Week nights he sleeps in town.
Seeming nakeder each weekend, in the bluebook-blue nightgown,
His wife cuts the daffodils—
The Sunday scissors shine and glint like the onset of chills.

Backed up love kills
The loving eye with its quills.
Once, his nerves would have stood and stared, prongs on a mace,
His meatless Jansenist hooked face . . .

Spawning salmon's face, the lippy death's-head
Fighting starvation to get to its deathbed.
Around the lawn, sparrows flit through the thaw
Trailing rabbinical beards of straw.

His favorite magistrate—favorite piece of justice:
Fielding committed a T. Jones for assaulting a bawd with his cutlass.
The lean law
Warbles the galliambic scripture through lips fat as pads of a paw.

And law-hagged America dreams on, with disgust, of a hairy,
Plenary,
Incessant lust,
A God-like black penis, a white buttocks-sized bust.

A large, slow tear, a hangover,
Rolls down his cheek, magnifying each unshaved pore . . .
Now the dark rose-pimples come up from so low,
Like pebbles tossed at a dark window!

From the judge's seat, a world of widow's peaks!
Where the lying defendant shrieks,
"Your Honor, I believe! Help thou mine unbelief!"
And slavers with hate and grief.

FROM *Final Solutions*

Plaintiff is awarded the judge! Passerine,
Perched on branch and vine,
Plaintiff spreads its smallish wings—
Brownish white, whitish brown—and sings.

THE HEART ATTACK

(An old man's dream, terminated by a heart attack: he dreams he hears a long-dead mistress haranguing him.)

You may forget: as I crouch near
Your love-sleep, yours on hers, that knife
You shaved me with is all I hear—
The scraping, this way, that way, like your breathing. Life
Has one career, and mine was bare.
You can't dig out the veined and knotted world despair
Tucked in your senses. Death slits you unbound.

I watch you drag yourselves around
The streets. If slovenry is mashed
And washed away, the stocks compound.
But tell it to the marsh mosquitoes and the gnashed
And Nile-green waste the gutters pass.
Bedded on tissues of roses, this still is Sybaris;
And even roses bruise your fulsome flesh.

Are hook-nosed stallions wearing mesh
Caparisons still taught to dance
To flutes? We saw them once—like fresh,
But this time virgin, Vestals—horse-hierophants.
What when Crotonian or Celt
Masters the flute and trips the brawny Romans, svelte
And all, into their fancy horses' pies

Of filth? I slit my wrists. Your prize,
Queered, arrow-eaten legionnaire,
Just back from Hatra, boy-starved, flies
To watch the lions get a Roman—daily fare
In Rome like pasta: armpit air,
A crush of bodies, fear. The one time we were there
You gagged and nearly fainted. Fail to feed

FROM *Final Solutions*

The raving masses all they need
Of vomit from the state's gorged throat,
And they may use you as the reed
To tickle up a gladiator. You still dote
On walks and naps, on simple toys,
Silk fans that needn't keep the flies away. Your joys
Are simpler than the wax work of the bees

Housed in the propped-up laurel trees
On your estate. You suck that child,
And think of me. Once, while a breeze
Feathered the sapling laurels, I found a bee the mild
South wind had injured, which, while my palm
Softly lifted it to its hive, woke from its calm
And stung its puny life into my hand,

And died—leaving me to demand
My vengeance from your whimpering lips
Which sucked the poison. Old men stand
That poison till they die. A bee, that fingertips
Deep sweetness, gives up sweets to spend
Its deadly, bitter ardor. Letting go's the end.
The rest is free, the rest of it is free,

That swells the schooner, pulls the sea
Out calm while lip-fresh Venus bathes
Close to the beach where a flower and bee
Barter the short summer, and land crabs back down the paths
Of slime where Pompey's tubas spray,
And ladies split their wishbones for Marc Antony.
You know Augustus banned adultery—

You could be blackmailed. You should see
Her gnawed-down thumb nails. Do you shake
The stars out of our Forum tree
With that poor girl? Or can't you now? They used to streak
Above us grinding in the grass,
And light us to the sunrise Tiber, where I'd pass
An hour, in silver, washing you away.

You *made* me love it. But the way
You nibbled, nibbled, in the pool
Near Acragas that August day.
And after, clinging to the bottom to stay cool,
I watched your body from below,
So papery and small afloat. I'd wondered how
Men drowned—and then you woke up, coughed, and smeared.

You made me. But your mouth is reared,
It waters for me, and my rut
Is dry. You liked it with your beard
Between my clenched thighs; now I'm willinger to shut
It all in with you. Ear to ear,
You swell—till pulsing like a baby, you burst clear—
You suck for air. Your girlfriend shrieks with fear.

DAYLEY ISLAND

Gulls spiral high above
The porch tiles and my gulf-green,
Cliff-hanging lawn, with their
Out-of-breath wail, as
Dawn catches the silver ball
Set in the dried-up bird bath
To scare the gulls. My slippers
Exhale lamé.

I was egged on by old age—
To sell that house,
Winterize this house,
Give up my practice . . . that
You, Pauli, gave up
At Belzec, our son at Belsen,
And one at Maidenek,
Our last at Maidenek.

Below the cliff, the shallows
Tear apart, beating
Themselves white and black,
While the sea's smooth other edge
Towers, reddening,
Over the surfacing sun.
I rise early, always,
Earlier each day . . .

Holding on.
But it's the island that's locked in
By the sea—a case
Of vaginismus, Pauli—
Except for the one bridge
To the next island. I'm free—
Dayley's first once Jewish,
Nonpracticing analyst:

Old, but she has no helper;
Station wagon, but
She's not a tourist; poor for
An island Venus or matron.
The man who sells me fish
Says he fought my Nazis,
The captured ones talked
Just like me—I'm somebody.

Last week—March-cold
In the middle of August,
Snow-blue, high, thin skies—
I drove the hour to Brunswick
To drop my suits at
Maine's Only Chinese Laundry,
A down-easter's,
With a Negro presser.

The man was just then off
For Hagard to shoot rabbits
For the reward,
Three miles off Dayley's east shore.
Years before,
A mainlander
Had loosed two white rabbits
There; now it was theirs.

Frail, pink-veined, pale ears,
And pink as perfect gums,
Pink eyes, rose noses, as if
Diseased—I'd been there.
The lead-gray Yankee owner,
After the shotgun blast,
Strode forward, gathered the bunch,
And one by one, grabbed each

By its hind legs while it sobbed,
And swinging it against
The bare lawn, slapped it dead,
And swung it to the shrubs.
I left the cleaners wanting
So to tell you. The sun's
Well up now. Our blue carpet's
Fading evergreen, Pauli.

THANKSGIVING DAY

I was the only child,
And a first boyfriend's brother,
Dead—in a shell-shocked truck
Crash, I think—in Sweden,
Couldn't make the war matter.
We wore parachute
Synthetic silk ball gowns
That year, at the Assemblies,
Which, looking back, all seem
A shifting, newsreel gray.
All I remember is, no one
Liked Truman, that there was
No gas for cars to speak of,
That the good things, my mother
Said, were rare-red and rationed.

The boy who would be my husband
Lived six blocks away,
And I didn't know him. Where
I lived, and where he lived,
And where we live now, you
Can see the bay apartments
And the crumbling prewar pier
And wharves—there, unused,
Before we could see that far.
One year, a new police
Patrol boat docked there, later
A small yawl. But the red iron
Pier understructure, resoldered
And buttressed, rusted and fell through
That year, and no one walks there.

FROM *Final Solutions*

2.

There's a small park near the wharves,
And a playground—
But no lovers, never children.
A few old folks sunned there.
Some see the gangs, some hear.
On summer vacations from Ann Arbor
We used to walk there.

The one water fountain
Was a lush affair
Between two angels, fat as Paradise,
Nubile, and male and female,
Holding winged hands around
A base of rose stone,
While from heaven above, an aquiline
Brass bird, a green dove,
Gargled up, it seemed,
All the city's water,
Year after year.
It was never turned off,
And stood a foot deep
In pond-green watery refuse,
And was never used.

We'd thought of getting married there.

3.

The warped, smutted kitchen window
Ripples the blue fume of November
Over the shore apartments and the wharves.
The window wavers in the oven's heat.
The street flows like lava, and the playground.
My baby stirs. Time to eat for it.

Cuddled in me—lovely! It will
Die in me, I know it will.
My child is breathing in my life,
Its heart is pressing on my heart.
You won't be here if you die on me
Before I have your child.

It's why I'm here.
To spoon the drugs up to your lips,
Be near your sleep,
Make you live an extra week.
What we have to bear
Will take two months, no more.

It can't feel you at all:
It rots the stitches and the lymph strings,
And gums you . . . dressing;
You go down rich, changed, sea-green
As tomalley. Cancer.
Balls of your groin, heart of your heart.

I feel you. The oven bell
Dings, and you call—the front door bell;
And in the hall, Papa and your mother
Gabble about our unborn daughter or son.
A perfect bird. Fatty sweat
Gleams on its bursting goosepimpled breast.

A YEAR ABROAD

(In A.D. 9 Q. Varus marched three legions into an ambush in Teutoburg Forest. "From ancient times onward the circumstances surrounding the end of Roman rule in Germany have been an occasion for prejudice and rhetoric. Varus was made the scapegoat for the miscalculations of Roman policy; the contrast between the inertia or benevolence of Varus and the energy or perfidy of Arminius, between the Roman governor and the native prince, was drawn in vivid colours, and artfully employed to personify the opposition between civilization and freedom.")

Holding his breath, he watched the whole wing flex
And flex and saw the bouncing jet pods stream
With condensation as they plowed through clouds.
He saw the stewardess back down the aisle
Smiling at seat belts. His lap was headlines—now
Another Electra had burst in two and still
No planes were grounded. Down there somewhere crowds
Hushed in the bars: the un-trust-busted Yankees
Were squeezing a World Series in the till—
Millions puffed and stared, the beer suds spilled.
The diplomatic pilot dipped a wing,
Lufthansa's bow to the United States . . .
His Volkswagen was waiting. If he drove
On through the night, by dawn he could salute
The Arch of Titus with his German plates.

Cologne he knew—Jew-baiting mothers who
Just couldn't get enough and chewed their hair.
Roman Agrippina had been born there.
Nineteen and weeping for perfection, he'd
Been lost each morning. He would wake with a start
Pacing along a lot that faced the Dom.
Powdered bricks had made the ground lip-red,
Electric bells bonged in the shaved-off belfry.
He'd watch the pigeons rise and settle, rise
And settle, gobbling, then he'd go buy bread.

Cologne to Wolfsburg for the People's Car,
Through Lippe, *Saltus Teutoburgiensis*.
Though it was Varus who when Herod died
Crunched up Judaea, from Teutoburg Forest he
Would bear the Eagles of Varus back to Rome:
History's straight-man, ambushed by his aide,
His trusted German, into suicide,
Bald, civilized, delicious—never praised,
But chosen by Augustus. Rome gawked, amazed . . .
The NATO general salutes the prizes.
His Holiness stops at *et credo*, and rises
To touch the braid and tatters. Washington
And Bonn have flown the long-lost Eagles home.
The place is crushed! the packed, cowed faces hushed,
Underdeveloped stomachs aching to cheer.

He heard the engines screaming for more air.
He pushed and drifted—waking smelled like steam.
Below him were the blank and linked-up roofs
Of suburbs . . . showers, crematoria . . .
The john tiles where his father's soft eyes worked
The crossword puzzle jackpots, poetry
Of Jews, ten thousand dollars for first prize.
Red bullets to the brain, the Seconal . . .
The world was turning into dawn, just as
The jet plane's sixteen landing wheels set down.

FROM *Final Solutions*

"THE BEAST IS IN CHAINS"

Waving *News of the World*, the other customer
Whines in his bib with laughter:
" 'The Nazi bombers still
Drop stink-bombs through the window,
But lobotomized now, she doesn't mind the smell!' "
The barber grabs me by the nose;
The blade flashes around my lips.

Leaving the Ritz, I watch the sun
Volley between the windows of the place Vendôme;
The column points the hour. My *Le Monde*
Is covered with bombs
Stuck like gum to café chairs and station lockers
Exploding in Paris, Oran, Le Havre.
I sit down in the Tuileries.

Kennedy banquet at Versailles.
A Russian, Gagarin, in space.
No one is here—a day
As bleak as Boston, despite the sun. I remember
My father saying, "What should we do?"
I was fifteen, my mother forty-three.
"This will be our decision."

Tumbling gold whorls of hair shaved back for the incision;
The skin, as always, Madonna-smooth,
Without a care, below the bandages;
Greener than ever, her eyes are open—
"How are you?" she asks, "how *are* you?"
And starts to smile, and is wheeled past.
My father's grief-stunned eyes clung to his face like starfish.

I recross the street: the zoot-suited Arab
Flashes his butter-blond Rubenses,
In black and white, sold by the pack,
As two more Black Marias
Bray through the rue de Rivoli
Toward place de la Concorde.
The column's shadow points the hour.

The plans for the place Vendôme
Called for a statue less than half its height.
Twelve hundred cannons seized at Austerlitz
Napoleon melted and wrapped around the stone
In a spiral of bronze. On the top he sits,
Surveying the City of Light,
Weighing the American flags brought out,

Those enormous banners, with outsize stars,
Stripes brighter than life, worth thousands of dollars.
They wave magnificence! Guarding the president,
There'll be the horsemen of the Garde républicaine!
Golden helmets afire, on chestnut stallions!
The West has bombed and bombed. Absinthe
Is now on Thorazine, the breaker of obsessions.

SPRING

Itching from Kotex pads, from green, polluted perch,
The Seine scratches itself lovingly along the quais—
Itching from the new spring!
Hot prickly yellow wool covers the evening.
The Eiffel Tower is full of hot air, full to bursting
Hearing the countdown
Start and stop again, then again.
Brains, thoughts swell,
Like bulls snorting out
Passionate red roses from black nostrils.

While passersby's eyes lock with theirs in various grips,
Young Americans
Are swigging French beer on benches by the river.
He is there. This is Lucifer's palace
For his angels' vices. At midnight, when Paris
Looks at her face in the mirror, she sees a buttocks,
And straps on a device. Green
Is rumbling. Like a cat's sharpening claws,
The cracks in the sidewalks
Stretch out and dig in.

2.

All startling legs and eventful spirit—
Corsaged handlebar, spring straw hat—
Bicycling on the flat through the snow
To Sever Hall, to recite her Sappho.
On hair like Hera's, black swansdown,
She wore white ribbons freshly ironed.
Unmarriageable Minoan eyes,
All intuition, delicately lidded.
The way she walked,
You'd have thought her body talked.

Those Harvard years
His ego hovered like a hummingbird,
Wingless, songless—halfway
Between his knees and shoulders.
Perhaps it wanted to embrace the universe.
Closing his eyes to caress
This girl or that, he saw stars.

Time the leukotome!
Softly slicing
The frontal lobes. That girl,
Bashed in by his love,
Happily married now . . . ?
He tries to remember what was happening:
The taste of zinc—the sight, without the sound,
Of thousands of hands clapping.
The empty beer bottle slaps the water
And sinks, hiccuping whitecaps.

3.

Along the row of square, snow-white igloos
The white chestnut tree blossom clusters
Sift through each other
In the damp light and few breaths of air
Like the slow shuffling of a tambourine.
Even ugly new buildings here are rare.
Compared to French windows, these are loopholes.
The tight, washed rooms are small enough for nuns—
Small for maid's rooms! There are no closets.
Room after room is stained and pervaded
By traditionally ugly, self-absorbed,
Talmudic-brown armoires.
One shelf of each supports one kepi, at least—
A son's or father's—a beaked pillbox
Banded with gold or silver, police or army,
To keep the armoire company
With the nineteenth, the last French century.

There are no shutters. Everywhere,
Even just across the street,
Faded shutters are drawn.
Orange rungs climb the Persian carpets,
Scale *sujets religieux* and mount the sideboards.
The family, if it's home, is in the bedrooms.
The maid has turned the kitchen light out, it is so hot.
She cuts up cucumbers with the butcher knife
In thick, crude slices, a folded soaked zero
Under each arm, her neck shining.
Her old buttocks and vagina contract.
She has a vicious, weakly mind—
Sympathized with, it comes off on your hands.
Or is it a mind too generous, too deep for her,
Always in the clouds, straining to rain?
Outside, he is passing by,
His eyes on the ground, on his way home.

4.

Greeting the opening door,
Drafts dash around the room,
Like a terrier sprinting in circles
Around its home-from-work owner.
The lampshades bow like tutus.
Fresh air—but freshened where?
The lace curtains billow like the Graces' nightgowns,
Then split and kick the cancan—
Higher! Nearer—
No, farther away, farther:
The click of heels.
The air has stopped, stands still.
Across the way, a light goes on and off,
But a girl with a chiffon scarf
Was standing by the window.
Not a cloud, not a thought of rain.

The great night is pacing the slot above the street,
And down into the street, back and forth . . .
Like Hamlet sweltering in velvet Elizabethan mourning.
His head is in the sheer, temperatureless stratosphere;
His heart is smothering.
The dark is clear.
Still, some of his thoughts connect,
And are stars.

AMERICANS IN ROME

Below the window wine-washed Rome
Is drying and the concrete lane
Weaves in the rose direction home
Southwestward. I'll take her off to Ischia and Spain
And marry her, and make her love
Her rashness. Then we pause—we stay where they smile clove
And garlic in the earthy air. We'll stay,

We'll mend the bedsheets when they fray
Ourselves, and seize the hours and work
Them into full-lipped ovened clay
Vessels of content. Her shy, bare fingers jerk
The satin ribbons and unbox
My saved-up present to her, a snakeskin purse which locks
Inside it the love poem I want to read.

"Only I don't intend to plead
With you to listen. Don't I know
The Fathers say I'll never lead
You to the altar? Let them go—and even so,
You love them, don't you? And you dare
Not love me just for wanting you alone? Then swear
You couldn't love the others and be true

To me—swear something or we're through."
But that's not all. You were so shy
A girl, a child. Where is she? You
Have lost her here. How can I convalesce what I
Corrupted when infection struts
Around this city whose street lights are sidewalk sluts?
She sits there glowering at the shadow-moths

Her thumbs twiddle around the oilcloths
Soiling the walls. The curtain's sleeves
Of mellow vespertine blue sloths
Of air are all my twenty-two years of life receives
From life, besides a wobbly bed
And tabletop and chairs. The poor are richer dead . . .
Yet my starved spider dangling from the wall,

My seeing-eye, wants nothing at all
Except what gives itself away
By moving, and only wants what's small
Enough to count as riches. Where's the charm to lay
Between our pillows? It's not grace,
Not the unspoken tenderness—or in the place
Of tenderness a tepidarium.

You venture so much and you come
To loathe life's honey on your hands—
And once love worked like a green thumb
In the hot weather. And she longed for Rome. Rome stands
For hope—pocked, wired, original,
Electric as a honeycomb or a staked skull.
And all those blue-eyed souls blinded by thorns,

All the poor souls loving suborns
And scales down to the irony
Of middle age, can kiss the corns
Of gold from Peter's toe, can give to piety
Their ego, for amnesia.
That jet plane's vapor trail is time's aphasia
Coiled over St. Peter's—but that tail will crack

The silence. Then it all comes back:
The glaring doorway and the door
Open, her husband—and the black
Missal the priest held: *"Paid?* She's *paid?* And you're some whore?"*
There is no God. They taught her wrong,
The smooth-faced Sisters. Depilation kept them strong,
But lessons can't fit Spellman's corpulence

Through the bright groove the penitents'
Blue knees carved to an altar rail
In stone Trastevere, where rents
Split with indulgences, where love hangs on its nail.
I turn the light out . . . I am sure
Of nothing—just the moon, brassiered and soap-sleek, pure
Perfumed Spellman, stinking with allure.

THE WALK THERE

As he approaches each tree goes on,
And the girls one by one
Glance down at their blouses. A nun,
Then six or seven, hop in
A cream station wagon,
White-beaked blackbirds baked in a pie.
In his mind is
The lid of an eye
The dark dilated closing behind him.

Levy. Arched eyebrows and shadowed
Moist eyes. An El Greco. Swart, slim.
He's late to her. He thinks of her, waiting,
Limb by limb.

Her defenselessness and childlike trust!
Smiling to be combed out
And parted—and her lust
Touching the comb like a lyre.
To have been told by her not to trust her!

And he distrusts her.

And everywhere he sees
Hunchbacks and addicts and sadists
In braces in the cities,
Roosting in their filth,
Or plucking the trees,
In New York for true love,
In Boston for constancy.
You can be needed by someone,
Or needy, thinks Levy.

They clutch their loves like addicts
Embracing when they see
Hot May put out her flowers.
Or clutch themselves. They can't shake free.

He thinks of the time
He lived by her calendar
When she missed her time.

She gave the child a name.

When she bled, she laughed and gasped
Tears warm as pablum
On his wrists. But that is past.

Levy feels his body
Moving in front of his last
Step. He sweats, and thinks
Of the rubble massed
On Creusa behind Aeneas's
White-hot shoulders and neck.

Addresses
And clothesline laundry swelled
Like pseudocyesis—
That's what he has to pass through.

His tie is her blue,
And a new lotion gives him an air
Of coolness. He combs his hair,
And tries to smooth his hair.

He'll be there,
The husband. She'll have left him asleep—
A nap, beyond the top stair,
In darkness.

Light, light is in the trees
Pizzicato, and mica
Sizzles up to his knees.
A dozen traffic lights
Swallow and freeze
And one by one relay red red
Like runners with a blank message.

I hate her, I hate her, he said
A minute ago. Curls cluster
Levy's dark head.

TO MY FRIEND ANNE HUTCHINSON

Now the green leaves of Irish Boston fly or wither
Into bloodred Hebrew, Cotton Mather's fall.
When this morning the end-of-it-all
Siren, out of its head,
Turned inside out, hell-red,

Anne, you touched my wrist, you touched your cross,
The Fine Arts' reproduction. It must have broken—
On and on and on sang the siren,
Like a hebephrenic
Bleeding noise from each second's pinprick.

Our hearts stopped. The cars zombied on
Through the synchronized lights;
Monosyllabic shapes,
Devoid of intonation as ghosts, deaf to melody,
Like melodic dysprody.

One more terrible redeemed day is risen!
A siren wails that it is noon.
You who are ill, Anne, soon
Will withdraw to your therapy,
Vainly again to seek succor:

Passing the trees, the fall smells in their war paint
And feathers—the statue of Mather,
The marble head bent seeming to ponder
The leaves on Moses' tablets like a shroud;
He wears his curls

Like a lion in a sampler,
And hungers to be president of Harvard—
But his hand is gently raised to heaven
Where his late wife is
Whose soul was pleasant as a rose:

Passing a nailless printed finger
(It asks, Do you know about Christian Science?),
Anne, passing a mother on a billboard
(She asks, Have you called Mother
This week long distance?).

Your breath stops . . . glued to the black leather,
Staring off into no hope, into space:
The way a fiancée
Stares past the left hand she holds up
At a distance from her face,

And the plastic groom figure
On the cake, the way he stares
When the bride begins to cut!
Between the unreal and the next world, stretched taut,
Anne, you are trying to talk, wide-eyed and hollow-eyed,

Bright starving eyes! Like sections
Of a tapeworm, the anacoluthons
Break off—fed
On your daily bread
Dread.

Yet you wear the cross,
The red saltire x,
And a Ban the Bomb button
On your blouse.
Said Endicott at the trial of your namesake:

"She saith she now suffers and let us do what we will
She shall be delivered by a miracle.
I hope the court takes notice
Of the vanity of it
And heat of her spirit."

You hear the helicopter:
The moth wings–against-a-window purr
Of a cat squinting with pleasure.
It hovers nearby,
A winking red eye.

Green helicopters patrol the mushroom-colored sky.
The sunstruck State House dome is ringing
The thin air with gold quoits. The end is winging
Nearer. Your lips part;
As if I, your one friend, might be late.

You are drunk
With being loved, the demands!
Drunk that night, while your husband slept in a stupor,
Your red-hot cigarette marked and marked and marked
His palms and the backs of his hands!

Over your bed is tacked the little print of Mather.
His wig is white as a lamb,
But evilly parted in the middle,
His flesh shines like marble or cold tallow.
He has anosognosia, he is incapable

Of knowing he is ill.
Aspiring to be less *Magnalia* and more direct,
He sees the witches' moist red and black parts
Joined mutually to infect;
Championing inoculation, he dreams of wet warm hearts,

Their extinction! Their annihilation!
You say he dreams of Mistress Hutchinson,
When the Bomb had descended and was in her heart,
That "peculiar indwelling of the Holy Ghost,"
When the Voice was in her ear,

When, all soul, without soul-space
Left for sanctification,
"At last she was so full she could not contain
And vented her revelations . . .
That she should come into New England

And should here be persecuted,
And that God would ruin us
And our posterity and the whole state
For the same." Banished as one seditious,
Indians stretched her apart piece by piece.

Even her shade has disappeared.
She is revered
Only by you alone,
Anne, no one even knows that she was here.
Her sweet heart and sweet mind and sweet flesh and soul are one,

Like the air with the wind, as if she had never been born!
You walk through the burning Common,
Past the low terror of the Ether Dome,
You walk over the rooftops of Charlestown,
You walk over the Mystic River, and think of the One!

The Voice! It speaks of a wordless converse
Between airy, sweetly singing
Silent invisibles intermingling—
In bliss! within a sunbeam!
Within a single atom!

The mind stops . . . mind and body
Longing for order and mystery,
To be as a cloud, pure as a Taj Mahal
Of grief for a cherished soul,
Floating over beautiful wine-colored October.

FROM *Final Solutions*

AFTER THE PARTY

A window sighs.
The row of houses stipples and sways
As if seen through a windshield after a downpour.
A brownstone tries to say something:
But the chimney is too small,
Is intimidated by the dark,
Its fireplaces never used.

Under the street light,
I take out the booklet
Of shadowless photographs
Drained soft beiges by reproduction:
Slave-bangles, kohl eyes—the partner,
With cracked patent-leather hair, in his socks and garters,
All aloofness, good posture, chin in the air,
Forty years ago. My glasses bite
The bridge of my nose
As I stare into the dustless room.

Is he her lover? But cheats on her . . .
And she's had others.
Her veil-gray fingertips brush my eyelids, my lips.
And will have more.

The cathedral clock has just struck three, or four;
A car parks in the piles of leaves.

I think of the flower-fresh wide-eyed gaze of Greece—
Garlanding what it sees.

Convinced life is meaningless,
I lack the courage of my conviction.

THE SICKNESS

The way a child's hands stare through glass
Under the frost, pining so much
They lag behind the child, they pass
Their two hours, patients and their visitors, and touch
Each other's hands with all their love.
The huge scarred Chinaman, a yellow boxing glove
(His neck and head), spreads out his wife's left hand

Just so, and strokes her wedding band,
A lion lapping at a thorn
In his own paw. Alone, I stand
By the wall scribbling with my finger Pound's forlorn
Hymn, "What thou lovest well remains . . .
What thou lov'st well . . ." They don't allow us pens. Bleak grains
Of sunlight cross the floor, as the sun leans

Inside the tall barred windowscreens,
While the river escalates downtown
On flattening steps of foam. "I cleans
Yo hans, I cleans you fresh blue sunshine," Chas, his brown
And blue eyes tilting madly, sings.
The gulls, their own white tracers, dip through spumy rings
For rubbers, fish, and rubbish. Pudgy squabs

Peck the yard's pebbles. Each head bobs
Like a cork floater. *From these stones
Give us our bread, Lord*, each craw sobs.
"Shall not be reft from thee"—rose lips and flinty crones'
Lips peck their husbands' lips, the priest
Who came is going. Eyes and tongues and ears, like yeast,
Swell through their sockets as the studded door

Opens and buzzes closed for more
Long hours. When washday's down the drain,
Comes Tuesday, two o'clock to four,
Though some of them won't come if there's a washday rain.
Priests, girls run down—the hours just run.
No heliotrope, I watch that dead gray door. The sun,
The flexed life-dealing sun's too strong, the sun.

2.

Bottlegreen grass in Central Park,
The early light streams. Lying like
A lover near her boy, a girl,
Pre-Raphaelite in profile, pearl-
Smooth lips, nose and brow, and the passive
Long eyelids and lashes of Melancholy pensive—
And when she rises and walks away
A borzoi and its soft sashay
On slender white paws comes to mind.
We lay there like a heart, our mind
Off to our right the blue lagoon,
Free still of sailboats, just free of the moon,
Our south, the red and brown brick zoo.
But that was then. This now is Bellevue,
And God knows where the girl is, a ruined
Wax mask, waist-down a shiftless hot wind.
Dear heart, those times that were sweet milk
For our pale bones, and in the clock spun silk
For our chapped skin, like dice have scattered.
I'm like that lady-killer Bluebeard,
Dead, but to my last wife's dust,
All Bellevue-blue obsessive trust,
Repeating like an old blind cock,
"Dear heart, the light streams down on Central Park."
It's not my mind. Shouldn't that show
Have gorgeous Desdemona snow
Othello, ax him and then fly,
Black circles under each blue eye,
My dear? And our Miss Liberty,
Lounging beside the door, our trusty p.t.,

Will she be had, will she give in
To the Red Bear and live in sin,
And then Red China break the door?
Divorce, adultery, and war
Thrive. "Let live, sleep late, leave the lark
To cry, The light streams down on Central Park,"
You'd say—but some say, "Miss the slut
A little while, poor soiled girl." What
Else is there but—to live—to care
For something flashy made of air
And lose it to the wind, and sue
For breach of promise with faked death in Bellevue
Or the sex pen? But I don't know.
The smile that builds the cretin's brow,
The tenderness one gives and gets,
And lives off, with stale cigarettes,
And what old people keep of fleece
And breath, aren't they some help? They give some peace.
One man here said, "Don't play dead—die!"
But others try life, try dope, try
The fairy bars, join the Reserves,
Or take the wife their life deserves.
He said we're locked together like rhymes,
Us and our loved-ones, in bad times,
And the live whole halves of our heart
Shall, wind or bomb, be smithereened apart.

3.

Like a gray cat tied to the tarred stump of a tree
At night, the hall hides, tries its length, slinks back. It climbs
Piles of back stairs down from the dark street. Finally
The kitchen. Just to waste the steak here would take lifetimes!
There's that much, and all much too gamy to be good—
Blue tons braised, baked, broiled, or basted violet. Pie-eyed
Waiters dump it on castered slabs they wheel inside
The banquet room. They breathe here. No one else could.
The air's close as wet wool. On the last door's a hide,
White once, now orange, lettered GRAEFIN SEIDE'S PRIDE.
In the room, jet columns lace the floor and balcony

From which low music flickers on the parquet wood
Through massive fuming candelabra. Easily
A dozen colored footmen hum along the walls,
Among them grown men dressed like Philip Morris boys,
Smooth moon-faced fairies, serving trays to him. He stalls
Over each choice until—this the fat king enjoys—
Their hands start shaking, picks some favorite *saignant* dish
He's had prepared, and motioning away the rest,
Pokes it, and slurps his fingertip, and smiles—"Deeelish . . .
Deeelicious!" Sweating, finished, he sheds his green vest
And rolls his saffron blouse's sleeves up to his armpits—
Slowly, because of the stiff spangles—even so,
They slip out of his fat gold fingers—and just sits,
Just strokes his lapdog, slowly—no hour hand's so slow.
The candles huddle, soughing, in the brain-gray gloom,
In their pale light. His gold knuckles gleam. Not a sound.
   Don't make a sound, here's your last chance. Take it
   And run for it down the wrong hallway, the one
   That's never used, and don't look back. You've missed
   The worst of it just barely. You *have* to know!
   Is what you're going to say. Well, things like a girl
   Exposing herself in various poses to
   A vast steel machine and its little red eye
   Which stares and stares and never goes off. Enough?
   Behind her, behind where she spreads herself out
   Nude in her stockings and black garter belt
   On the Persian carpet, its pile the silencer,
   Is another huge heavy machine, this one
   Entirely hooded in black leather except for
   Its appendages, mantis-like chrome arms
   Which operate on her face with silver knives,
   Finally leaving only her eyes. Enough?
   Well, like the room where priests walk on the ceiling,
   Nuns on the floor, looking for each other
   In pitch-darkness with great blind eyes on stalks,
   Like dandelions. With their charcoals they scrawl
   Messages they of course can't know the others
   Can't see, all being deaf-mutes, on the damp walls.
   Enough? One last thing, then, and the worst.
   In about an hour the Royal Servitors
   Of the Commode come in and fold a silk screen,

Tall and lavender, with various seals
And names sewn into it, like Eurydice, Gandhi,
Nietzsche, Troilus, Dulles, Pola Negri,
And others—they fold this screen around the fat king,
Who is seated. Under it you can see
The pairs of slippers, the Servitors at attention
On triangle bases. Then they emerge, the screen
Is folded back, and in the pot are gold bees,
Honeybees, millions of them, which rise and join
The millions and millions of them on the ceiling
That you thought were highly overwrought
Gold work. They made the low music that you heard.
No one eats honey here—it drips down the walls
And columns, it hangs in the air—so it happens
Sometimes that a live man is selected
For his weakness to come and gorge, to swell up
Half dead on the sweetness that famishes,
And all the while he dies the honeybees feed
On him with their stingers, until in ecstasy
He does die. You were lured here for this purpose.
Get outside. It is morning on Eighty-sixth Street
Where you live. The painted clock outside
The jeweler's window happens to have the right time,
Six o'clock. A girl with crooked stockings
Walks on the feet of a goddess to the bus stop.
An opening window flashes light out over
The street like a big white bird. Coming home,
After a rainy night in Central Park,
Behind his old friend, his old suffering mare,
A horse-cab driver, looking straight ahead,
Smiles quietly, just because it is morning.

INDEX OF TITLES

INDEX OF FIRST LINES

INDEX OF TITLES

INDEX OF FIRST LINES